WE BAND OF BROTHERS

A biography of Ralph Honner,
soldier and statesman

PETER BRUNE

ALLEN & UNWIN

First published in 2000

Copyright © Peter Brune 2000

Allen & Unwin
9 Atchison Street
St Leonards NSW 2065
Australia
Phone: (61 2) 8425 0100
Fax: (61 2) 9906 2218
Email: frontdesk@allen-unwin.com.au
Web: http://www.allen-unwin.com.au

National Library of Australia
Cataloguing-in-Publication entry:

Brune, Peter Franklin, 1951– .
    We band of brothers: a biography of Ralph Honner.

    Bibliography.
    Includes index.
    ISBN 1 86508 285 6.

    1. Honner, Ralph. 2. Australia. Army. Infantry Battalion, 39th.
    3. Soldiers—Australia—Biography. 4. World War, 1939–1945—
    Campaigns—Papua New Guinea—Isurava. 5. Honner family.
    6. Ireland—Genealogy. 7. South Australia—Genealogy. I. Title.

940.5426

Set in 12/13 pt Bembo by DOCUPRO, Sydney
Printed by Griffin Press Pty Ltd, Adelaide

10 9 8 7 6 5 4 3 2 1

We few, we happy few, we band of brothers;
For he to-day that sheds his blood with me
Shall be my brother . . .

Shakespeare, *Henry V*

For the soldiers of the 2/11th, 39th, 2/14th,
2/16th and 2/27th Battalions—Ralph's brothers

FOREWORD

L ieutenant-Colonel Ralph Honner is one of the great figures in Australian military history. Yet he never commanded large-scale forces, and indeed he commanded an Australian infantry battalion for little over a year before he was wounded in action. In military jargon, he always commanded at the tactical level.

War is fought on many levels, each of which demands different skills and qualities. At the tactical level, soldiers confront the enemy in a personal way, pitting their courage, strength and wits against their foe. Here commanders direct the battle, deploying their reserves, leading by example and maintaining their soldiers' morale. At this level, too, soldiers endure the extremes of weather and terrain, suffer wounds, illness and psychological stress and, ultimately, lose their lives.

Commanders at higher strategic and operational levels are more remote from the battlefield. Often they do not have to lead men in battle. Rather, they decide where the battles are to be fought and how the tactical forces are to be supplied. In the long run, success in war depends on the quality of planning at this higher level. At times, however, outstanding performances and sacrifices by those at the tactical level can rescue a campaign from disaster caused by errors of planning and direction at the higher level.

The fighting withdrawal by the Australian soldiers on the Kokoda Trail in 1942 was one of those occasions. It was crucial to Australia's security, for if the Japanese forces had reached

Port Moresby they could have mounted air raids on northern Queensland and, who knows, the Japanese high command might have reversed its earlier decisions not to land troops in Australia. But the Allied high commanders had misjudged the enemy, and had deployed insufficient troops.

The successful defence of Port Moresby, fought along the narrow, winding, heartbreaking Kokoda Trail over the towering Owen Stanley Range, hinged on several key battles, but none more so than the battle at Isurava at the end of August 1942. The 39th Australian Infantry Battalion, composed of inexperienced young militiamen, took the first shock of this battle alone. Exhausted from six weeks in the jungle, disheartened by constant withdrawals before a superior enemy, the battalion was reinvigorated by the arrival of Lieutenant-Colonel Ralph Honner as its new commander. Newly promoted, he had just flown from his home state of Western Australia to Port Moresby and had then marched over the mountains to reach his command.

Few battalion commanders in Australian history have fought a more important battle than that conducted by this mild-mannered lawyer and part-time soldier on the Kokoda Trail. His battalion defended Isurava until reinforced by the more experienced 2/14th Battalion. Both battalions then held Isurava against great odds for a priceless period of several days. It set the tone for the series of bitter defensive battles that denied the Japanese the chance of reaching Port Moresby.

Honner was not just a capable commander: he was a man of integrity, honour and faith. He needed to be, as he led his men through events of such stress that they were to dominate the memories of the survivors for the next half-century. This biography is a reminder that in the long run wars are won by the skill and loyalty of commanders at the tactical level. It is also a reminder of the quality of the men who were brought up in the Great Depression, sacrificed six years of their lives during the Second World War and then, carrying their wounds, helped shape and build Australia in the second half of this century. Peter Brune has captured the heroic quality of Honner's achievement, and in so doing has paid a fine tribute to a great Australian.

David Horner
Professor, Strategic and Defence Studies Centre
Australian National University

CONTENTS

ACKNOWLEDGEMENTS

The research for this book was made possible by the generous grant and the support of the Deputy Chief of the General Staff, now Deputy Chief of Army. I thank him sincerely.

I am indebted to Professor David Horner for his selection of Lieutenant-Colonel Ralph Honner as one of the subjects for the Australian Army's Military History Series biographies. Although this series has now ceased and this book is not part of it, Professor Horner has at all times offered astute advice and encouragement.

To Ralph Honner's children, Richard, Brian, Margaret and John (and Richard and Brian's wives), I owe a debt of gratitude I shall never be able to repay: their support at various times has included unrestricted access to Ralph's papers and family photos, constant meetings and interviews with me, and a harassment of their privacy through the medium of the telephone, with seemingly endless questions from Adelaide.

I should like to thank Lieutenant Ken Johnson, 2/11th Battalion, for his untiring work in the organising of interviews and written material, and his time spent in reading the work from a 2/11th perspective.

I have had the pleasure, through this book, to renew a working relationship with a number of 'Those Ragged Bloody Heroes'—Keith Lovett, Stan Bisset, Doug McClean, 'Judy' Garland, 'Kanga' Moore, Hugh Kelly, Jack Sim, Noel Hall, and many others. I thank them for their untiring efforts in my search for Ralph.

To Neil McDonald I owe special thanks. Neil interviewed Ralph in 1985 for the research for his *War Cameraman: The Story of Damien Parer*. Our paths have repeatedly crossed during our research and writing and I have found his counsel invaluable.

To Bill Edgar, Brigadier Arnold Potts' biographer, who combed Hale School's archives on my behalf, I offer sincere acknowledgement and thanks. I also appreciate the support of John Honner, Ralph Honner's nephew from Perth.

I should like to record my appreciation to Ian Bowring, my publisher, and Ann Crabb, Simone Ford and all at Allen & Unwin for their support and encouragement.

I am indebted to the Australian War Memorial for permission to use a number of their photographs; to Dr Peter Stanley for permission to use extracts from the official histories; to the 39th and 2/14th Battalion Ex-Servicemen's Associations for permission to quote extracts; to Neil McDonald for permission to use extracts from his work; and to Jay Wheeler for his expert assistance with the maps for this work.

To my daughter Kylie and my partner Meredith, who have made no small number of sacrifices for this work, I wish to record my gratitude.

I should like to sincerely thank Humphrey Tranter, of the Flinders University of South Australia, for his expert knowledge and advice concerning Ralph's education and writing style.

Last, I hope and pray that I have done justice to a great Australian—warts and all—whom I was privileged to know, to work with, and to greatly admire. My thanks go to Ralph.

Peter Brune
March 2000

MAPS

ILLUSTRATIONS

1

BORN OF THE GREAT HUNGER

. . . chivalry is both rational and far-sighted, for it endows the side which shows it with a sense of superiority, and the side which falls short with a sense of inferiority. The advantage in the moral sphere reacts on the physical.

Liddell Hart, October 1925[1]

For those who were familiar with this soldier's journey, his immaculate last parade bore all the obvious signs of his distinguished service. Three illustrious Australian infantry battalions were represented—their emblazoned battle honours ample testimony to both the critical and diverse nature of his splendid service. The soldier's granddaughters adorned the coffin with his country's flag and his medals, testimony to the nobility of the warrior; with his walking stick, evidence of the price the warrior pays; and, with the yellow and blue flowers of the Western Australian football team he had supported from afar, a symbolic link with both his home state and original battalion. His grandsons were to be the pallbearers for the journey that this faithful Christian soldier hoped to be his final and yet eternal reward.

Politicians, statesmen, church representatives and veterans were in abundance at this gathering, but none could have been prepared for the dramatic entrance of a representative of this warrior's former foe. Amid the hushed formality of the occasion,

an uninvited Japanese veteran approached the coffin, stiffly
bowed, then approached the front pew and, with a further
formal bow, presented a letter of condolence to his family. Even
in death, this distinguished soldier's faith and moral strength
stood above warfare and its victors and vanquished.

Above all else, Lieutenant-Colonel Ralph Honner, DSO,
MC—the stubborn defender of Isurava and the stirring victor
of Gona—was in all likelihood the last Australian chevalier. This
is his story.

The Ireland of the mid-1800s was a land of long-endured
political and social repression, of economic exploitation, and
therefore a land of little real hope. Families of farmers who had
for generations owned and tilled their soil for measurable gain
had been reduced to downtrodden tenants. Roughly four out
of five of them were classified, according to the 1841 census,
as being class 3 families—people who were often illiterate and
without capital or land.

Such Irishmen worked a small plot of soil, varying in size
from a few acres to less than one, and relied overwhelmingly
on the potato harvest. Potato crops were not the prime agri-
cultural pursuit by chance: they were easy to sow, to nurture
and to harvest; they provided a magnificent source of nourish-
ment (all that was required without supplement by other often
unavailable crops); and they afforded tenants the opportunity to
venture elsewhere for work and further income.

The Great Famine of 1846/47 (the Irish called it *an Gorta
Mor*, the Great Hunger) was the ruination of 19th-century
Ireland, as it attacked the potato, the basis of existence for the
poorer Irish. The blight turned both the flower and stalk black
while the buried foodstuff became putrefied. A million Irishmen
succumbed. In some cases, despite efforts to grate the diseased
potatoes, boil them and squeeze them through fabric and then
make cakes, the results were catastrophic. The fit often survived
the recipe, but the old and the very young just as often lost
the fight.

If a million Irish died as a result of the famine, then a million
more gave up their homeland forever. The New World beck-
oned for those who could raise sufficient capital and Glasgow
and Liverpool for many who could not. For the majority of the

emigrants, the United States of America provided perceived salvation, in the form of unskilled work in its teeming cities and a priceless political voice and measure of social freedom. Transportation to New South Wales still often awaited political prisoners and criminals.

John Honner (pronounced 'Honour') lived in the heartland of southern Ireland, near where the county borders of Offaly (formally King's County), Leix (formally Queen's County) and Tipperary meet. There, in 1858, a decade after the Great Famine and the resultant mass exodus of many of his countrymen to the New World, he too made the momentous decision to leave his homeland.[2]

But while many of his countrymen chose the American version of a renewed life in the New World, Honner, at 46 years of age, sought more than the opportunity of unskilled work in an American city—he longed for the chance to farm and eventually purchase his own land. The young colony of South Australia seemed to offer the potential fulfilment of such a dream, a dream held chiefly for the long-term benefit of his seven children.

There were a number of other reasons for his choice. The first is, perhaps, a little obscure. The name Honner is in fact English, not Irish. It seems likely that an English Honner would have had an Irish estate bestowed on him centuries before, in recognition of war service. The fact that a long succession of Honner Christian names are English—Richard, John, William, Henry—would seem to support the theory. However, inter-marriage, the adoption of the Catholic faith (or at least, initially, a greater acceptance of it), and many generations of life in Ireland had markedly diluted that English predominance. Thus John Honner might not have been as greatly influenced as many of his countrymen to sever all ties with British influence.

The second reason was more pragmatic. The sea passage to North America was a risky undertaking, as the conditions were often appalling and the authorities, chiefly the ships' captains, were under few regulations or penalty for either the survival or the condition of their charges on arrival. By contrast, the sea voyage to South Australia guaranteed the travellers a ship's doctor, who examined and treated them both before embarking and during the voyage.

However, John Honner's decision must have been decisively

fortified by the fact that his daughter Mary had married one
Timothy Feehan and emigrated to the colony some time before.
Under the South Australian colonisation scheme of the time,
settlers could nominate friends or relatives in Britain, deposit
sums of money in the Colonial Treasury and thereby gain
passages; or, if private funds were unavailable, potential emigrants could apply for free passages.

The emigrants were required to be of high moral character
and to be prepared to work for four years as tradesmen, farm
labourers, servants, or in other nominated occupations. Miscre-
ants who challenged the emigration cycle of labourer and
potential landowner by moving to the goldfields or by specu-
lation through land purchases were required to repay the cost
of their voyage.

Edward Gibbon Wakefield's model of systematic colonisation in South Australia must therefore have appealed greatly to
John Honner. It offered the chance to labour for the eventual
(and plausible) dream of land ownership; it had proclaimed
religious tolerance; it offered a safe and comfortable passage (for
its day) to the far distant colony; and, at the end of his hopes
and dreams across the other side of the world, a cherished
member of his family awaited him, a firm foundation and
helping hand to establish his family in a new land.

While their daughter Mary awaited them in South Australia,
John and Mary Honner and five of their other six children,
William 20, John 15, Johanna 13, James 11 and Kate 10,
embarked on the 949-ton *Utopia* bound for Adelaide on
28 March 1858. The *Utopia* carried 342 emigrants who had
made some financial contribution to their passage: 32 married
couples, 90 single men, 55 single women, 28 boys and 29 girls.
Seventeen married couples, nine single men, twelve single
women, nine boys and twelve girls sailed under free passage.
Three boys were either born in port before embarkation or
during the voyage, while three others died during that passage.
One girl also died and one was born during the journey.[3] Given
the conditions, the length of the voyage and the standards of
hygiene and food during passages of those times, the survival
rate on the *Utopia* was impressive.

John Honner's second-eldest son Richard, 17, and his wife
Sarah, 20—Ralph Honner's grandparents—were forced to stay
behind. They embarked on the 1156-ton *Frenchman* on 1 June

1858, as Richard had contracted measles. Mary, the couple's first child, was born during the voyage. The *Frenchman* carried 416 emigrants to South Australia, of whom seven died in transit.[4]

The newly arrived Honners almost immediately moved to a place called Little Gorge near Yankalilla, about 80 kilometres south of Adelaide, to join Mary Feehan. While not being allowed to own land, they were able to lease a farm some small distance away in the Little Gorge–Second Valley district, known as Bishop's Flat.

John Honner contracted pneumonia while clearing land at Second Valley and passed away in 1875. By this time two of his sons William and John and their sisters Ellen and Kate had moved to New Zealand. Johanna stayed in South Australia, James married a local girl, and Mary and Timothy Feehan remained in the area for some years.

From the time of their arrival in South Australia, Richard and Sarah Honner continued to aspire to the realisation of John Honner's dream of land ownership and long-term financial prosperity and security. During the period 1858–73 Sarah bore Richard ten children—Mary (born on board the *Frenchman* on the voyage to South Australia), Bridget, John, Edward, Richard Jnr, William, James, Joseph, Robert and Joseph (the first-born Joseph died in infancy).[5] The family historian recorded that:

> . . . Richard moved on another five miles to Rapid Bay. He built a slab hut of split sheoak to house his family who made the journey on foot, accompanied by a cow and a goat—to be joined by a second goat captured from a wild flock. The years of unremitting toil continued—even for Sarah and her children who could help with the cows and goats, the pigs and the poultry. Sarah made butter and packed eggs; Johnny, old enough to sit on a horse, rode in to Yankalilla with a basket of butter and eggs balanced on the saddle in front of him, while his sister Bridget trudged beside him to shop for the household necessities that would return in the same precariously balanced basket.[6]

Richard supplemented his gradually increasing farm income with regular sojourns to the Lower North region of South Australia, where his persistence in mastering sheep-shearing slowly paid dividends: within a year his daily tally grew to 90.

Faith, hope and material abstinence produced gradual prosperity which saw the purchase of drays for his farm work and a cart for, among other things, the journey of his children to the Yankalilla convent for their Catholic education.

Within seventeen years of his landing at Port Adelaide (half of his life to that time), Richard Honner and his wife Sarah, through sheer hard work and thrift, had accumulated the impressive sum of 1280 pounds for the purchase of 640 acres at Brentwood in the Minlacowie district of Yorke Peninsula. The Honners were to become land-owners.

The trek to Brentwood was undertaken in three stages. Late in 1875, Richard and his second- and third-born children, Bridget and John, journeyed by road with ten bullocks, two horses and three drays. Along the way they stopped at Virginia, where they visited Sister Mary Laurentia, Richard's first-born child (one of Mary MacKillop's early companions), and reshod their bullocks and horses. On arrival at Brentwood the three Honners built a stone-and-pug house and a number of farm sheds, and began the enormous task of fencing and clearing the land in anticipation of cropping in 1876. The second stage of the journey was undertaken early in 1876 and saw the embarkation of Sarah and her remaining six children by ketch from Port Adelaide. The final stage of the journey saw Richard and his 12-year-old son Ned complete a 640-kilometre round trip from Second Valley to Brentwood with the family's horses, cows and steers. Their substantial pig population was slaughtered and brought with them for a monotonous but staple pork diet.

The family migration from the Yankalilla area to Brentwood on Yorke Peninsula established a family dynasty.

From Brentwood, as it became established, it was natural that the process of expansion should continue, to provide for the seven sons as they grew to manhood. Land at Arthurton (now 'Roscrea Hill') was acquired in 1881. Then two properties at Maitland were added to the family holdings—'Glenanaar' in 1886 and 'Ynoo', with its old station homestead, in 1888. If there was not yet land for all there was work for all. Crops were still sown by broadcast and reaped by hand. Stone picking was an interminable drudgery, the clearing of the ground providing the material for the construction of paddock walls and farm buildings. No less monotonous than the work was the food—home-killed pork was the staple diet . . .

It was at Maitland, at 'Glenanaar', that he [Richard Honner senior] built his fine stone home and saw out his years surely satisfied with his life's work. He died on June 19, 1928, shortly before his 88th birthday on the anniversary of the Battle of the Boyne . . .

His wife Sarah, who was older than he was, had predeceased him in 1924.[7]

If Richard Honner Snr had faithfully carried his father John Honner's dream of land ownership and prosperity from Ireland to South Australia, then his devout Irish Catholicism was no less part of the legacy. On 6 July 1928, the South Australian Catholic paper *Southern Cross* attested to his religious piety:

His was a rugged personality, like unto that of Moses, made gentle by the Gospel of Love. His spiritual outlook was almost Jansenistic, strong, unswerving from tradition even in the knowledge of obedience being best. Strong, dominant, defiant, uncompromising, he faced his Catholic duties and obligations with a conservatism that made even the unchanging Catholic Church seem for the moment, changeable in comparison.[8]

Richard and Sarah Honner's dream of a network of prosperous properties on Yorke Peninsula for their seven sons was destined to be only partly realised. The farms prospered and five of the seven boys aspired to their parents' dream. But two of their sons were restless souls and unsuited to the cause.

Richard (Ralph Honner's father) was the third-born son— attractive, over six feet in height, straight-backed, solid in build and athletic. And he was most definitely restless and free-spirited. Richard was the son who always chose the most spirited mount and challenged it to the limit, who swapped mounts out of his father's view when allotted the most docile of horses, who loved a quiet drink and a yarn, and who stole away late at night for mischief. He was in the habit of awaiting domestic tranquillity after the Honner family had retired for the night and then slipping out of his bedroom to attend dances and all means of social interaction. He was caught at least once:

Richard had been in the habit of going off to dances around Maitland . . . after their parents thought the boys were in bed. This night he went off to a dance in Moonta and while he was away a traveller knocked on the door. He was lost, so they gave him some supper and invited him to sleep in the

spare bed in the boys' room. The seven boys slept in there.
For a joke, the boys showed the stranger Richard's bed. All
was quiet until he returns on his horse sometime around 3 am.
When he climbs up onto the roof and lets himself down onto
his bed, with a drop of about three feet, the stranger woke
up with a start and yelled . . .[9]

Richard and Robert soon tired of gathering stones on
paddocks and awaiting their turn for a property on Yorke
Peninsula. They decided to dig for more immediate wealth in
the goldfields of Western Australia. And perhaps their parents
thought a period away from home—where hard work, increased
responsibility and isolation from their loved ones were the order
of the day—might temper their restlessness. When they arrived
in Esperance, the arid, harsh land to the north cooled their
enthusiasm for mining, with the result that both took jobs in
that thriving port. Richard settled down for some time as a
shop assistant. However, when the Perth–Coolgardie railway
line was completed, the resulting demise of Esperance as a
goldrush port saw the brothers return to Adelaide. It is not
known how long they stayed in South Australia, but the period
could not have been fruitful as Richard and Robert decided to
set sail for Fremantle. But it would seem that the Honner
brothers left more than their family on Yorke Peninsula—a
number of broken hearts was a further legacy. But, in Richard's
case, one such heart would not be denied.

Eleanor McMahon was born at Killinkere, County Cavan
in Ireland, on 16 September 1866. Her father Patrick and
mother Elizabeth were extremely poor tenant farmers. The
marriage produced eleven children, four of whom died in
infancy. The small farm could not be expected to support all
seven surviving children as they reached adulthood, and
Killinkere did not abound in opportunities. The four eldest girls
decided to emigrate to Australia and one son and a further
daughter to America.

Annie and Bertha McMahon were the first of the four to
leave for South Australia and Eleanor and May followed, probably in much the same fashion as had the Honners (the first
two assisted the second). Annie was a dressmaker, Bertha and
Eleanor were trained schoolteachers, and May was a lady's help.

The newly arrived McMahon women were country girls by

birth and country girls by nature. May married and settled at
Booleroo Centre, about 240 kilometres north of Adelaide;
Annie married a mail-coach contractor and settled at Maitland;
Bertha taught at a one-teacher school near Maitland before
marrying and residing in North Adelaide; and Eleanor taught
at the one-teacher school at Arthurton on Yorke Peninsula.[10]

On Friday evening 10 February 1893, Misses Bertha and
Eleanor McMahon, among other young damsels, were cordially
invited to a function held by the Committee of the Bachelor's
Club of Arthurton. Dancing was to begin at 8 pm. The invitation
was signed by Richard Joseph Honner.[11] It is unknown whether
or not this was the first meeting between the 27-year-old Honner
and Eleanor McMahon, but it is the earliest surviving record of
their social interaction. Eleanor had endeared herself to the
community and had also painstakingly saved her money, acquiring an impressive glory box.

It is known that Richard Honner came back from Western
Australia at least once to his family's Yorke Peninsula properties.
Love must have bloomed (very strongly at least on Eleanor's
part), because in early 1899 she applied to the South Australian
Education Department for a transfer to Western Australia. On
3 June Miss McMahon received a letter from that department
stating that:

> I beg to inform you that a memorial has been received from
> parents of children attending the Arthurton school asking that
> you may *not* be transferred. What are your wishes in the matter
> now?[12]

Eleanor left the Arthurton community with a framed address
and a solid silver tray and tea service. The framed address read:

Dear Miss McMahon,

> We the pupils of the Arthurton Public School, learn with
> sincere regret that you are leaving the District.
>   We feel however that we cannot allow you to depart from
> us without testifying to your courteous demeanour; kindly
> attention; great care and interest ever manifested towards us,
> in the discharge of your Scholastic duties.
>   We therefore beg of you to accept the accompanying
> Souvenir, not because of its intrinsic value, but as a volun-
> tary expression of the regard and esteem in which you are held
> by us.

Constable Richard Honner, Fremantle Mounted Police.

> Wishing you every happiness and prosperity in the future.
> We beg to subscribe ourselves . . .[13]

The letter was signed by all fifteen students.

On 14 March 1900, Eleanor was posted to the Number Two Mill School, Jarrahdale, a timber mill town in the hills southeast of Perth. Her wage was to be 110 pounds a year with a lodging allowance of 15 pounds per annum, provisional on her receiving satisfactory reports.[14]

While Eleanor was occupied in gaining her teaching transfer, Richard Honner had been busy in gaining a secure job with prospects of advancement. His athletic prowess and superb horsemanship saw him accepted into the Western Australian Mounted Police and posted to Fremantle on 2 December 1899. By this time the couple had been separated long enough, and on 12 September 1900 they were married in Fremantle. Richard was 35 and Eleanor 34.

Eleanor was to bear Richard five sons in five years, followed by a daughter, but her responsibilities amounted to much more

Eleanor McMahon.

than maternal ones: she brought the marriage great love and devotion, stability, her savings and glory box, and a sturdy Catholic faith. Her sons were named accordingly—Corentin Valery Honner (12 December 1901) was born in lodgings at Hill Street, and Richard Aniceti Honner (17 April 1903), born at Holdsworth Street, Fremantle. Both places were close to the Fremantle police stables. Eleanor later bought a house in Higham Street, Fremantle, and it was here that her third and fourth sons were born, Hyacinth Ralph Honner (17 August 1904) and Clement Wilfred Honner (2 October 1905). After Richard Honner qualified for a police home in a two-storeyed terrace block in Henderson Street, Fremantle, the home bought in Higham Street was rented out. The last two children, Forrest St Alban (12 December 1906) and Mary Sadie (22 June 1909), were born in Henderson Street.

Hyacinth Ralph Honner was born into a devout Catholic home. His Christian name 'Hyacinth' is derived from the Catholic saint of the same name who travelled and preached extensively in Prussia, Pomerania along the Baltic, in Denmark, Sweden and Norway. Saint Hyacinth became known as the 'Apostle of the North' during the 13th century. Saint Hyacinth's feast day is 17 August, Ralph's birthday. Ralph's brothers were also named after Catholic saints whose feast days coincided with their birthdays.

Mary Jeffs, Ralph's sister, remembered her mother:

> She was about five foot four and a kilo heavier than my father when they were married . . . she had lovely skin and beautiful hair, so long that she could sit on it. She had a burning accident six months after she was married in which one side of her hair was destroyed, so she had it all cut off to grow again, and I have that beautiful wavy hair in a box, nearly a century old. My mother had a good sense of humour but was more of a home body. She was very practical and would tackle any job that had to be done. I think my mother would have had more influence on Ralph when he was young . . .[15]

Given Ralph's Irish Catholic roots, the fact that his mother was of critical influence on his religious and, in turn, his character development is hardly surprising.

Cardinal Moran, speaking at the Australasian Catholic Congress held in Melbourne in October 1904 (two months after Ralph's birth), stated that:

> . . . woman's sphere was in the home, where she reigned as the queen and mistress, surrounded by her loving husband and little children. All the good that was in a man was due to his mother, for to her God entrusted the moulding of the mind, as well as the safeguarding of the infant intellect.[16]

Patrick O'Farrell, in his book *The Catholic Church and Community: An Australian History*, went further:

> It was commonly argued by clergy in Australia that, through devotion to Mary, the church had made a great historical contribution to improving the status of women, from that of degraded exploitation, to that chivalrous regard characteristic of the Middle Ages when 'woman reached her true level, enthroned as queen of the home'—a depiction which quite ignored the active woman saints. Then came the Protestant Reformation which, in spurning the veneration and cult of the Virgin, led to a degeneration in women's social and domestic position—so went the Catholic argument.
> . . . Catholic self-satisfaction in this regard obscured within the church the fact that all the denominations—including the Catholic—in the nineteenth century were moving towards a

stress on the martial virtues—fighting for the faith, heroism in its service, courage in its defence.[17]

Such a view of the world had been brought to South Australia by Ralph's great-grandfather, John Honner, in 1858; Ralph's grandfather Richard had not merely carried the faith but had given it an almost new dimension in piety; and, when his wayward, restless son and namesake had wandered to Western Australia and sought his fortune, along had come the austere, steady and devoted Catholic, Eleanor McMahon.

It is highly unlikely that the good cardinal and Mrs Richard Honner were in direct communication, but it is accurate to say that she modelled Cardinal Moran's views in a most strict and enthusiastic manner. The rosary was said every night before bed and in transit to all social functions, and prayers were said kneeling by the bed—a practice that was to survive with Ralph for the remainder of his life. Mother ruled the roost with a quiet and yet utterly determined Catholic hand. And 'the roost' included father, whose former free spirit and contacts within his varied and action-packed life as a police constable were curbed, in some measure at least, by the constraints of a strong-willed woman who administered the family investments and provided him with a modest weekly allowance.

The qualities of quiet, inner conviction, resolution and religious faith were ingrained in Hyacinth Ralph Honner by his mother, and would remain as the pillars of his existence. The future teacher, husband, father, lawyer, soldier, statesman and political figure were life's varied manifestations of those unshakeable roots. In a rough draft found in his papers and written in the last years of his life, Ralph had a fond recollection of his mother and early home life:

> Eleanor was now receiving rent from her Higham Street property and Richard was able to buy a forty acre farm three miles out of Fremantle. It had a small house, with no running water, no bathroom, no gas, no electricity but a brick chimney and a stove for cooking. In the next paddock was a well, windmill and tank for water and a shed for a cart and horses and feed. Richard trenched one section to plant an orchard, cropped a larger paddock for wheat, hay and chaff for his horses and grain for his pigs . . . slaughtered on site by Fremantle butchers as soon as they were big enough for sale. And the pigs were fattened on a boiled diet of discarded market

Richard, father, Ralph (between father's legs), Clem, Forrest, mother, Coretin (photo c. 1910).

vegs [sic] and fruit and swill from a string of hotels and restaurants in Fremantle. A man was employed to make the evening round to collect the discarded food and cart it to the farm.

During the years 1909–1911 Eleanor spent much time living at the farm with her four younger children (the two eldest boys were with her sister Bertha in North Adelaide). She could oversee the work in the piggery and lead her young brood out through the surrounding woodland to cut rushes to cover the floors of the sties. But she also showed them the flowers and the stars and, one clear night in 1910 took them out on to the high parapet of Richard's orchard trenching to gaze at Halley's Comet with a wild surmise.[18]

Ralph was six years of age.

In 1912 Eleanor Honner's investments allowed for the purchase of 3000 acres of land 8 kilometres north of Dalwallinu (about 200 kilometres north of Perth). The land was of only average standard and comprised only '23 per cent first class land'.[19] The orchard just out of Fremantle was leased out, and the long-term Honner ambition now became that of farm-owners. Perhaps Richard and Eleanor were thinking of their children's future, but it is highly likely that the attraction of rural life ingrained in both their pasts had caught up with them. In order to develop their new purchase, it was decided to lease the farm but live as close as possible to it.

On 21 May 1913, Richard Honner was posted to the police station at Three Springs, about 315 kilometres north of Perth.[20] That town was a small rural community of about 1000–1500 people serving a relatively prosperous farming hinterland. The railway to Geraldton ran through the town, which consisted chiefly of a general store, post office, boarding house, smaller shops, a hotel, bakery, bank, school and approximately twenty houses.

The police establishment at Three Springs consisted of an office that doubled as a courtroom, a one-room lock-up and a modest police house. Richard Honner's area of jurisdiction extended in a rough rectangle from Arrino, about 16 kilometres northwest of Three Springs, about 100 kilometres south to Gunyidi, across to South Dalwallinu, and thence about another 100 kilometres northwest to Bowgada—a massive area for one constable and his horse and cart.[21] Each year Constable Honner had to collect statistics, which involved a three to four week expedition from farm to farm. Young Ralph accompanied his father on a number of occasions, as it gave mother a break and provided father with company for the numerous nights spent camping out. Richard's other tasks included riding over the Wongan Hills to the Mullawa railway line construction to intercept 'sly groggers and two-up school promoters'[22] and investigating lost, stolen or damaged property within his area.

The Honner family's religious needs while at Three Springs were accommodated by Father Scanlon, 'an old saintly priest'[23] who journeyed from Dongara (near Geraldton) once a month to celebrate mass and give religious instruction to the Catholic children in the playshed at the state school. He arrived by goods train at midnight every fourth Friday, trudged with case in hand up to the galvanised iron church and slept in an attached room.

Mary Jeffs (Ralph's sister) remembered fragments of the Honners' period in Three Springs:

> When we were in Three Springs there was a railway strike on
> and the hotel was out of bread and flour. Dad mentioned Mum
> had just got a bag of flour so she baked for the hotel for as
> long as needed. She also won first prize at the Three Springs
> Show for butter and some were not pleased about that as she
> was not a farmer's wife.[24]

Life was strict and frugal: material possessions were scarce and
highly valued, each and every penny was hard-earned, accumulated
keenly, and spent with considerable prior thought. The boys'
clothes were made by mother, pillowcases were starched, the
bedsheets were patched until the sheets were just patches, everything had a place and there was a strict place for everything.[25] And
while motherly love abounded, it was not demonstrative—unless,
as on one occasion, the young Honners were chased home by
bigger boys. Mrs Honner confronted the enemy at the gate with
a threatening look and an intimidating kettle of boiling water. The
enemy retreated.[26]

In short, Eleanor Honner's devout and dour view of the world
was translated to her child-rearing and, as a consequence, such
character traits were implanted into the young Hyacinth. He was
a quiet boy, eager to learn (he was reading all manner of labels
in mother's cupboards and was a fluent reader before he began
school), and was eager to please, but there was always an
emotional barrier, a difficulty in expressing love and affection
in an open, unrestrained way. Throughout his life, people were
to admire the man, his principles, his deeds and service to both
the individual and community, but there was always that private
wall in relationships, a wall not easily scaled.

Social functions in Three Springs were rare, but the local
Catholic Ball provided Eleanor with the opportunity to hang a
4-gallon kerosene tin of milk in a copper of boiling water and
make her much-sought-after 'Zuare, Coffee and Chichory'
supper beverage.[27] Christmas and birthday presents were rare,
according to Mary, although Ralph once maintained that he
did remember a popgun for his birthday at approximately eight
years of age.[28]

Ralph's state school education during this period and his
class 6 year at the local Catholic school (three Dominican Nuns
from Dongara opened the school in Three Springs in 1916)
made it abundantly clear to his mother, the former teacher, that

her third-born son had very real potential as a scholar. Three Springs might have offered her husband and family a stable income and the opportunity to rent Eleanor's Fremantle property and purchase and live near the family's newly acquired farm, but life in that rural outpost could not facilitate the adequate education of a gifted son. The 12-year-old Hyacinth would have to go to Perth.

2

LIFE IN EPIC TERMS

Those who are concerned with the practical questions of
defence ought to realise the practical importance of ideals.

Liddell Hart, August 1936[1]

As the First AIF were busily engaged in adding Bullecourt,
Messines, Ypres, the Menin Road, Polygon Wood and
Passchendaele to their list of battle honours in 1917, Ralph
Honner had moved to Perth and enrolled at Perth Boys School.
It is highly likely that his parents had decided to place him at
that school for his class 7 year to consolidate his education to
a point where he might gain a scholarship to the prestigious
Perth Modern School the following year.[2] He boarded at
Goderich Street, East Perth, which left him with approximately
a 20-minute walk to school. Ralph won a scholarship and duly
enrolled at Perth Modern School on 5 February 1918 and
boarded at Coghlan Street, Subiaco, which entailed a 15-minute
walk to his new school.[3]

Although only a boy during the Great War years, the scale
of sacrifice made a strong impression on him. He recalled the
seemingly endless columns of casualties in the newspapers and
the memorials that sprang up in country towns across Western
Australia.[4] When he entered Perth Modern School, three of its
assistant masters were on leave with the AIF.[5] The school stood
in grounds of about 12 acres on the heights of West Perth, and

contained 'a fine cricket ground with turf wickets',[6] two asphalt tennis courts, two large grassed playgrounds for the girls, and a miniature rifle range for the cadets. It had an enrolment of 400 students. In its official information booklet for 1918 the school also boasted impressive buildings:

> . . . thirteen class-rooms fitted in the most modern style, Art Room, Library, Physics Laboratory, Chemistry Laboratory, Science Lecture Room, Biology Laboratory, Museum, Kitchen, Laundry, Dining Room, Workshop, Gymnasium, and various rooms used for administrative purposes. There is also a finely proportioned Assembly Hall. The Lavatories, etc., are all connected with the deep drainage and sewerage system.[7]

Page twelve of the school information booklet also stated that:

> As there is a tendency for girls to suffer in health from the strain of school work, it is the aim of the school to give them an opportunity to indulge in regular exercise in the open air . . . During the winter the hockey field provides opportunities for those who are strong enough to enjoy the game . . .[8]

One of the 'stronger ones' was one Marjory Collier Bennett, whose combination of good looks, hockey skills and grit and determination was to make an eventual impact on the boy from Three Springs. And there were two other students at Perth Modern School who were eventually to strike long-term friendships with Ralph Honner—Paul Hasluck and H.C. 'Nugget' Coombs. However, at this time Ralph was not the strong, athletic young man of his later adolescence but a retiring, short, thin boy dubbed 'squib' and 'swot' by his peers.[9]

It was at this juncture that his Christian name began to cause him some anxiety—'some' being much more than normal. Hyacinth Honner was misplaced, for the times, in a home economics class. He detested his Christian name, found it an acute embarrassment, and must have wondered why his Catholic mother could have given him such a uniquely Catholic name in such a Protestant-dominated world. The young, impressionable student took to transforming the first initial of his name into a box with an 'X' inside it. To complete the transformation, a similar pattern was formed at the end of his surname to give the impression that the boy was named 'R. Honner'.[10] But there

were further problems of a more enduring nature. His sister
Mary remembered that:

> When Ralph was boarding in Perth, I think he was very
> lonely. One place he was at he was so cold in winter, he had
> to take the table cloth off the table and add it to his bed
> clothes . . . my mother taught Ralph and me to knit with
> turkey quills and string and during the school holidays Ralph
> used to knit his socks with turned over tops. At Modern School
> he was the only boy in short pants and I think that was a sore
> point. He was small and didn't do his growing until he was
> seventeen.[11]

The quiet, reserved and undemonstrative 13-year-old boy from
Three Springs was over 300 kilometres from home and could look
to absolutely no-one for immediate emotional or material support;
he was acutely embarrassed by his first name; there was a hint of
deprivation at his lodgings; he wore short pants and home-made
socks; and, above all, his physical appearance was hardly imposing.
What was 'swot' to do? The answer was simple—'swot'. It was
not a question of acquiring mere solace in books, but more a
matter of accumulating knowledge, inspiration and sheer enjoy-
ment from them. By his fifteenth birthday the young student had
read the complete works of Shakespeare.[12]

The boys at Perth Modern were required to study English,
French, Arithmetic, Algebra, Geometry, History, Geography,
Physics, Art, Workshop, Physical Training and Cadet Training
during their first year, and then take either another science
subject or another language in their second and third years.[13]

Ralph's school records for his first year show his parents'
address as 'Police Station Three Springs' and 'farm Dalwallinu'.[14]
At this time, Richard Honner and his sons were spending
as much time as possible attempting to establish their property by share farming. During his first school year in 1918,
Ralph's April report stated that he was 'a good type of lad and
a promising student'. Subsequent reports in August and December acknowledged his distinctions in maths, history and
geography.[15]

During his early Perth Modern School days Ralph's parents
allowed him a shilling a week pocket money. He kept a ledger
of his spending and preferred to spend his allowance on neces-

sities, such as elastic for his shorts or wool for sock darning, rather than on frivolous items such as sweets.[16]

On 28 October 1918, Ralph received a third visit during school time from his father. But on this occasion Richard Honner had journeyed from the Beverley Police Station, not Three Springs. Richard Honner's posting to Beverley, about 125 kilometres east of Perth, thus entailed a much longer trip back to the farm at Dalwallinu than had the journey from Three Springs, but the higher pay and the fact that the property was still share farmed seemed adequate compensation. A measure of Richard Honner's standing as a police constable can be gauged from the certificate of appreciation presented to him by the citizens of Three Springs. It stated in part:

> We learn with pleasure that your transfer to Beverley means promotion for you. In this regard, you have the double consolation of knowing that you have advanced in favour with the superiors of your department, without forfeiting the good-will and esteem of the citizens among whom you have lived.[17]

Ralph's school reports for the period 1918–22 show a consistent pattern of high attendance, visits by his father on average three or four times during his school year, and distinctions in all subjects except maths. His final report states that he 'should do well and should now specialise in English and History'.[18] It was sound advice, and he took it.

A further critical change came over the Honner family during Ralph's last year at Perth Modern School. On 25 July 1922, Richard Honner resigned from the Western Australian Police Force.[19] The circumstances of that resignation are clouded in some mystery. Ralph's sister Mary remembered that at Beverley the children had 'fowls, a cow and a police horse to feed morning and night'.[20] However, it would seem that the police horse had an additional quality—speed. 'Candidate' had been selected by Richard Honner not only for police duties but, with young Clem Honner as jockey, for its racing potential. Perhaps Clem and Candidate achieved too much success, as it is known that 'the powers that be found out'.[21] Richard's resignation did not coincide with a completed year of service (in terms of holiday pay), and it is therefore likely that his resignation was encouraged. Further, the generous Richard had gone guarantor on two occasions for friends in Dalwallinu and

had lost a considerable amount of money honouring his obligations.[22] Eleanor Honner's reaction was predictable. All family
monies, investments and bookkeeping duties were now totally
(not mostly, as had previously been the case) under her jurisdiction. Richard received a payout of 471 pounds, 16 shillings
and 10 pence,[23] and the Honners moved to 'Cheltenham Park',
the family property at Dalwallinu.

Three critical events shaped Ralph Honner's life during the
period 1923–25: the extraordinary impact of his tertiary education; the gradual emergence of the athlete; and, last but not
least, the love of a woman that was to variously transcend or
surmount depression, war, religion and intermittent separation
for most of their life together.

In 1923, at eighteen years of age, Ralph entered Claremont
Teachers College and, as a consequence, undertook a Bachelor
of Arts degree at the University of Western Australia. It was
not an uncommon career path for the times for students without
financial means, as bonded student teachers could look to all
educational fees being paid by the government in return for a
period of teaching service after graduation.

For his Bachelor of Arts, 1923–25, Ralph majored in English
and Modern History. But such study became no mere path to
an academic qualification and a teaching career but rather the
lofty illumination of his Catholic ideals. His courses of study and,
it will be shown, his subsequent behaviour and writings reveal
an extraordinary grounding and influence in two key concepts—
the age of chivalry and the epic. And the historical and literary
background from which they emerged was strictly Catholic,
having flourished when Europe was called Christendom.
Honner's university courses, reading lists[24] and comprehensive
samples of his writing drew the following observations:

> It [his Catholicism] would have opened his mind certainly
> to the Catholic Middle Ages in his history and literary stud-
> ies . . . if you're a Catholic and particularly a Catholic who's
> over about fifty, you're half way there . . . half way to an
> understanding of the Middle Ages. There's no Australian lit-
> erature here, it's all English English. There's no American
> literature. A bit of Chaucer, Shakespeare, Milton, Byron,
> Macaulay—you wouldn't get Macaulay nowadays—Ruskin,
> you wouldn't get him nowadays, Pope . . . Wordsworth,

Carlyle. He'd have loved it! It's based on British models very closely.[25]

In *Chivalry: Its historical significance and civilising influence,* Dean Kitchin remarked that:

> At its highest, and in theory, chivalry sets before us the perfect gentleman—gently born, gentle-mannered, truthful, faithful, courteous to women, pure, brave and fearless, unsparing of self, filled with deep religious feeling, bowing before God and womenkind, but haughty in the presence of others.[26]

Ralph Honner aspired to all of the above qualities, although he might well have been described as aloof, distant and even shy, rather than haughty. In the present age, where chivalry is considered by many to be worthy of disdain, largely irrelevant, and the concept of the Holy Grail is more the realm of Monty Python than of the Crusades, Honner appears lost in a far-gone age. But the age of chivalry gave shape to Ralph Honner's unshakeable, immovable set of Catholic ideals. The barbarism and strict social-class division and the fact that the human deed often failed to reach the exalted heights of the ideal were not the issues of chivalry to Honner: it was the purity of the ideal and the heroism of the quest that mattered. The second exemplar that shaped Ralph's view of history in both its past and future forms was the epic.

An epic is a long narrative poem written about a momentous, serious subject and concerned with a heroic or quasi-divine figure on whose deeds depend the ultimate fate of a nation or mankind. Honner read and was captivated by the great epics: *The Song of Roland, El Cid, Paradise Lost, The Iliad* and, of course, by what he considered the ultimate epic—the epic of Christ. The critical point is that Ralph Honner lived a dream of chivalry and the epic. He had a view of life as being both beautiful and tragic. You had, he believed, to live and die—with absolutely no half-measures—by what you believed in.

Thus, when Ralph Honner went to war, he sought to re-enact the great epics and, crucially, he saw his soldiers in that exalted light. It is no mere coincidence that his children were to be named according to his Catholic and epic ideals—Richard Michael Honner, 'Michael' named after St Michael; Brian Roland Honner, 'Roland' from the *Song of Roland*;

Margaret Cecile, 'Cecile' after the martyred patron saint of music; and John Roderick Honner, 'Roderick' from *El Cid*. Ralph Honner, and later his children, would have privately rejoiced that St Hyacinth had not claimed an epic. In a strong measure, Ralph's writing style also reflected his education. Humphrey Tranter:

> . . . the style is a bit old fashioned and flowery, but that's partly the man and partly the period—not entirely the period because contemporaries of his had a more straightforward, more Australian style. Honner's style is Edwardian, and in fact, it's more English than Australian I think . . . there's a lot of Bible in it . . . it's strongly adjectival . . . it's a mannered style and it draws attention to itself, you notice it.[27]

Ralph Honner's Edwardian writing style was, therefore, an extension of his ideals and epic view of the world and life. When he journeyed to the Middle East, Greece and Crete with his 2/11th Battalion, led the 39th Battalion in Papua and the 2/14th Battalion in New Guinea, he was in fact acting out his own and his soldiers' romantic epic. It will be shown that very many of his deeds, and most certainly his writings, illustrate the point. But there was a further aspect to both the man and his writing. Humphrey Tranter:

> Oh certainly he was a romantic, there's no doubt about it! The man has a very deeply romantic imagination. Mind you the word romantic is not a very precise word. What we really mean is that this is a man with imagination, a man who could make imaginative leaps, a man who could connect . . . history has got to be based on facts, but facts aren't enough to write history with. You've got to interpret it and interpretation involves imagination; it involves making imaginary leaps.[28]

The second major event during the period of Ralph's tertiary education was his rapid transformation from the frail boy of Perth Modern School ('squib') to the accomplished athlete during the 1920s. The remarkable quality of that transformation was that it was self-induced.

During his last year at Perth Modern School Ralph experienced a rapid, if late, physical growth spurt. By the time he entered teachers' college he stood just on 6 feet in height. And he experienced a unique body-building course by modern standards: not that of the modern gymnasium with its weight-lifting programs, or aerobic classes or isometric exercises, but the demanding and exacting test of Albert Facey's Australia. Farm life at 'Cheltenham Park', Dalwallinu, during the early 1920s was one of the last vestiges of pioneering Australia.

The land at Cheltenham Park was mainly small scrub and gimlet, and used more for wheat-growing than grazing. The Honner homestead was a small four- or five-room weatherboard dwelling with an iron roof and rainwater tanks.[29] Ralph's nephew John (Clem's son):

> The land was rolled on by a big roller about three metres long and two metres high. This would break down all the scrub or bush and it would be burnt when it was all dead. The big trees were cut down with an axe. Water was always short and a lot of time was taken up carting water from the Government Dam. At Daly [Dalwallinu] there was not a lot of sheep. Cows for milk but mostly cropping up to 3000 acres of wheat. Prior to 1926 Grandpa and the boys put the crop in and took it off. The farm was just average farm land, but by very hard work and thrift they got a living.[30]

Ralph's holidays were spent working on the farm. There was land to clear, fences to erect, crops to be harvested, and wheat to be bagged, sewn and taken to the railhead by horse. Each bag weighed about 180 pounds. At night the four boys often played cards by hurricane lamp. Ralph seemed always to win at bridge as, according to Clem, 'after a few hands had been played Ralph could tell exactly who had what and what cards were to come because he could remember all the cards'.[31] And mother's influence still prevailed. John Honner recalled an incident with his father Clem many years later that personifies the Honner family attitude to life:

> . . . one day I was going out in the ute to get Clem who had taken our Caterpillar Bulldozer out to do some clearing. Apparently a stick came up & punctured the radiator. Clem had taken it off & had carried it almost all the way home, about one-and-a-half miles before I met him. The radiator & surround would have weighed about 180–200 lb. Dad had it on his shoulder like a bag of wheat. When I asked him why he didn't wait for me & just walk home . . . he said simply, 'that his mother never raised a JIB'. ie., a Jib was a horse that wouldn't pull . . .[32]

'Jibs' were not contemplated in the Honner family. There was an expectation, an unspoken demand, that quiet, resolute forbearance would tame the land and both endure its hardships and facilitate humble thanks for its gifts. Ralph's time at university thus nurtured his intellectual and spiritual self and strengthened his body. But what of the heart?

His sister remembered visits by Ralph in Perth during those years, usually on every second Sunday—and 'usually with a lady friend'.[33] There must have been some romantic interaction during this period, but each relationship could not have lasted for long. By the end of his time at university, a woman named Marjory Bennett had entered his life.

Marjory Collier Bennett was one of eleven children (two died in infancy) born to Thomas and May Bennett. She was born at North Perth on 4 September 1905. Her father saw service as a postmaster in a number of country towns in Western Australia and she, like Ralph, had gained entrance to Perth Modern School by scholarship. While at Perth Modern, she boarded at Malcolm Street, Perth, with her sisters Gwen and Pauline. Ian Bennett, Marjory's brother, remembered his sister as 'very lovable, affectionate, vivacious . . . always bubbling over'.[34] Ian Bennett:

> The story goes in the family . . . that she took one look at Ralph at Perth Modern School, and said, 'I'm going to marry him, and that's for sure!' She'd made that announcement to her sisters.[35]

Years later, when Marjory went to a Perth Modern School reunion, one of the subjects under discussion was 'who had married whom'. When Marjory's turn came, the response was, 'Not the boy with the dirty knees!'[36] The 'boy with the dirty knees' became 'My Ralphie' in a relationship that was to last 69 years. And the boy who kept himself on a shilling a week and also kept a ledger at Perth Modern School would spend the rest of his life being remembered as a smart dresser, always immaculately presented. Times were changing. It was not as if Ralph had much money, but dressing well had become an understandable priority. John Honner, Ralph's son:

> According to dad, the first time he took notice of Mum was when some of his mates at teachers' college came back and said that this Marjory Bennett was a real tiger on the

hockey field. And dad liked courage and liked guts and I think from that moment on their lives were bound up with each other.[37]

Marjory was to represent her state and achieve All-Australian status as a hockey player. An early example of the Honner sense of pragmatism and a feel for tactics in the field came during a series of wet, muddy hockey matches that Marjory participated in during their time in Teachers College. Ralph suggested that the use of 'sprigs' or 'stops' might alleviate Marjory's difficulty in staying on her feet during matches. The theory was acted on: the on-field success was startling, but 'Ralphie' drew the ire of the opposition and spectators alike as having instigated an unfair advantage.[38] It is not known whether the tactic was withdrawn or adopted by all.

Ralph and Marjory became unofficially engaged in 1925. Both began their teaching careers in 1927 (it would seem that Ralph completed his Bachelor of Arts in 1925 and then completed his teaching qualification the following year). He received notification of his first teaching appointment while on holidays at Cheltenham Park in early 1927. The letter was addressed to 'Miss Hyacinth Honner' and advised 'her' that 'she' was to teach at Kalgoorlie. This was the last straw. He is reported to have said to his mother, 'Mum, they think I'm a sheila!'[39] The author has been unable to find any further written or oral evidence of 'Hyacinth'. From this time on, the man's name was 'Ralph Honner'.

It is known that Ralph taught for some time at Kalgoorlie and Marjory at Pinjarra. But in mid-1929 Ralph was offered the position of Senior House Master at the prestigious Hale School in Perth. The offer was fortuitous, as Ralph had decided to pursue a career in law. The position at Hale School would allow him to attend evening lectures at law school, maintain his living as a teacher, and receive free board and lodging as the school's house master.

In a letter dated 1 August 1992 (sixteen days before his eighty-eighth birthday), Ralph wrote to Bill Edgar, the archivist at Hale School. The letter is both a comprehensive description of the school teaching structure during Honner's time, and a remarkable illustration of his memory:

In 1929 Headmaster Le Couteur appointed me Senior Housemaster . . .

The following table correlates class nomenclature. I can't remember whether Hale form numbers were Arabic or Roman [Honner then outlined the classes in detail]. The only year with sufficient numbers to form two classes for compulsory subjects was the Junior Certificate year. The brighter boys were selected for 5A; the rest went into 5B. With 5B as well as 5A allotted to the Junior year, the Sub Junior class was called the Remove. Although Mathematics, Sciences and Languages demanded a two-year syllabus for the Leaving Certificate, the humanities—English, History, Geography had a one-year syllabus. Numbers were low in the depression years and 6A and 6B were combined into one class for those humanities, the boys doing a Leaving Certificate course of study each year they were in the class—and taking the Leaving examination in their first year in it if they wished . . .

I also added the book-selling job . . . The Headmaster decided on the year's books. I ordered them and the stationery, and sold them to the boys from the book-room in which they were stored. There was a continual negotiation with changes and additions of stock and reconciling of accounts, and stock-taking reviews . . .

There was no school library . . .

There were young ladies teaching the smallest boys. They did not share the Masters' Common Room opposite the Headmaster's Office. Each form had a form-master (or mistress) who monitored attendance and collated examination marks for his form—for reports, promotions, prizes. I was form-master of the Remove. I taught its English, History, Geography, Mathematics as well as Geography in 6A, 6B and 4A and English in 5B and (after Clarke's departure in 1931) 6A and 6B.[40]

There were 35–40 boarders during Ralph's time at Hale School with fees set at 30 pounds per term. Two tennis courts were on the school grounds and a football and cricket oval in Kings Park;[41] there were four dormitories: one was empty, and one each for the junior, intermediate and senior boys; and the food was adequate, although the boys were 'always hungry'.[42] Time was allowed on Sundays for students to walk in Kings Park with relatives, 'except when we nicked out to the movies under the lap'.[43]

Ralph's Hale School students called him 'Reg', the reason

Some of Hale School's masters (Ralph is second from right).

for which the author has been unable to establish. Dr J.B. Craig
was a boarder at the time:

> Always dignified, reserved & slightly aloof, he was a man I
> greatly respected and admired . . . about six feet tall, hair short
> & swept back . . . always immaculately groomed & dressed,
> head held high & with a handsome face & direct clear eyes
> with a firm look but not unkind or uncaring in any way, but
> perceptive & knowing. He was engaged to marry . . . an
> extremely beautiful & nice girl in WA whom we had seen
> with him, & were all very jealous! This, of course, raised his
> standing in our eyes, very much! . . .
>
> If one 'got the cuts' from Reg, you NEVER came back
> for more! for he hit hard & very accurately. I got one lot from
> him (for what I thought was not my fault, but saw that he
> had to take action), 3 on the tips of my left hand fingers—*right*

on the tips, each time. Boy, they hurt!! But, he *did* only give me three, not six, & there was no viciousness or anger associated. It did me more good than harm & I certainly didn't look for more ever again.[44]

Keith Prescod, a 'Dago' (the boarders' term for a day student), also remembered 'Reg' as well dressed, quiet and reserved.[45]

Ralph Honner was destined to meet some of his ex-students on the battlefields of the Middle East and, for some of them, in tragic circumstances at Gona Mission some twelve years later.

During the period 1929–32 Ralph taught at Hale School, supervised his young boarders and studied for his LLB degree, which was conferred in 1933. Interspersed with these activities, he pursued his love of sport with a consistent passion. He would later write:

> I represented the University in a variety of sports and competed in the highest grade in the State in three of them, Australian Football, Rugby Union Football and Athletics. When the University A.C. [Athletics Club] won its first premiership of the W.A. Amateur Athletic Association in 1930 I was its President. The standard of Australian Football is too high for a University to be able to compete in its top grade, but I played 'A' Grade football for Claremont in the W.A. National Football League, starting in 1926 and finishing in 1932. Thereafter, until war broke out at the end of the 1939 season, I played for the University in the W.A. Amateur Football Association, being selected as a centre, in the state amateur sides of 1934 and 1935. My one year of competition Rugger was 1929 when we played that game on Sundays for relaxation after Australian football on Saturdays; but when the Rugby Union games were changed to Saturdays in 1930 I had to forego that pleasure.[46]

Ralph's years at Hale School were not without controversy. In a letter dated 6 June 1992, Ralph described his brush with authority 62 years earlier:

> I had three Junior Housemasters under me on slave wages (they were inexperienced) and when they had their salaries cut 10% in 1930 (depression) and were told to go and live elsewhere during school holidays at Easter (I was not affected, spending my holidays as usual at Rottnest with Marjory) I went to bat with the Head on their behalf and they retained bed and board privileges. But Le Couteur recommended to

Ralph as best man at Clem's wedding (Ralph is third from left).

his successor, Buntine, that I be sacked as a trouble-maker. Buntine did give me notice of the sack but changed his mind and promoted me to Senior English Master.[47]

In 1933 Ralph began his articles with the prestigious Perth law firm of Parker and Parker. It was a tough time. The nation was still in the grip of the Great Depression and young lawyers completing their articles were paid a pittance. His relationship with Marjory had now been in existence for some eight or nine years and, while both desired marriage, money was always the prohibiting factor, as female teachers were compelled to resign

Marjory Honner.

their teaching positions on marriage. But on 2 June 1934, Reverend Father Kelly presided over their wedding at St Patrick's Catholic Church in West Perth. The ceremony took place in the sacristy, as Marjory was not a Catholic, and few resources were allotted to the wedding as neither family—given the large number of siblings in each—could afford much. Ralph was 29 and his bride 28.

Mr and Mrs Ralph Honner settled into marital bliss at Nedlands in Perth. Ralph's sister Mary often stayed with them and remembered that they led a very spartan life. Ralph used to go to work with his Gladstone bag and buy shopping articles that were on special which Marjory had previously identified. There was no radio, as the Honners could not afford the licence.[48] Mary Jeffs:

> He and Marjory were terribly poor when they got married. She said that if only Ralph had told her how things would be, she would have saved instead of spending. My mother often tried to lend Ralph a little money from her private source, but he always said no. If he couldn't live on his own, how could he pay back a loan? Marjy said they would be on their uppence, and along would come a couple of pounds from

Mum for someone's birthday or something. They had a very hard life but a very happy one for starters . . . they were a real team. I never ever heard them have a cross word . . . and I remember Marj saying once, 'You can't argue with an Honner, they just won't play!'[49]

Two of Ralph's children were born at Nedlands before he went to war—Richard Michael Honner (28 April 1936) and Brian Roland Honner (14 June 1938). By the time the Second World War began in September 1939, Ralph and Marjory Honner were really only just getting on their financial feet. If Ralph Honner's Catholic upbringing and the chivalric and epic aspects of his education had given him a vision of life in those terms, then his participation in history's greatest confrontation was about to provide him with an opportunity to re-enact that vision.

3

IT'S A CONFIDENCE BUSINESS

I couldn't do anything but join up because seeing the war coming, I had gone back into the militia in 1936; I had gone back to brushing up my French, German, Spanish and Italian and although I was over age, over 35, to be a junior officer in the AIF, I think if I hadn't made strenuous efforts to get in, I could hardly have held my head up again.[1]

Honner's statement, made in 1985, is a masterly piece of understatement. His devout Catholic upbringing had produced within him an unshakeable, lofty moral code, while his comprehensive study of European history and literature would shape its no less exalted expression, be it in deed or written word. The two had inculcated in him an ideal of service—great or small—free of personal gain, degradation or disparagement, for the weak by the strong. Adolf Hitler was a modern-day Apollyon, an incarnation of the devil, and just as Bunyan in his *Pilgrim's Progress* had created the noble warrior Christian to combat the devil, so it was Honner's duty to embark on his modern-day crusade.

Ralph Honner's joining of the Second AIF in October 1939 was no impulsive, rushed affair: it was neither a pursuit of nor a longing for adventure, nor for economic gain, but rather the perception of the duty of the citizen. The Second World War was, perhaps, the most clearly defined of conflicts, where the issues were relatively precise. Therefore, in Honner's eyes, service in Europe took the form of an obligation. The fact that he had rejoined the militia and had 'brushed up' on his European languages reflects both the sincerity and breadth of that preparation.

But Ralph Honner went to war with a further quality—an extraordinary sense of history, in both its actual and mythical forms, and a priceless ability to identify parallels between its past and present. It will be shown that the momentous events in which he participated were interpreted by him on a far more comprehensive scale than mere battles.

Two of Honner's languages were to prove militarily advantageous, but his Spanish and French were destined to prove inconsequential. It is interesting to note that Japanese was not considered to be part of his linguistic preparation for war, as, like that of most Australians, his cultural, political and military perception of the world looked almost exclusively to Europe.

The 6th Division was the first AIF formation raised. It consisted of the 16th Brigade, formed in New South Wales (the 2/1st, 2/2nd, 2/3rd and 2/4th Battalions), the 17th Brigade, raised in Victoria (the 2/5th, 2/6th, 2/7th and 2/8th Battalions), and the 18th Brigade, formed in Queensland (the 2/9th and two companies of the 2/12th), in South Australia (the 2/10th), in Tasmania (the remainder of the 2/12th) and in Western Australia (the 2/11th). Lieutenant-General Sir Thomas Blamey was chosen to lead the division. He selected Brigadier A.S. ('Tubby') Allen to command the 16th Brigade, Brigadier Stanley Savige to command the 17th Brigade, and Brigadier Leslie Morshead to command the 18th Brigade.[2]

When the 2/11th Battalion was raised in October 1939, its heritage could be traced with great pride by Western Australians over a short but illustrious service. On 13 September 1861, the Metropolitan Rifle Volunteers was raised in Perth. This unit was the direct ancestor of the 11th Battalion (the City of Perth Regiment). In recognition of the distinguished service of various contingents in the Boer War, the battle honour 'South Africa 1899–1902' was awarded to a number of Western Australian units before World War I, including the 11th Battalion.[3]

At the outbreak of the Great War, the 11th Battalion was raised in Western Australia. As part of the 3rd Brigade AIF the battalion was among the first to land at Anzac Cove on 25 April

Lieutenant-Colonel T.S. (Tom)
Louch, MC, ED, QC.

1915. The 11th Battalion was awarded 23 battle honours, of which the Somme 1916–18, Pozieres, Bullecourt, Ypres 1917, Menin Road, Hazebrouck, Amiens, Hindenburg Line, Landing at Anzac and Defence of Anzac are emblazoned on its regimental colours. The unit's proud name continued through the interwar years as the 11th Militia Battalion.[4]

The original CO of the 2/11th Battalion was Lieutenant-Colonel T.S. (Tom) Louch, MC. Captain Darrald McCaskill, 2/11th Battalion:

> A very good man. I don't suppose you could get a better commander . . . a bit cynical, he'd been through the mill of course and was a bit cynical of the bureaucrats . . . he was extremely efficient and very thorough and looked after his people well.[5]

Louch, a Perth lawyer, had served with the 11th and 51st Battalions during the Great War, and at the time of the formation of the 2/11th Battalion was CO of the 16th Militia Battalion. He would later write that:

> Major Sandover commanded the H.Q. Wing, Captain Heagney A Company, Captain Norris B Company and Captain Honner C Company. Half the remaining officers came from the 16th Battalion and the remainder from the list given me by the DAAG. I did not fill all the vacancies at the time, but

left room for the promotion of some ten or more from the ranks of the Battalion.[6]

Louch did not mention that the then Lieutenant Honner was not his first choice as OC C Company. He had originally sought a fellow 16th Militia Battalion officer, Captain Arnold Buntine (the then Hale School principal under whom Ralph had worked), but when that officer decided his place was at Hale, Honner had become the next choice. Louch must have had some contact with Honner, as the offices of Parker and Parker were directly across Howard Street in Perth from Robinson, Cox and Wheatley, in which law firm Louch was a partner.[7]

The 6th Division AIF was to nurture many outstanding leaders for subsequent AIF and already established militia units. Of the original officers of the 2/11th, thirteen were destined for brigade or battalion command or staff appointments. Two points are worthy of mention concerning the quality of the original officers of the 6th Division. The first is that, on the whole, COs were able to select their junior officers from local knowledge of militia formations. Such selections usually proved succinct. Second, the early Middle East battles were destined to provide a very good chance to weed out the few poor choices— both officers and other ranks.

While the other two company commanders were simply allotted their recruits (at the beginning of the war each battalion raised three, not four, rifle companies), Lieutenant Honner instigated a rather unique process of selecting his soldiers for C Company service. Lieutenant K.T. Johnson, C Company, 2/11th Battalion, remembered that:

> Honner, in selecting the soldiers coming in, went for largely Kalgoorlie people, they were miners and had earnt their living on the end of a shovel. He wanted to know in questioning them, did they play sport, football, and what club . . . then he got quite a few out of the Great Southern (we call the Great Southern going down from Perth to Albany), farming people. There'd be fifty soldiers . . . coming in, and they were going to be allocated A, B, C . . . so he'd say, 'Well, he looks a likely type, we'll grab him.' And, 'Have you got a mate?' So we finished up with a lot of Kalgoorlie people.[8]

Honner's selection process was not perfect. Four men were dishonourably discharged by the end of January.[9] But the

overwhelming majority of those soldiers were magnificent physical specimens, mainly within the 25–30-year age range. Honner
served with three battalions during the war and fought alongside
many more. Although he might be accused of the not unusual
bias that most company commanders felt for their troops, he
often spoke with great affection of the immense physical bearing, stamina and fierce individualism of his C Company, 2/11th
Battalion. He had hand-picked a magnificent body of men and
he resolved at once that his was the responsibility to weld them
into an elite company.[10]

If their commander had joined the AIF for the perceived
duty of a citizen, had 'brushed up' on his four foreign languages,
and had come to serve others and the nation, a number of his
other ranks had less lofty ideals and were far less articulate.
Private Harry Johnson, MM, C Company:

> They were all volunteers . . . very free spirits, they were fairly
> strong and tough, a lot of them were miners and workers from
> all around the place, come from up the bush . . . I was sworn
> in about eleven o'clock on the eleventh day of the eleventh
> month. We came down from Kalgoorlie, a train load of us,
> and picked up a bloke from Northam on the way through.
> We marched out and this bloke was blind drunk and he had
> a pot hanging around his neck . . . we didn't even know what
> a German looked like . . .[11]

Corporal Cecil Rogers, C Company:

> I joined because there were three of us . . . we used to go
> to parades once a week, once a fortnight . . . we were issued
> with a uniform and a rifle and we used to get it thrown up
> to us that we were bloody chocolate soldiers and the day that
> war was declared the three of us, we got our heads together,
> we said, 'Right! It's been good enough for us to do military
> training, it's good enough for us to enlist!' We put our names
> in right from the start.[12]

Corporal Bernie Rogers, C Company:

> I was happy to swap a trip around the world at the army's
> expense in return for carrying a rifle for them.[13]

Nor were educated, cultured or sensitive minds the inventors
of Lieutenant Honner's nickname: he was, much to his later

Corporal Harry Johnson, MM,   *Corporal Bernie Rogers,*
C Company, 2/11th Battalion.   *C Company, 2/11th Battalion.*

amusement, christened 'Jump' as a suitable prefix to his surname.[14]

The first draft of volunteers were sent to Northam Camp, about 96 kilometres due east of Perth. The camp was in such an early stage of construction that the first rifle aiming rest built was made from 'borrowed' timber and nails from the YMCA hut under construction nearby.[15] The battalion was at Northam for only three weeks before receiving orders to join its other 18th Brigade battalions in New South Wales. Service dress was issued just prior to embarkation, and the battalion arrived first at Rutherford and then Greta in the Newcastle district, some 125 kilometres north of Sydney, in mid-December.[16] It was during the voyage to New South Wales that Honner officially assumed the rank of Captain, with effect from 13 October 1939.[17]

The battalion's training at Greta was handicapped by a lack of war equipment; as a consequence, a number of the free-spirited 2/11th recruits took some time to settle down. Lieutenant-Colonel Louch:

> Discipline has to be maintained . . . however, occasionally a glint of humour relieved the proceedings. Private B came

before me charged with having used offensive language to the
Sergeant of Police at Greta; and when asked what he had to
say, his reply to the charge was: 'I only done one thing wrong.
I forgot to call the bastard Sir'.[18]

When the 16th Brigade departed for the Middle East in
January 1940, the 18th Brigade occupied their former camp at
Ingleburn. The 2/11th was stationed at this camp for about
eight weeks and received two or three 30-cwt trucks, a few
Bren guns, a Stokes mortar and an anti-tank rifle. No ammunition was provided for the anti-tank rifle or the mortar.[19] The
provision of equipment for the AIF in Australia at this time
thus severely prohibited training, and it was anticipated that
formations would complete training in the Middle East.

The 2/11th returned to Perth at the end of March 1940,
engaged in a brief exercise, and sailed for the Middle East
on 20 April 1940 on the British troopship *Nevasa*. Lieutenant-
Colonel Louch recalled the voyage:

> The ship had little refrigerated space, and had been used to
> making comparatively short journeys with not more than four
> or five days between ports, so that it could take on water and
> fresh provisions. When the war broke out she had finished her
> useful career and was about to be broken up. Instead she was
> diverted at the last moment and sent to convey troops from
> Australia to the Middle East—a task for which she was quite
> unfitted. She carried only a skeleton crew—mostly Indian—and
> the Standing Orders provided that so many men were to be
> detailed for duties that I noted in my diary: 'It would seem
> that the troops are expected to do nearly everything except
> navigate the ship and fire the boilers'.[20]

If the 2/11th Battalion's voyage to the Middle East was an
uncomfortable one, then a demand placed in transit on the
corporals of C Company by their OC was even more so.
Corporal Bernie Rogers was one of them:

> He [Honner] was so keen on perfection that on the boat going
> over . . . he got us corporals all nine of us, and said he wanted
> the nine best corporals in the battalion, and while we had been
> promoted to corporals he wanted to make sure that he ended
> up with the best, and he wanted our resignations, that he could
> hold and use if we didn't measure up to what he believed.

We were young and enthusiastic in those days and we signed the forms.[21]

Honner had no right—moral or legal—to make such a request, and, had there been a complaint, the enthusiastic captain may have found himself in a deal of trouble. Ralph would have been only too well aware of his transgression but, no matter, he *was* going to have the best possible junior leadership for his other ranks.

On 19 May 1940 the battalion arrived at Kilo 89 in Palestine. This camp was destined to be its home for six months. It was joined by the 2/4th and 2/8th Battalions to constitute the newly formed 19th Australian Infantry Brigade. Before the 2/11th had left Australia, the Army had decided to reorganise its structure. Each infantry brigade was required to reduce its strength from four battalions to three. As a consequence, the 16th, 17th and 18th Brigades were each required to furnish one battalion to form a 19th Brigade. The 16th Brigade surrendered its last numbered battalion, the 2/4th; the 17th Brigade likewise supplied the 2/8th; but the 18th Brigade, as part of the third convoy to the Middle East, had been diverted to England. The 2/11th Battalion therefore took the place of the 2/12th as the 18th Brigade's contribution to the new formation. Originally formed to act as the first brigade of the 7th Division, the 19th Brigade was now incorporated back into the 6th Division.

The anticipated equipment that had retarded the training of the 6th Division in Australia was not yet available in the Middle East. Lieutenant-Colonel Louch:

. . . the Ordnance cupboard was almost bare . . .
    For a long time our only vehicles were a taxi-cab from Jerusalem with an Arab chauffeur, and a hired truck. Eventually all our vehicles came from Australia.[22]

When the 2/11th Battalion began training in earnest, C Company, as a matter of pride (and astute leadership), was required to march further, march faster, and dig in when its march to a venue was completed, no matter what the time of day or the physical state of the troops. Although 35 years of age, the non-smoking and frugal-drinking Honner 'could march all day and at top pace—he was at the top of his form'.[23] Equipment was rotated by company, which allowed for improved section, platoon and company training.

The 2/11th had occasional leave during this period, which inevitably included some frequenting of brothels by various members of the battalion. Honner, as did many officers in the division, had the occasional task of supervision of both the premises and the soldiers. When discussing this time in the Middle East the author, tongue in cheek, felt obliged to ask the obvious question—did he indulge? The answer was immediate and sincere: 'No, first on moral grounds, and secondly, Marjory would have known'.

In November 1940 the 2/11th moved to Burg el Arab about 48 kilometres west of Alexandria, where a divisional exercise was undertaken. The 16th and 17th Brigades were given the task of attacking the 19th at Burg el Arab. The exercise was to be made 'as realistic as possible'.[24] From positions about 3 kilometres south of the railway line the 2/11th could see the 17th Brigade concentrating about a kilometre-and-a-half away in likely preparation for an all-out attack the next day. B and C Company patrols sent out during the night raided a 17th Brigade battalion HQ on two occasions. When one of Honner's patrols raided it a third time, the battalion CO bitterly complained that he 'had been assured by Captain Honner that he would not be captured again'.[25] If the exercise was realistic, the reaction of the brigade commander was no less so—the thrice-captured battalion commander was removed before his battalion went into action at Bardia.

During the period of training before Bardia a strong emphasis was placed on aggressive night patrolling, of which accurate navigation was a prime part. Honner and C Company, 2/11th Battalion, regularly practised the procedure, and when the company commander was less than satisfied with his own performance another aspect of his style of command became apparent. Private Harry Johnson, MM:

> . . . one of the Jump's blinkin' top things was navigation. On one occasion we went for a march, a night march and he took us out—our company lines were all on the south edge of the battalion area and he took us out for about three quarters of an hour turn left, another three quarters of an hour turn left again, and marched us back. And it was pitch dark, you couldn't see two blokes in front of you and when we came

back to the camp area we came into a transport platoon . . .
we came in through lines to our end . . . and he lined us up
and apologised for hitting the camp in the wrong place. About
two hundred yards.[26]

On 9 December 1940 Lieutenant-General O'Connor's British Western Desert Force, consisting of the 4th Indian and 7th
Armoured Divisions, attacked the Italians at Sidi Barrani in
western Egypt. After two days' fighting, the Italian fortress fell.
In the light of this stunning victory, General Iven Mackay, who
had replaced General Blamey as GOC 6th Division when the
latter had been given the 1st Australian Corps command, was
ordered to move his division to relieve the 4th Indian Division
and assume the right flank of the British advance. The next
objective was the coastal Libyan town and port of Bardia. The
16th Brigade moved out along the desert road on 12 December
followed by the divisional HQ and the 17th Brigade on
22 December. The 19th Brigade—of which Honner's 2/11th
Battalion was a part—was to follow later. Brigadier Robertson
was to move his brigade by sea from Alexandria to occupy
Bardia should the Italians decide to evacuate that position. But
the Italians had decided to stay and fight. Bardia was to be the
Australian Army's first action of World War II.

To defend Cyrenaica from British invasion, the Italians
fortified the two easternmost coastal towns of Bardia and
Tobruk. Bardia lay about 24 kilometres across the Egyptian
border while Tobruk lay about a further 96 kilometres west.
Part of the town of Bardia lay on the top of a cliff overlooking
the northern part of the bay, and the remainder of the town
lay below the cliff on the harbour. The Official Historian, Gavin
Long, described the Italian Bardia defences:

> At great expense of labour, steel and concrete, they had dug
> a defensive line in the form of an arc eighteen miles in length
> round the little harbour and garrison town . . . they consisted
> of an almost continuous anti-tank ditch and behind it a double
> line of underground posts, the front line being linked by rows
> of barbed wire. The posts in the forward line were generally
> about 800 yards apart and were protected by their own
> anti-tank trench (later found to be connected by a roof of
> thin boards). They were armed with one or two 47 mm guns
> and from two to four machine-guns. The guns were fired
> from concrete-sided pits connected by trenches with a deep

underground shelter which occupied most of the area of the
post . . .

Four hundred yards behind the forward line lay a second
arc of posts, similar but lacking an anti-tank trench and
sometimes without wire . . .

Within this perimeter aerial photography revealed a considerable array of artillery, estimated at 110 guns, and some
long stone breastworks. Each flank of the line lay on the inner
bank of one of the steep-sided wadis carved into the cliffs
forming the coast from Salum northwards, but elsewhere the
posts were in flat, almost featureless ground offering little cover
to an attacker, and few landmarks.[27]

British and Australian intelligence estimated that the Italian
fortress contained about 25 000 soldiers.

The Australian attack on Bardia envisaged Brigadier Allen's
16th Brigade moving before dawn on 3 January 1941 from a
position about 1600 metres from and parallel to the Italian posts
of 45, 46 and 47, which were positioned about 3 kilometres
south of the Tobruk–Bardia Road. Through the 16th Brigade
breach, Brigadier Savige's 17th Brigade was to exploit with two
battalions while its third battalion was to hold the right flank.
The 19th Brigade was to constitute the divisional reserve. The
Australian 6th Division saw its baptism of fire at Bardia as a test
which was to be evaluated against the superb record of the
First AIF.

The initial results were stunning. The 16th Brigade swept
through the Italian defences and almost immediately found that
the collection and supervision of its demoralised enemy presented its greatest problem: the anticipated 25 000 Italians were
actually 40 000 in strength and they were surrendering in
enormous numbers. It is at this juncture that a certain degree
of controversy entered the Bardia battle. When the 17th Brigade
sought to exploit the 16th Brigade's success, its progress was
not as speedy as anticipated. Gavin Long would later write:

During the morning of 4th January while Savige was planning
to end the Italian resistance in the pocket his brigade had now
surrounded, by making a night attack from the north and west,
he did not know that, at the same time, MacKay's staff were
writing orders for an attack through his area next morning by
the fresh 19th Brigade, with tanks and behind an artillery

barrage. While this attack was being made Savige's battalions were to stand and watch the new troops pass . . .

In effect, the tired but resolute 17th Brigade had been halted.[28]

Brigadier Robertson chose the 2/11th Battalion to lead the attack, with his 2/4th ready to exploit and his 2/8th assigned to protect the left flank and clear the coastal area. Captain Honner could not have known when and where the 2/11th Battalion would first go into action, but he had taken precautions to ensure that his company would be the first involved—he had extracted a promise from Louch.[29]

The biographer is blessed with a subject who had a determination to record both his and his men's actions for posterity (and for his future use) in as much detail as possible. Ralph Honner's letters to Marjory during his Middle East campaigning begin and end with words that portray his deep and abiding love for his wife, but the substance of that correspondence constitutes a meticulous diary of his experiences that were added to soon after the war by separate notes, and also classified by an intricate cataloguing system that was in turn used to write a series of detailed articles for publication. These letters, written in Ralph's immaculate handwriting, contain some 600–700 words per page and number, on average, three to four pages. The chivalrous soldier had certainly gone to war in 1940, but the astute, painstaking scholar and writer were no less part of the journey. His first letter is a case in point: it begins with 'My best beloved' and concludes with 'It's growing too dark to write sweet, so on the wind I whisper "I love you"— O wind carry those words home to my true love—and say so long. Ralph'. Two large kisses end the work, obviously intended for sons Richard and Brian. Between those two romantic efforts is to be found an approximately 4000-word Bardia diary (numbered B1–6) of Ralph's experiences of 4–16 January 1941. The handwriting is about 3 millimetres in height to facilitate the 600–700 words per page. To placate the censor, the 16th Brigade is referred to as the 'Push Brigade' (the letter 'P' being the sixteenth letter of the alphabet), the 17th Brigade became the 'Quiet Brigade' ('Q' being the seventeenth) and the 19th Brigade became the 'Shock Brigade' ('S' being the nineteenth).[30]

Lieutenants K.T. Johnson (left) and Arthur McRobbie.

At about 7 am on Sunday 5 January 1941, Honner and his three platoon commanders, Lieutenants McRobbie (13 Platoon), Johnson (14 Platoon) and Bedells (15 Platoon), set off in the company utility to examine the ground 'over which we might be expected to attack'.[31] The utility arrived at the Scemmas Wadi, where it encountered a portion of the front line of the 2/5th Battalion. Through a misunderstanding, Honner got back into the vehicle and proceeded to cross the flat, featureless no-man's land. While looking for the now non-existent forward elements of the 17th Brigade (he had just left those), he decided to drive to a line of telegraph posts that he concluded might be useful as a start line for an attack. As he jumped from the still-moving utility, compass in hand and eyes fixed on the line of telegraph poles, he quickly realised that he had landed on the edge of a wadi. Ralph's Bardia letter to Marjory:

> . . . we saw we were in the middle of an Italian artillery battery with 100 men within a hundred yds of us. I leaped back to the truck and got my pistol while Katy Johnson seized the driver's rifle. At that the four nearest Italians put up their hands—they couldn't see we were alone as they were in a gully and we had just driven up to the edge of it. I yelled 'Avanti'—advance—to the dagoes—and up they came.[32]

Lieutenant Jack Bedells.

Honner's driver, Private Quinlan, was ordered to immediately turn the vehicle around and leave the engine running while the four prisoners were loaded into the back to ensure that the party would not be fired on as they beat a hasty retreat. Honner had therefore reconnoitred the ground over which he would soon stage an attack, and had returned with four prisoners in the process. It is suggested that, on balance, if the enemy had been German or perhaps other Italians, Captain Honner's short military career might have come to an abrupt and embarrassing end.

When Ralph returned to Battalion HQ, Lieutenant-Colonel Louch had only just received orders for an attack, which was set for 9.15 am. C Company on the left and B Company on the right were to comprise the advance, followed by A and D Companies. Six infantry tanks were placed in support under Honner's command. Louch could have requested an alteration to the artillery timetable, but he was reluctant to do this as he had seen, during his World War I experience, the consequences of meddling with such plans at the last minute. This was explained to Honner and his platoon commanders.[33] Louch therefore decided that C Company would have to keep to the artillery barrage plan regardless of time. It is at this juncture that Captain Honner's demanding standards of physical fitness and training were to pay off. Ralph to Marjory:

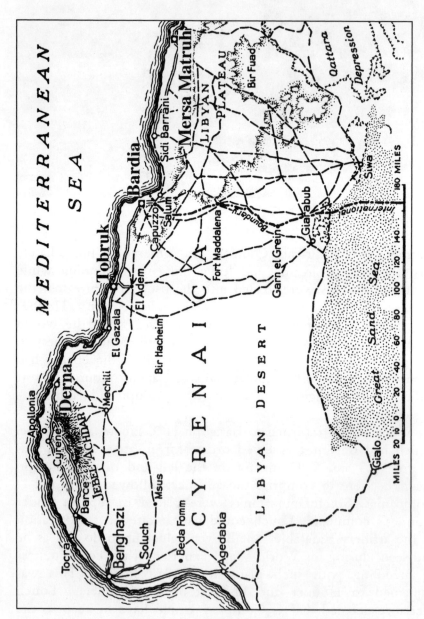

Bardia.

> We had to cross a line three miles away at 9.15. It took me
> 15 minutes to get back to my company—half-a-mile away—
> give orders for the attack, and get the company moving. That
> left us half an hour to do the 3 miles and we just managed it.[34]

Honner's C Company soldiers were equipped with their weapons, 100 rounds of ammunition, four grenades per section, steel
helmets, one day's ration of bully beef and biscuit, respirators,
a haversack, and some wore long underwear and balaclavas. To
have double-timed their way to the start line over 3 miles and
then gone straight into battle, at a solid pace, was a magnificent
feat.[35] As the company moved forward, past about 100 prisoners
Honner's small reconnaissance party had 'captured' earlier that
morning, the six tanks were joined and a brief liaison occurred
concerning proposed tactics and communications. As B Company was well to the rear, C Company assumed the advance—
'120 men on a thousand yard front'.[36] As the artillery creeping
barrage concluded, the Italians took their turn:

> When our barrage ceased and left us in full view of the enemy
> posts ahead, their artillery opened up with such accuracy that
> we were sure they had previously registered on the line we
> were crossing. The shells dropped across the two leading
> platoons and my small command party between them. I was
> buffeted by the blast but kept my feet. I could not see through
> the dust to my left, but to the right, where the three sections
> of 15 Platoon were moving in their wide arrowhead formation,
> I was horrified to see first two sections and then the third
> blown over. As nothing moved in the dust I thought, 'This
> is it—one platoon gone—how long will the rest last?' But after
> a moment the dazed sections scrambled to their feet and
> hurried forward to regain their alignment with the left
> platoon.[37]

Although the Italian artillery very quickly acquired a reputation
for docility, Honner's artillery barrage experience of 5 January
1941 at Bardia was burnt into his memory, and would influence
his planning at Gona Mission a little under two years later.

When a hail of machine-gun fire then greeted the further
advancing C Company, it went to ground. Honner castigated
them, pointing out that there were no casualties and that, even
against high-volume fire, fast, dispersed, orderly movement
would minimise casualties. And if the enemy were inexperienced

and panicky and therefore forgot to lower their sights, the danger would decrease as the advance gained ground. Few of the other ranks—and their platoon commanders—would have heard those words of wisdom, but some did and many also embarrassedly witnessed their leader on his feet while they had gone to ground. The reaction was infectious. C Company rose and pressed on.[38]

When an Italian post was located, the section or platoon commander rushed to the tank and, 'pointing his rifle, with his steel helmet on the bayonet, at the enemy position',[39] the tank either induced the enemy to surrender or kept their heads down as the infantry fired and went in with the bayonet. Lieutenant Johnson remembered banging on the tank with his rifle butt. He was told by an irate tank occupant that rifle pointing and hitting tanks were unnecessary risks—a phone was positioned at the rear of each tank.[40] Johnson's experience is a damning indictment of hasty tank/infantry liaison during, rather than before, battles are engaged.

The unchanging pattern of conflict had been determined. The Italians at Bardia used their artillery with mixed results. Although the 17th Brigade suffered casualties, the quality of that artillery was not great; their machine-gun fire was reasonably dense but they failed to readjust sights as the Australians gained ground, and when the enemy drew close with supporting tanks and demonstrated a resolve to come on with grenade, rifle and bayonet, the Italians lost the will to fight. A new flag was briefly flown at Bardia over many positions during the three-day period 3–5 January 1941. It was white.

Honner described the demoralised Italian prisoners as 'a long broken column winding back like a great segmented serpent over the sky-line to the rear'.[41] Ralph to Marjory:

> The only thing that held us up was dealing with prisoners. They had to be disarmed and with large batches that meant a platoon was held up. But I always swung up the reserve platoon to keep up the two platoon front while the prisoners were being sent back—leaving instructions for the third platoon to follow. Towards the end we outstripped the tanks and over the last mile the wadis were so steep sided that they couldn't possibly follow us. So they swung off to the right . . . to clean up the enemy infantry. Jack Bedell's platoon [15 Platoon]—then in the rear—followed them because of the volume of machine-gun fire pouring into us from our right

flank. He covered about 9 miles in the advance whereas we only had 7 miles to reach our objective—and the sight of the cool blue sea.[42]

The tanks and Bedells' platoon overcame anti-tank fire to silence Post 8 and then closed in on Post 11, which was a half kilometre further south. Although the Italian commander had fought stubbornly against the 2/6th Battalion earlier, he now capitulated. Bedells was then ordered to withdraw his tired platoon, leaving the 2/6th to disarm the enemy. The post contained 350 Italians, including 24 officers, two field guns, two three-inch mortars, twelve medium and 27 light machine guns and 325 rifles.[43]

C Company's objectives had been gained. Captain Ron Horley's A Company, which had been following Honner up, now journeyed into the southernmost area of the Bardia perimeter and captured the last Italian post. Private Harry Johnson, MM, remembered the journey back:

> I know we ran out of water and we were all pretty thirsty. And on our way back we . . . went back towards the fence and we came on an Iti blinkin' fifty gallon keg of wine . . . I put me tin hat under and got it full of wine . . . you tried to drink out of a tin hat . . . it filled both ears! I know we also picked up a general and two or three of his girls . . .[44]

Perhaps Honner's Bardia letter to Marjory best sums up both C Company's battle and his own performance:

> Our success was due to the speed and resolution shown in the attack but our comparative freedom from casualties was miraculous all the same. All officers, NCO's and men behaved splendidly. If I take any credit it was for keeping up the speed of the attack. I moved in front between the two leading platoons and kept the boys on the run through shell-fire and machine-gun fire which looked and sounded bad but wasn't hurting anyone.[45]

Honner's repeated reference to the 16th Brigade as the 'Push Brigade', the 17th as the 'Quiet Brigade' and his own 19th as the 'Shock Brigade' reflects more than an alphabetical code for those formations in his self-censored letters. Such references are also testimony to the fact that the fog of war often creates

reputations that are not always fairly earnt. The Bardia experience of the 17th Brigade's 2/5th Battalion is a case in point.

In its operation designed to exploit the startling 16th Brigade
success on the first day, the tanks attached to the battalion had
failed to arrive to provide the success that Honner's C Company
had received; Italian artillery had fired most successfully on
the 2/5th's first attack; and, crucially, the battalion's newly
appointed CO and a number of its officers were casualties during
that baptism of fire. Honner rightly assumed some credit for
maintaining the impetus of his C Company attack at Bardia. The
2/5th Battalion had experienced a less fortuitous beginning to its
campaigning. Further, the 6th Division staff—particularly Berry-
man and Vasey—were critical of Brigadier Stanley Savige's 17th
Brigade command performance. On 6 January, Vasey wrote that:

> The Battle of Bardia is over and I have dealt with more
> prisoners than I have ever thought of. We haven't counted
> them yet but the estimate is 25–30 000 . . .
>
> Tubby and his fellows [16th Brigade] did excellently. Not
> so Stan and his [17th Brigade]. Had Iven any real go Stan
> would get a bowler hat.[46]

Savige in turn was critical of the manner in which the divisional
plan had fragmented his force and provided inadequate tank and
artillery support.[47]

The so-called fog of war had thus been kind to the 16th
and 19th Brigades, and it had been kind to Captain Ralph
Honner—his astute, aggressive leadership and, most definitely,
his determination to be right up near the front in this, his
company's first action, had been complemented by his splendid
artillery and tank support and by poor enemy artillery and
machine-gun fire. The Official Historian recorded one 2/11th
Battalion casualty for the battle. Given the intensity of the fire,
the ground gained, the posts captured and the prisoners taken,
it was a dream start by Honner to an illustrious career.

The 2/11th's stunning success at Bardia at such frugal cost in
casualties sat most comfortably with all except the battalion medical
officer. Lieutenant-Colonel Louch would later write that:

> 'Killer' Ryan, the RMO, had established his RAP at a con-
> venient spot under the bank of the Wadi we had crossed at
> the foot of the first hill; and had prepared to receive and treat
> anything up to one hundred wounded. When none arrived he

got worried and thought he must be in the wrong place. So he left his RAP and set out to have a look for patients. This was understandable, but he should not have done it.[48]

General O'Connor's next objective was the capture of Tobruk, chiefly because the acute shortage of transport within his command had meant that his force were short on petrol, water and ammunition. Many of these demands had been supplemented by captured Italian vehicles and supplies, but as his line of communication lengthened, so his supply problems magnified. The capture of the port of Tobruk would enable him to move supplies by sea direct from Egypt. Gavin Long has recorded that:

Documents captured at Bardia and interrogation of prisoners had given him a fairly clear picture of the garrison of Tobruk. On 15th January it was estimated to comprise 25,000 men, including General della Mura's 61st (Sirte) Division, two additional infantry battalions and 7,000 garrison and depot troops with some 220 guns, 45 light and 20 medium tanks, the whole force being under the command of General Petassi Manella, the commander of the Italian XXII Corps.[49]

The ground at Tobruk was not unlike that of Bardia with flat, hard ground sloping down to the coast and covered sparsely with short clumps of camel bush. A number of ravines stretched from the coast about 3–4 kilometres inland.

The Italian defence of Tobruk relied heavily on 128 concreted underground posts protected by barbed wire entanglements spread along a semicircle about 48 kilometres long. The same-shaped Bardia perimeter had contained 80 posts spread over about 27 kilometres of ground. The British Staff considered that Tobruk might be an easier job than Bardia, given that there were fewer of the enemy at Tobruk protecting a larger perimeter.[50]

The 19th Brigade led the approach. By midday on 7 January the brigade was facing the eastern Tobruk perimeter with Lieutenant-Colonel Ivan Dougherty's 2/4th Battalion within about 1600 metres of the coast, the 2/8th Battalion in the centre and the 2/11th Battalion on the left flank. The following night the 2/4th gained the western bank of the Sidi Belgassem Wadi and the 2/11th sent out a patrol that reached the Italian anti-tank ditch.[51] Ralph's detailed account to Marjory continued:

8–9 Jan. We moved up each night and dug in each night. Each morning our water was ice and our groundsheets were

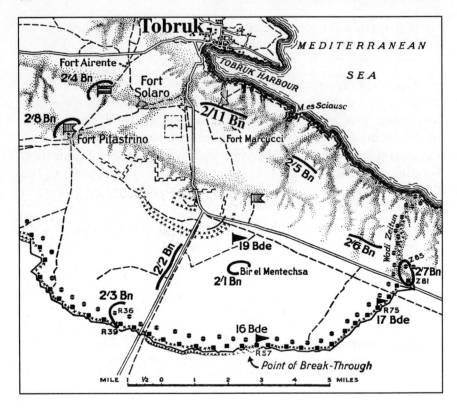

Tobruk.

ice-jackets caked with a quarter of an inch of frozen dew—a nice sort of eider down to sleep under.

10 Jan. C Coy moved forward a mile ahead of our leading troops and dug in within 1500 yds of the enemy defences . . .

14 Jan. We moved back to the battalion's back area and I got 3 pints of water in which I shaved (first shave since 6 Jan), bathed all over, and washed my dirty socks (3 pairs). I'm afraid I didn't get all the soap off.

15 Jan. Our brigade was relieved by the Quiet Brigade and we moved in the evening to our brigade reserve area a few hundred yards from the sea. It was a filthy day and we arrived covered in dust. My hair was a solid cap of red earth interlaced with hair.

16 Jan. I managed to get 10 mins in the sea and a few minutes bare to the wind and sun . . .

Friday Jan 17. We have marched away from the coast again . . . I have a match-box full of Italian pips for Richard and will try to post them tomorrow if I can. I think we are to be

*14 Platoon, 2/11th Battalion, overlooking Tobruk Harbour. Lieutenant
K.T. Johnson is standing behind the soldier front centre (13). (AWM)*

rested tomorrow and then I expect that Sunday will be a
repetition of the Sunday a fortnight earlier [when Honner's
C Company had first gone into action at Bardia].[52]

As at Bardia, the Australian 6th Division plan for the assault
on Tobruk envisaged a concentrated breakthrough by the 16th
Brigade and a movement through the breach and exploitation
by another—this time the 19th Brigade. But on this occasion
it was hoped that the enemy artillery could be assaulted and
silenced far quicker than had been the case at Bardia. Posts
57–59 were identified as the break-in area.

All went according to plan. The 16th Brigade's performance
was yet again exemplary. At dawn on 21 January its 2/3rd Battalion, although suffering some 50 casualties, forced a breach in
the Italian line and its sister battalions, the 2/1st and 2/2nd, also
managed to secure their objectives. Lieutenant-Colonel Louch:

> The advance to the first objective was in the nature of an
> anti-climax. It was just a long walk. We met with no oppo-
> sition and suffered no casualties. There was some random m.g.
> fire as we crossed the Bardia road, but no one was hit. The

2/4th Battalion on our left had an equally quiet passage; but the 2/8th on their left struck a tough snag in a series of heavily fortified posts manned by men who were prepared to fight and did. In the battle the 2/8th suffered 100 casualties before winning the day. It was just the luck of the draw . . .

Red Robbie [Brigadier Horrace Robinson] had been occupying the centre of the stage all morning, and he was in his element dispensing hospitality, and—as commander of the 19th Brigade—receiving congratulations from all and sundry on having taken Tobruk.[53]

Years later Honner would state that:

It's a confidence business; all war is a confidence business. If there isn't confidence in your mates and your leadership, and your weapons and your training, you're not good soldiers.[54]

Ralph's C Company, 2/11th Battalion, had made a most impressive start to this 'confidence business': there was definitely confidence within the other ranks in each other; there was great confidence in the company commander and his platoon commanders, as they had led by example with great dash and determination; and, most of all, providence and sheer good luck had been their companions.

Ahead lay another coastal fortress, and this time Honner and his company were to lead the attack.

4

THESE WAR
CORRESPONDENTS
AMUSE US

On 22 January 1941, as Ralph Honner's 2/11th Battalion was entering the town of Tobruk, the British Chiefs of Staff had identified Benghazi as the next major objective. The capture of that port would facilitate the construction of a major naval and air base for long-term operations in the desert. General O'Connor decided to push inland to Mechili in the hope that he might rapidly outflank the Italian force protecting Benghazi. To this end, and believing that Derna, the next coastal town on from Tobruk, might be lightly defended, he issued orders for the armoured division to move west and an advance guard of the Australian 6th Division to move on Derna. The advance guard was commanded by Major MacArthur-Onslow of the 6th Division Cavalry.

While the commander of the 6th Division, General Mackay, considered that a squadron of the 6th Cavalry with some artillery, machine gunners, engineers and detachments of other troops might be sufficient to capture Derna, he also ordered the 19th Brigade to advance towards that location, absorb the advance guard, and 'facilitate attack by 6th Division or attack and occupy the town'.[1] Official Historian Gavin Long:

> From Tobruk the bitumen road ran along the coastal shelf through Gazala and Tmimi, skirted the Gulf of Bomba . . . and, leaving the coast, travelled across an open plateau to

Derna. West of the road as it nears that town the country is
cut by the Wadi Derna, which reproduces on a vastly larger
scale the wadis which had protected each extremity of the
semi-circle of posts at Bardia and Tobruk; this ravine travels
about twelve miles south and south-west from Derna before
it turns west and loses itself in the uplands. Near its mouth it
is, in some places, a mile wide from lip to lip, and the banks
so steep that they descend 700 feet in a horizontal distance
400 yards. On the coast, for some thirty miles to the east of
the wadi's mouth, the plateau ends in an escarpment to Derna,
which was built on a mile-wide ledge at the mouth of the
wadi; then it travelled along the narrow shore for five miles
before winding up the escarpment again into the Jebel Achdar.[2]

On the afternoon of 24 January 1941, the 2/11th Battalion,
acting as the 19th Brigade advance guard, began its movement
west. By noon the following day the battalion was halted by
Brigadier Robertson and ordered to leave their transport. Robertson informed Lieutenant-Colonel Louch that MacArthur-Onslow
had reconnoitred the Derna aerodrome and had come under
light-artillery and machine-gun fire from the hangars. Given the
6th Division's experiences at Bardia and Tobruk, Robertson felt
sure that a vigorous and speedy company assault would cause the
Italian defenders to either withdraw or surrender. Subsequent
events were to prove Brigadier Robertson's appreciation as based
more on wishful thinking than on sound reconnaissance. The
Italians had held much of their fire to mask their dispositions and
strength.

Louch's plan envisaged Captain Egan's D Company attacking
on the right flank, Captain Horley's A Company to the left and
Captain Honner's C Company to make the frontal assault on
the drome and hangars. Ralph Honner in 'The Capture of the
Drome at Derna':

The undulating ground of the first two or three miles provided
adequate protection if we needed it, but all was peaceful except
for a few stray rounds of artillery fire. Then we came to the
last of this cover marked by a stone wall stretching away to
the right . . .
A broad plain stretched before us, seemingly as bare as a
billiard-table except where the road, raised a few feet above
the level of the plain, ran across its centre from where we
stood to groups of buildings either side of it about three miles

away. In front of the buildings on the right of the road were
a few aeroplanes, marking that part of the plain as the Derna
aerodrome and the first big building beyond as a hangar.
Immediately behind the buildings, high ridges ran east and west
from the road, looking down from their dress circle position
over the houses in the stalls at the performance on which we
were just ringing up the curtain.[3]

The fact is that Brigadier Robertson's orders contradicted the
basic principles of war. Ralph referred to the operation as 'folly
to go forward without first clearing the ridges and the buildings
from the flanks', but also added that 'we had our orders'.[4]
Although on this occasion the Italians were to give a far better
account of themselves, it should be stated that seasoned, disci-
plined and motivated troops could have rained such a volume
of fire from that high ground and over such flat, featureless
ground, that staggering casualties and no objectives gained
should have been the result. It would seem that Brigadier
Robertson's liking for surrender ceremonies and the acclaim that
accompanied them had outweighed his military prudence.

As Honner's soldiers passed the last cavalry outpost, they
were assured that all was quiet ahead except for some sporadic
artillery fire and the sighting of two Italian motorcycle machine-
gun outfits some 800 metres away beside the road.

Ralph spread C Company well out with Lieutenant McRobbie's 13 Platoon on the right flank and Lieutenant Bedells'
15 Platoon on the left of the road. Company headquarters and
Lieutenant Johnson's 14 Platoon moved behind, accompanied by
a three-inch mortar detachment moving alongside the ditch by the
road. A Northumberland Fusiliers' truck was also moving some
distance behind 15 Platoon. The Italian motorcyclists, deployed
under a culvert, put up only token resistance to the company's
progress, and soon offered themselves as prisoners of war.

With the ridges still out of range, 'we were pummelled by
tracer and high explosive, and were soon coming up against a
wide wall of heavy fire . . .'[5] The company were forced to
ground and continued their movement—except for 15 Platoon,
which was pinned down—slithering along on their stomachs
over thorns and prickles. And it was here, as the company slowly
gained ground, that Honner's C Company sustained its first
killed in action, as a bullet pierced a soldier's helmet, killing

him instantly. This slow, time-consuming and uncomfortable approach was to last four hours. Ralph would later write that:

> We couldn't get low enough. The haversacks on our backs were the highest objects that moved through the horizontal hail of lead, and the contents of more than one were riddled, though their owners went scatheless. That night they were to find their mess-tins punctured, their bully-beef and biscuit minced by metal fragments, their cutlery inartistically twisted, and their groundsheets or spare socks with undesigned ventilation. My haversack was unharmed but a broad webbing strap to which it was attached was half-severed, my steel helmet was dented on one side, and something had seared a shallow furrow across the back of my right hand.[6]

Honner decided to mount an attack aimed at the centre of the Italian defences. He sent a runner across the road to order Bedells and his pinned-down 15 Platoon to push on, while at the same time McRobbie's 13 Platoon was to advance with covering fire from Johnson's men. But Ralph's chief concern was close support. His mortar detachment had declined to offer covering fire because they had been unable to find a covered position. This was, perhaps, a little unenterprising, as they might have chosen to fire briefly and then perform the same operation as the infantry—get down fast or use the partial cover provided by the turning bays and the shallow ditch. And that detachment was further handicapped by the fact that the barrel, baseplate and bipod restricted the number of bombs they could carry. The Fusiliers were worse placed, as they were both out of range and lacked a covered position (and would have had to remain more upright and therefore vulnerable during their fighting).

Honner ran back to the mortar truck and offloaded six bombs in two carriers and gave the driver a message for headquarters requesting artillery, tank and/or carrier support. He was unaware that the British tanks had been called away to the south and that the 6th Division's artillery had yet to arrive. Nor did he realise that Bedells had been unable to advance from his position. Returning with the mortar bombs, Ralph ordered the detachment to move along the shallow ditch adjoining the road.

It was at this juncture that the Italian Airforce intervened in the battle to the Australians' advantage. As McRobbie and Johnson's men inched forward, a number of planes dropped a string of bombs well forward of the Western Australians, which conveniently manufactured a wall of dust. C Company's slow slithering instantly became a desperate foot race—except for the luckless Bedells, whose platoon front was not enveloped by the dust—which saw the soldiers cover a vital 400 metres of priceless territory before the enemy could again force them to ground. Lieutenant K.T. (Katy) Johnson:

> Two of McRobbie's platoon, Corporal Bremner and Private Graffin with a Bren gun, went ahead of their platoon and there were little parking bays on this road which gave us a little bit of extra cover and the edge of the road also gave us a bit of cover. And they went on some hundreds of yards but were masking the fire of the rear people. I had Honner's OK to go forward and stop Bremner from going any further forward. When I got there and asked him what the hell he was doing, he said, 'We thought if we could get up closer to the hangars we would reduce the number of casualties in the company'.[7]

Bremner, Graffin and Johnson were soon joined by Honner. Ralph ordered the mortar brought forward and told Graffin to fire his Bren gun and thereby draw some identifying Italian counterfire. Ralph to Marjory:

> The Bren was fired at them and brought immediate retaliation on us. This was what I wanted. The enemy were firing tracer and each burst was a luminous stream which showed where the gun was that fired it. I sent for the two platoons to come up alongside us as the sun went down and they arrived about 6 pm or a few minutes before.[8]

The Italian fire had disclosed two machine-gun positions in two white buildings to the right of and beyond the hangar.

The mortar detachment arrived without its range-taker and therefore without range-finder, but although the task of firing accurately was most difficult without the sight and in the failing light, the bombs kept the Italians' heads down. C Company rose and attacked. Lieutenant K.T. Johnson:

> At this stage with 15 Platoon still pinned down to the left rear, he [Honner] switched McRobbie's platoon across the road and he brought me forward to act as a firm base and provide covering fire for McRobbie's platoon to come in on an angle. At this stage there's a shout, 'McRobbie's been hit!' So the platoon comes to a grinding halt. McRobbie had been

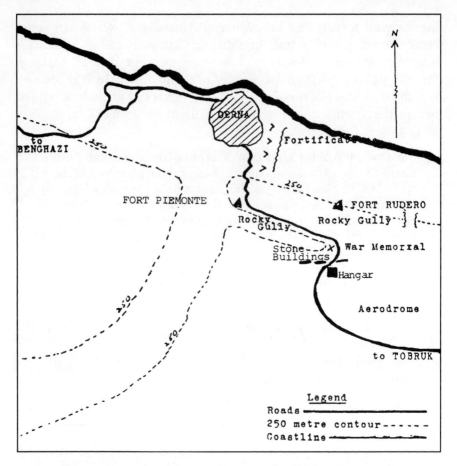

Derna. (Map courtesy 2/11th Battalion. Not to scale)

hit in the water bottle and the liquid in the darkness, they
didn't know whether it was water or blood . . . and Honner
says, 'Well get up and go!'[9]

Despite the fact that the 'water wound' had numbed his leg,
McRobbie and his platoon rose and pressed on. It was only a
temporary delay. During the final dash an Italian truck could
be heard pulling out with the last of the guns from the hangar
area.

C Company grenaded the hangar and the nearby houses but
the Italians had left. Moments after Honner and his men had
captured the hangar, an Italian motorcyclist rode to the door of
the building with a message from the Italian company on the left
of the road. McRobbie brought the unsuspecting Italian off his

cycle with a pick handle. What followed astonished Honner's men. Lieutenant-Colonel Louch:

> . . . the cyclist . . . burst into a torrent of abuse in the Australian vernacular. He turned out to be a market gardener from Perth who had been visiting his relatives in Italy and had been conscripted when the war broke out. I handed him over to the Intelligence people: but he had only recently come to Derna and could give no information of any value.[10]

With the capture of the hangar, Bedells' 15 Platoon and the Fusiliers rejoined the company. Ralph deployed 15 Platoon forward round the white houses, McRobbie's 13 Platoon on the left of the hangar and Johnson's 14 Platoon to its right. The company did not dig in, as they found the Italian network of weapon pits more than adequate. Some time during the night two phone lines were brought forward, one from battalion HQ and the other with the artillery FOO (Forward Observation Officer). Honner learned that supporting artillery now lay about 8 kilometres to the rear and would be available by morning.

Although Honner's company had therefore penetrated the Italian Derna defences at their centre, the enemy still held ground overlooking the Australian flanks.

The still of the night was periodically punctuated by activity on the ridges some 600 metres to the front of C Company. Tanks could be heard moving between the harbour and the buildings, and a half-hearted infantry attack was mounted. Ralph thought it more likely that it was a patrol to ascertain the Australians' strength and dispositions. The Italians withdrew after a brief exchange of fire.[11]

While C Company had been thus occupied on 25 January, Captain Egan's D Company had managed, without loss, to reach its objective—the edge of the escarpment overlooking Derna and the coast.

Before light on the 26th, Ralph joined his forward platoon in the company of the artillery officer. It was not long before four tanks moved on C Company's positions. They were met with fire from three anti-tank rifles, two Vickers guns and nine Bren guns. By the time they had moved to within 80 metres of the Australian positions, one of the four tanks had been set on fire. Three withdrew. The Italian guns in the Derna forts now began to shell Honner's positions and did not slacken until

answered by the distant 6th Division artillery. By 8 am, that
fire had been subdued enough for Ralph to send a platoon off
on each of his right and left flanks. The Italians withdrew. What
Ralph called 'the battle for the drome and the ridges' was
complete. But Derna cost Ralph Honner his first significant
casualties—on 25 January 1941, C Company had lost two killed
and 21 wounded.[12]

On Australia Day 1941, as C Company rested from its
capture of the Derna drome and ridges, the 19th Brigade's
2/4th Battalion was endeavouring to establish itself on the
Derna Wadi and block the two roads leading to Mechili, while
the 2/8th Battalion was ordered to push in between the 2/4th
and 2/11th Battalions and move along the road into Derna.
Louch was also ordered to advance on the town. He sent his
B Company (Captain Shanahan) to advance on Fort Rudero,
to either capture it or facilitate its capture. D Company (Captain
Egan) was sent down the escarpment to the east of Fort Rudero.
Lieutenant–Colonel Louch:

> **27th January**. In the morning a well planned and neatly
> executed surprise attack by B Company . . . overran and cap-
> tured Fort Rudero with 290 prisoners and five field guns . . .
>
> With the capture of Fort Rudero we got a grandstand view
> of the edge of the scarp of the town of Derna, and the
> defensive preparations which had been made on the eastern
> side which had held up D Company . . .
>
> **28 January**. The whole of the escarpment had now been
> cleared of the enemy; but the shelling by the guns on the far
> side of the Wadi Derna continued and at times was really
> heavy . . .
>
> **29 January**. The 19th Brigade plan for the 2/4th and 2/8th
> Battalions to move on Derna on the west side of the Wadi
> Derna had had to be abandoned because they had been unable
> to effect a crossing. On their left the 17th Brigade had had
> much the same trouble . . .
>
> So far as we were concerned the 29th was a comparatively
> quiet day; but when evening came there was an intense
> bombardment.[13]

At dawn on 30 January 1941, Lieutenant–Colonel Louch received
a delegation of Arabs, informing him that the Italians had left
the town of Derna and requesting he organise an end to the

THESE WAR CORRESPONDENTS AMUSE US

shelling. A patrol confirmed that the enemy had indeed left and the 2/11th immediately occupied Derna. Ralph to Marjory:

> I made the commandant's mansion my headquarters and bil-
> leted my company in its spacious apartments. Mussolini had
> stayed there. We had it to ourselves except that half a dozen
> war correspondents came in to type on the great table in the
> council chamber—fifty could sit down at the table with com-
> fort and the high-backed chairs were ranged around it. Their
> occupants had fled that morning and now the typewriters
> clicked out the story of their going. These war correspondents
> amuse us. We have seen reports from Australia of Bardia—
> mostly in praise of the Victorians (the Quiet Brigade) who did
> nothing, and the New South Welshmen (the Push Brigade),
> who did a damn fine job and deserve all the praise they
> get. But apparently no one knew we existed—in Australia.
> However the English and foreign correspondents followed
> 'C' Company round after they heard about us at Bardia—from
> the tanks and the artillery and the English machine-gunners
> who watched us and said we were bloody lunatics.[14]

It was a sore point. Ralph's ongoing criticism of the 17th Brigade is overstated and simplistic. Had Arthur McRobbie, K.T. Johnson, Jack Bedells or, for that matter, Ralph been killed or badly wounded in the first stages of their campaigning at either Bardia or Derna, as had various officers of the 2/5th Battalion at Bardia, then C Company's performance might not have been as impressive. When the company had gone to ground without casualties at Bardia, it was Honner's cool and resolute presence that had moved them on; when McRobbie's soldiers had gone to ground and had showed little inclination to move after his 'water wounding', Honner had again been present to restore the advance.

But Honner's criticism of the war correspondents—and, later, of the Official Historian—was not without substance. Gavin Long claimed in his first volume of the official history that, as Honner's C Company went into battle at Derna, '. . . the Western Australians who, alone among the infantry battal-ions, had had little fighting at Bardia or Tobruk, went into their first real action'.[15] Ralph and his C Company's Bardia experience had been their first 'real action'. It seemed to Ralph that the Victorians had received perhaps too generous praise and his deserving troops none. And it will be shown that, when Honner attempted to right the wrong before Long's volume went to press after the war, Long displayed a lofty, masterly indifference to their correspondence and Ralph's meticulous evidence.

However, the performance at Derna of C Company and its OC was not lost on Lieutenant-Colonel Louch. In his recommendation for a Military Cross for Ralph, he wrote that:

> During the attack on the aerodrome at DERNA on 25. Jan. 41 this officer led his company with conspicuous skill and complete disregard for his personal safety. Under his leadership the company debussed and advanced without artillery support across several miles of perfectly flat country in the face of heavy enemy m.g. fire, artillery and Breda guns firing over open sights from the hangars and the ridge behind. By securing the Aerodrome that afternoon the way was opened for the subsequent advance on DERNA.[16]

As the 2/11th Battalion was busily engaged in 'guarding warehouses, food dumps, light and power stations, water works, flour mills, etc., to prevent looting by the Arabs',[17] Ralph Honner had a chance meeting with an Australian cameraman from the Department of Information. Both men were devout Catholics; both were energetic and curious; both possessed a sincere and exalted sense of history; and both were determined to record and capture its Australian content. Their meeting at Derna evoked an almost comical re-enactment, but their meeting on the Kokoda Trail nineteen months later would record for all time one of the turning points in Australian history. Damien Parer would become the famous, award-winning observer and cameraman, and Honner was destined to be at the forefront of Parer's film content. Parer's biographer, Neil McDonald:

> After the Italians had retreated, Parer went down to the town. He introduced himself to Ralph Honner and asked him if he could take some photographs of the troops advancing into Derna. Captain Honner took an instant liking to the young photographer.
>
> 'He impressed me as someone who wanted to get on with the job, to find out what had happened and to report it' . . .
>
> But the soldiers started skylarking, prodding each other in the backsides with their bayonets. 'I was watching all this with some amusement,' Honner recalls, 'when, before I knew it,

Damien Parer's now famous shot of Ralph at Derna. (AWM 5638)

Damien had swung around with his camera and had taken my photograph.'[18]

There is a further adjunct to the encounter. Neil McDonald has recorded that after Derna, Damien Parer realised that to

capture authentic war film footage he had to be up with the
front line troops or, perhaps, ahead of them.[19] Ralph Honner
not only had, by the end of the fighting at Derna, developed
a habit of being right at the front of his soldiers' fighting, but
had also taken to performing tasks that might have been dele-
gated to others. Both men were therefore imbued with a lofty
sense of service. This common characteristic would eventually
cost one of them his life, and the other his combat career.

Ralph's Derna letters to Marjory now displayed the most
fluid nature of the distant pursuit of the Italian Army:

> **Saturday Feb 1**. Two days of beautiful weather and the nights
> so delicious that I hated leaving them to go to bed.
> **Sunday Feb 2**. We marched twenty miles climbing the lofty
> scarp west of Derna and slept in the open. An issue of new
> boots at Derna meant a crop of blisters among the boys.
> **Tuesday Feb 4**. We slept by the road near Slonta.
> **Wednesday Feb 5**. We slept in the mud west of Barce.
> **Thursday Feb 6**. After a night of rain we travelled through
> a day of it on muddy tracks to Benina where we slept at the
> aerodrome. That night we learnt that the enemy we were
> chasing . . . had vacated Bengasi [sic].
> **Friday Feb 7**. At first light our battalion became a flying
> column. We passed Bengasi and reached Ghemines to find
> the battle had moved on about fifty miles in the morning and
> as the armoured division had almost won it we stopped . . .
> that night we slept blanketless in the mud and rain outside
> Soluch . . .
> **Saturday Feb 8**. We travelled north past Bengasi and stopped
> where we are now. We are now in our third lot of billets
> since arriving in the area and today I am taking over the town
> guard from A Coy which has moved to an inland town.
> It is now **Feb 13** . . .
>
> Tomorrow perhaps I will have that long overdue wash and
> sit down and write to you. But first I wanted to let you know
> that all was well—and that he still lives and loves you who
> has loved you so dearly all these years. Ralph.
> P.S. Everyone you know is safe and sound.[20]

Gavin Long would later write:

> The campaign was over. In two months, for a cost of 475
> killed, 1,225 wounded and 43 missing or prisoners, O'Connor's
> corps of two divisions, extravagantly described as 'the Army

of the Nile', had advanced 500 miles and taken 130,000 prisoners, 400 tanks and 1,290 guns. It had destroyed ten Italian infantry divisions—the *60th, 61st, 62nd, 63rd, 64th;* the *1st, 2nd* and *4th Blackshirt, 1st* and *2nd Libyan*—and considerable armoured forces.[21]

On 8 February 1941, with the campaign all but over, the 2/11th Battalion moved to Tocra. Ralph to Marjory:

> I've saved all your letters and now I'm going to read right through them—the ones I've received on the track—the others are in the kit store—and see if I have any questions to answer. I've read them sweet and it is good to feel that you are chatting away to me from these pages even if I can't hear you. I'm glad the kids are well . . . how are Richard's knees these days? I've had no report for some time. And is Brian at all inclined that way? Young Brian looks the sturdier of the two in the snaps you have sent me . . .
>
> Just now a dozen little Arabs from about 2 years to 8 years are kicking and throwing a tennis ball around the market place—and there's a little black Brian or two conscientiously and happily chasing it up although they'll never catch up with it. And there are a couple of snowys among the Italian small boys who go for walks with their mothers—I don't know who or where their fathers are.[22]

The little, black Arab boys were not the only people playing from Tocra. From that centre, leave was granted to its deserving 2/11th soldiers. And a number of the 'deserving soldiers' had quite a time. Ralph to Marjory:

> I've had no trouble with them except a spot of drunkenness and absence without leave when we first arrived in this area—and they were angels compared with the general run. Up went five men on the mat before the colonel. He asked their ages—one was 23 and the others 20—only boys now and they joined up in 1939.[23]

In his notes written in the early 1950s as further elaboration to his letters to Marjory, Ralph referred to these young men: 'those dreadful drunks . . . had got a lift to Bengasi [sic] (without leave) to relieve the boredom. They had returned in the merry, friendly stage . . .'[24] Honner was not bitter about the absence without leave. But one of the men in question, during a

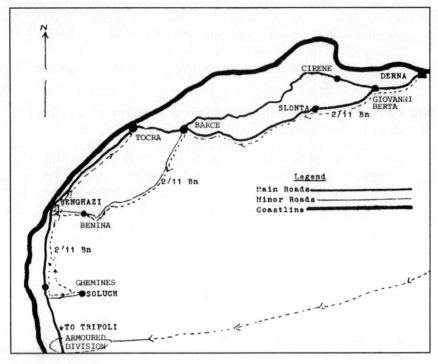

*Derna to Benghazi, approximately 250 miles (not to scale). (Map courtesy
2/11th Battalion)*

drunken stunt, accidentally killed himself back at camp—hence
the term 'dreadful drunks'.

Ralph Honner's final words to Marjory before his battalion's
departure from the North African coast reflect the formidable
esprit de corps and service of both his platoon commanders and
his soldiers:

> He [McRobbie] is the best platoon commander that ever
> walked this earth and his men worship him. And personally
> he's the most likeable bloke I've ever met. I've been lucky
> in my officers though their military knowledge has been inad-
> equate owing to lack of training and experience before
> appointment. K.T. Johnson the 20 year old is irrepressible
> and devoid of fear or nerves, he has an insatiable appetite
> for work or food—is never tired and always hungry. He and
> Mac are great company—young and keen and boisterous and
> always cheerful and confident. Jack Bedells—21—is more
> highly strung and a bit nervy—but in action he's game as Ned
> Kelly . . .

The 'C' Company spirit is something to be proud of—and these lads will face up to anything without hesitation—though thoroughly scared as they all were . . .

Now they're wondering when they meet the Germans.[25]

Captain Ralph Honner's fighting against the Italians at Bardia, Tobruk and Derna had given him invaluable command experience in offensive, fluid infantry operations. His ability to control his company actions, his ability to refine his fire and movement, his experience in infantry/artillery and tank coordination had all proved both beneficial and highly successful. And, on balance, it must be stated that the military quality of his enemy had facilitated the learning of those lessons at a very small cost.

Ahead lay the tests of the fluid fighting withdrawal in the mountains of Greece, and the set piece defence in the olive groves of Crete against a new enemy—and one that was to prove a far more proficient and professional soldier than the Italian.

5

THE MORNING HATE

On 11 February 1941, British Prime Minister Churchill and his Chiefs of Staff decided that General O'Connor's advance in the Western Desert was to be halted and a force sent to Greece in an attempt to resist the imminent German invasion, thereby perhaps to encourage Yugoslavia and Turkey to enter the war.[1]

Whether or not General O'Connor's startling success in the Western Desert would have culminated in the capture of Tripoli, before the arrival of General Erwin Rommel and his Afrika Korps in North Africa, is debatable. The Greek campaign was to provide perhaps the most striking example of Churchillian strategy at its worst: it severely debilitated the Western Desert Force and offered far too small a force for Greece.

On 17 February 1941, General Wavell, Commander-in-Chief Middle East Command, ordered General Blamey to Cairo. Two days later Blamey was informed that a force (code named 'Lustre Force') was to go to Greece and would comprise the New Zealand Division, the Australian 6th and 7th Divisions, 1st Australian Corps HQ and a Polish Brigade Group. Wavell planned to leave the 6th Division in Cyrenaica, send the New Zealand Division to Greece first, then the 7th Australian Division, and finally relieve the 6th in Cyrenaica with the newly formed Australian 9th Division. Blamey would have none of it. He insisted that the 6th Division was his only fully trained and equipped division, and should therefore be the first Australian formation to go to Greece.[2] Wavell eventually yielded.

The British effort during the Greek campaign was to operate under some major handicaps. The first was airpower. The German Airforce was to outnumber the RAF with 490 planes to about 80.[3] With their decisive air superiority, the Germans had the potential to attack Greek ports, shipping and the transport network, and achieve this against a token British air commitment.

The second problem was the state of the Greek Army. Although it had successfully defeated the Italian invasion of Greece from 28 October 1940, it was to prove no match for the Germans. It lacked decent equipment and its transport was outdated. Further, there would exist the obvious language barrier and poor liaison between the Greek and British forces.

The third problem lay in the Greek rail and road network. The area in which the Australians were to fight was served south to north by only one railway line, which ran from Athens to Plati before moving east to Salonika, west to Florina, and thence to Yugoslavia. This railway, antiquated and vulnerable to air attack, was at the time of the arrival of Lustre Force already being overtaxed by the Greeks. The Greek road system was also primitive. The Athens–Florina road was bitumen 'interspersed with stretches of macadam, often so narrow that two vehicles could not pass, particularly on hills and side cuttings'.[4]

The last major problem was more one of strategy. If the Germans overran Yugoslavia quickly, advanced from Monastir through Florina and thence to the Aliakmon Valley, and finally onwards towards the River Pinios and the Plain of Thessaly, they would effectively drive a wedge between the Greek forces and Lustre Force. This later transpired. Then, the rapidity of the German advance had the potential to outstrip the projected British build-up of its force from North Africa (which, when it did begin to arrive, would be further slowed by the poor Greek transport system). Gavin Long, Official Historian:

> By 18th March the 1st Armoured Brigade and about half the New Zealand Division were in Greece. The 16th Australian Brigade disembarked between the 19th and 22nd. For the men of the Australian division it was a swift transition. On the 8th March when the first 'flight' or contingent of Lustre Force

was landing at Piraeus, the 16th Australian Brigade was at
Tobruk, the 19th near Tocra in western Cyrenaica, the 17th
in position on the Tripolitanian frontier beyond Agedabia.[5]

With the German attack on Greece imminent, disturbing
news came from the Middle East. On 4 April after a short,
sharp engagement at Agedabia, General Rommel's Afrika Korps
entered Benghazi and thereby forced the 9th Australian Division
to withdraw to Barce. Wavell now requested that Blamey release
the 7th Division from its intended participation in Lustre Force
for operations in the desert. Further, the next day he informed
Blamey that he had deployed the 7th Division's 18th Brigade
in Tobruk. These developments were destined to further weaken
an already grossly outnumbered Lustre Force.

On 1 April 1941, the 2/4th and 2/8th Battalions, the 2/3rd
Field Regiment and the 19th Brigade HQ embarked on the
SS *Pennland* for Greece. Aboard was the new 19th Brigade com-
mander Brigadier George Vasey, who had replaced Brigadier
Horace Robertson after the latter's hospitalisation. Ralph Honner's
2/11th Battalion was to sail on a later convoy with the 17th
Brigade. The 19th Brigade, less the 2/11th, arrived in Piraeus on
5 April and began moving north. The next day the Germans struck.
Captain Ralph Honner was at this time still in camp 32 kilometres
west of Alexandria at Amirya.[6]

The 2/11th's Greek story is one of a relatively minor role.
As a consequence, given that the unit has yet to publish an
official battalion history, that the official historian has understandably mentioned the battalion's story sparsely, and that the
2/11th's Unit Diary is also of limited help, Ralph Honner's
detailed letters to Marjory provide the only substantial account
of his movements in Greece. They are now used in conjunction
with battalion interviews. Ralph to Marjory:

Wednesday April 9. In the evening we received orders to
move.
Thursday April 10. Reveille at 3 and we marched out of camp
at 3.45 arriving at the railway station at 4.15 for breakfast . . .

All morning and part of the afternoon troops kept arriving
and embarking. On our ship there were three times as many
troops as on the ship that carried us across the equator—and
there were 84 nurses . . .

Our crossing was mostly without incident—two nights and
two days of pleasant cruising. On Easter Saturday I wrote you

a long letter as we passed island after island on the approach to Greece—I left it unfinished. That afternoon we were taken off our ship in private yachts and landed at Piraeus about half a mile away.[7]

The 2/11th was forced to come ashore in this fashion as a result of a most successful German bombing raid on the harbour of Piraeus on the night of 6/7 April. The steamer *Clan Fraser*, loaded with TNT, exploded, causing the additional loss of seven merchant ships, 60 lighters, 25 caiques and an ammunition train and barge. There was also considerable damage to docks and adjacent buildings.[8] Ralph to Marjory:

> We moved by trucks through Piraeus and Athens to Daphni for the night—a lovely camp on a pine clad hillside.
> **Sunday April 13.** We woke in a glorious country with bracing air and everywhere the sight and scent of green and flowering things with the hills looking down on gardens and the Acropolis watching over Athens. In the afternoon we motored to the train, moving north through the cheering suburbs in the last hours of daylight and out into the lovely garden that is Greece. We slept on the train that night—Stan Wood, Jim Ryan, McCaskill and myself shared a compartment—no smoking for a change.
> **Monday April 14.** We woke in the Brallos valley with snow clad mountains towering over us. Through dozens of tunnels we shot on what must be one of the most picturesque train rides in the world—and as we came out of the mountains near Thermopylae to look down on the Lamia plain we little guessed that we should be back there within a week fighting off the pursuing Germans.[9]

By the time Ralph's 2/11th Battalion had reached the Lamia Plain on 14 April 1941, Brigadier Vasey's 19th Brigade's 2/4th and 2/8th Battalions had fought a number of desperate rearguard actions.

Vasey's first task was to take command of the defence of the Florina Gap with his two 19th Brigade battalions and the 1st Rangers from the 1st Armoured Brigade. On the morning of 9 April Vasey began deploying the 1st Rangers with the 27th New Zealand Machine Gun Battalion (less two companies) astride the road in the Vevi Pass. He deployed the 2/8th on the right and the 2/4th on the left. The 21st Greek Regiment was further to the left of the 2/4th and the 20th Greek Division

Withdrawal from Greece to Crete, April 1941.

was to the right of the 2/8th.[10] The plan was that Vasey's force was to hold at Vevi until the night of 12/13 April.

During some extremely tough fighting and operating in rugged, mountainous terrain, Vasey's force fought its rearguard

to Sotir—where Lieutenant-Colonel Dougherty's exhausted
2/4th Battalion fought a magnificent rearguard—before retiring
to the north bank of the Aliakmon River. In the process, the
2/8th Battalion had been broken up and had lost significant
numbers of men and equipment in the withdrawal from Vevi.
David Horner, in *General Vasey's War*:

> By now Vasey's brigade had been reduced to under 900 men.
> On 14 April the 2/8th Battalion reported a strength of eighteen
> officers and 290 other ranks. To hold this exposed position the
> 26th New Zealand Battalion was sent across the river to bolster
> the brigade, which was in a steep mountainous area all but cut
> off from the rest of the corps. Soldiers of the 2/4th Battalion
> on mountains at altitudes over 1000 metres could watch
> German planes taking off from their airstrip at Kozani 15 km
> to the north.[11]

While these events had been unfolding, Ralph's 2/11th Battalion had been assigned to Savige Force (Savige's 17th Brigade),
and sent to block the western approach to Larisa via the road
from Kalabaka. In the process, they were to cover the withdrawal of the British Armoured Division. Ralph to Marjory:

> **Tuesday April 15**. We moved north up the valley in the
> morning without contacting the Germans. In the afternoon we
> fell back to a holding position a few miles west of Kalabaka—
> and watched the thousands of plodding Greek soldiers moving
> down the road to the south. The war was now left to the
> British forces and we were to stay put until the main forces
> withdrew to the Larissa [sic] area.
> **Wednesday April 16** . . . more Greeks heading south.
> **Thursday April 17**. Ditto. And now came news that the
> British withdrawal to the Larissa area was completed and we
> who had been protecting the vulnerable left flank would soon
> pull out and fall back to save ourselves from being cut off.[12]

Although the collapse of the Greek Army had left the Australians
and New Zealanders in a most vulnerable position, the Greek
soldiers had won the admiration of the Australians. In a letter
to his mother on 29 April 1941, Lieutenant Arthur McRobbie,
OC Ralph's 13 Platoon, stated that:

> It would take a better pen than mine to give my opinion of
> these men. Personally I would have been proud to be killed
> in an attempt to stand by these Greek soldiers and save their

country from the Hun. Some of them had been four and five days without food, and during that time they had covered anything up to 150 miles after they had been cut off by a German push. They were footsore, hungry and weary, some even without boots and hardly able to walk . . . if that isn't guts I've never seen it.[13]

Ralph to Marjory:

> **Friday April 18**. Starting at about 1 a.m. we marched back through Kalabaka and embussed for the south before daylight. I had command of the rearguard—C Coy and some machine-gunners—and was last out—but the Germans did not press us. We stopped at a place called Sintomai—that's what it sounds like. I had no map and never saw the name. Before dark we crossed the river on a punt. Then the punt and the remains of the bridges were destroyed. We had to get through Larissa that night. Once more I was given command of the guard on the river and the rear guard of the brigade convoy. I had some machine-gunners and was to have a troop of anti-tank guns, but the latter did not turn up.[14]

By 2 am on Saturday 19 April 1941, all of the 2/11th had withdrawn except Ralph's rearguard. About ten minutes later he pulled his machine guns out and had them moving by 2.30 am. Within a further half an hour Ralph had extricated his last battle post off the river bank—four men with a Bren gun and an anti-tank rifle. The rearguard climbed onto the last truck and the company moved west to Larisa along a cratered road. Ralph to Marjory:

> As it turned out, peril came not from the ground but from the air. The convoy was held up by a series of bombing and machine-gunning attacks. My rearguard had just caught the main body when a couple of bombs dropped beside my truck. One of my lads had a piece taken out of his hand and the driver scored in the back and ribs. The spare driver took over. Then one of the company trucks broke down and I eventually had about 40 men aboard mine and dropped to the rear. At 2 in the afternoon they caught us alone in the middle of a flat five miles wide. They held us there till nearly 6 with our noses down in the mud of the wheat field round our truck. The rain came down and soaked us through and through . . .
>
> And the net result of that four hours strafing was that we were wet. The truck was covered in mud from . . . bomb

craters within fifty yards of it but there were only a few holes
through it. And the only damage to the men was a small list
of bruises from the flying clods of earth . . .

Our dispersion among the wheat had not hidden us but
had made us a bigger target and had saved us.[15]

Ever the romanticist, Ralph recorded that while 'waiting for
the end I had time to admire the magnificent poppies that
bloomed among the growing wheat—great crimson chalices that
bowed their sturdy stems'.[16] Others of his C Company had no
such inclination or opportunity. The occupants of one of
Lieutenant Johnson's trucks had gone to ground and sustained
four killed and five wounded by the bombing.

The rearguard drove through the plain and into the mountains of the Thermopylae Line, which had been selected as the
next defensive position. This locality was composed of a mountain barrier that ran from a mountain system to the east and
stretched to the sea in the west. It faced a flat plain divided by
the Sperkhios River, which ran through the town of Lamia.
The coastal plain was held by the New Zealanders, while the
6th Division was given the role of holding the inland route.
Vasey's 19th Brigade was allotted the task of holding the main
approach, which consisted of a winding mountain road of about
8 kilometres from the pass down to the plain. It is at this
juncture that the 2/11th Battalion rejoined its 19th Brigade.

When Honner arrived at the 2/11th positions near Brallos,
he reported to Lieutenant-Colonel Louch. He found his commanding officer in a distressed state and in pain. Louch's car had
been strafed that day by a German fighter, with the result that
his driver had been killed and his Adjutant, Bob Ainslie, slightly
wounded; Louch had pinched a nerve in his shoulder, causing
his left arm to numb. Ralph recorded that 'the experience was
too much for his indifferent health and he was sent to hospital
the next day'.[17] Louch's ill-fortune caused Major Sandover to
assume command of the 2/11th and Ralph to become second-
in-command. Lieutenant McRobbie was now to command
C Company and Lieutenant Johnson, who had previously been
selected to command the Mortar Platoon, rejoined C Company
as the officer commanding McRobbie's 13 Platoon.[18]

By 20 April the Germans had reached Lamia, about 15 kilometres north of Vasey's defensive line. The New Zealanders now

Major (later Lieutenant-Colonel)
R.L. Sandover,
second-in-command, 2/11th
Battalion. (AWM 21769)

began to fall back through the 19th Brigade's defensive position. The 2/11th was deployed as reserve just north of Brallos. General Mackay now made it clear to his brigade commanders that there would be no withdrawal, and that the real battle for Greece was about to be staged. It was at this juncture that Vasey's colourful language ably illustrated the position. David Horner, in *General Vasey's War*:

> Brigadier S.F. Rowell, the BGS of the Anzac Corps, visited Vasey during the afternoon [20 April] and recalled that Vasey asked: 'What's the policy Syd?' I said 'as far as I know George, it's to hold on'. He said, 'That's what I told my b____s. Here you ____ well are and here you ____ well stay. And if any ____ German gets between you and your post and the next, turn your ____ Bren gun round and shoot him up the ____'.[19]

Ralph to Marjory:

> **Sunday April 20**. In the early hours of the morning I sat down in the front of my truck to close my eyes for the first time since the night of Tuesday April 15. On Wednesday it had rained all night and—in the open—it was impossible to sleep. On Thursday I had just finished my tour of outpost duty round about midnight when we got orders to move and I had to take over the rearguard. On Friday night I still had the rearguard to organise and control and dared not lie down. So

early Sunday morning sleep came easily to a tired man sitting in sodden clothes.[20]

The fight to hold Brallos Pass began early on the morning of 21 April, with the German airforce strafing along the whole front. On 22 April an intense artillery engagement occurred between the 2/2nd Field Regiment's guns and the Germans. The Australians bravely carried on the uneven contest until their position and gun were destroyed. Late that day, however, Vasey received orders that Greece was to be evacuated and that the 6th Division was to be withdrawn, with its 19th Brigade ordered to hold its positions until the night of Anzac Day eve.

For Ralph Honner, participation in this battle was to have tremendous historical significance, in its past, present and future contexts. He was deeply aware of the past when, during the inspiring battle of Thermopylae over 2000 years before, Leonidas and his Spartan few had fought and died a glorious death against Xerxes and his Persians; he was now aware that history was repeating itself and that the Anzac Corps, of which he was a part, was once more creating a legend of bravery and sacrifice at famed Thermopylae by attempting to delay a modern-day superior-sized, encircling enemy. And, in an article years later, Ralph would draw a parallel between those famous Thermopylae battles and another remote mountainous pass—Isurava on the Kokoda Trail in Papua. Honner had a tremendous capacity to perceive the endless journeying of the eternal soldier.

During the morning of 22 April Brigadier Vasey visited the 2/11th to inform them that they might be required to return to the reserve position they had occupied two days before. Ralph to Marjory:

> **Wednesday April 23**. The move back came in the night. C Coy was heavily shelled as it moved into its new position but I knew where the shells were going and guided the Coy out of trouble. Two of its mules were blown to pieces and another had its legs broken, but a chip off the ear and a scratch on a hand were the only damages to men. I left them to go back to Bn HQ where I lay down at 5.30 a.m. and rose again at 6.30 a.m. to help McRobbie with his dispositions before the morning hate started.[21]

The battle for Greece had become very much 'the morning hate'. Weary soldiers had been required to fight, day and night,

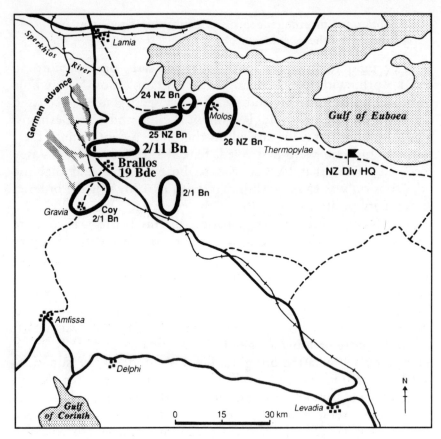

Brallos Pass, 24 April 1941.

against superior numbers, equipment and air power, only to be
confronted with a slow, cumbersome withdrawal and little sleep.
Early morning inevitably produced savage, accurate strafing and
bombing of the withdrawal route and its slow, snake-like
columns. There was little defence against that overwhelming air
attack other than to disperse and hope for the best—or perhaps,
as Honner did, to attempt to dismiss its venom by studying the
immediate flora. Anzac eve 1941 became the critical day. Ralph
to Marjory:

> Bombing and shelling and machine-gunning in the morning.
> Our battalion was left with a coy of another, a platoon of
> another, some machine gunners and some artillery to hold the
> enemy until after dark. The rest of the brigade had moved
> south to embark. Early in the afternoon the enemy attacked.

D Coy were forced back on the left and B Coy were being pressed back in the centre. C Coy stood unshaken on the right. A Coy were sent up from reserve to just rear of the front line between B and C to cover B's withdrawal. That left C in front with A behind them to the left. I dashed back and reorganised a second line with B and D Coy and a third line with a Victorian platoon, while a N.S.W. Coy covered our left. Darkness fell with the enemy pressing but still held in check. At about 9 we started embussing—the N.S.W. Coy was pulled in from the left flank, the Victorians lifted off the third line, A and C Coys brought back with the machine-gunners from the front line. Then I leapfrogged B and D Coys back along the road from corner to corner with a couple of Tom Bedells' carriers to protect their rear and we all got aboard and headed south. Ray Sandover had gone back to supervise the getaway leaving the organising of the holding force to me as soon as he had left orders for the forward companies to pull out at 9 p.m.[22]

Some concept of the immense strain that Honner must have been under is given by Lieutenant McRobbie's account of the last withdrawal under the intense and relentless pressure of the German air and artillery bombardment:

At this stage, I thought I was finished. My nerves were gone to pieces and I just shook like a leaf, and for the next two hours I fought like hell to get myself into shape. At this time, 'Katy' [Lieutenant K.T. Johnson] proved a rock of friendship, for he helped no end, and to him goes most of the credit for our day's doings.[23]

Ralph Honner's Greek campaigning was of paramount importance to his development as an eventual battalion commander. If he had demonstrated an ability to lead and control a company in action in North Africa, then this campaign gave him tremendous experience in the planning, coordination and control of the fighting withdrawal—and one conducted against a first-class adversary and under intense pressure. He had come through with flying colours. Captain Darrald McCaskill, OC A Company, 2/11th Battalion:

. . . Ralph Honner was in charge of the withdrawal on this particular night . . . his thoroughness payed off then . . . he was meticulous, his control was good, because we had to come back in section by section and not leave anybody behind; not

come back too far at once because then you get lost . . .
you've got to come back stage by stage . . .

He was approachable, very fair to people and had a humane
interest in his troops. He wasn't a fella who went out on the
tiles or anything like that, but he appreciated fun. He was a
very strong character who didn't fly off the handle, very well
balanced.[24]

Lieutenant-Colonel Louch, 10 June 1941:

Citation: WX15 Capt. Ralph Honner. Recommended for M.C.
This officer is the best Company Commander I have known
in this or the last war. Throughout the campaign he has
led his men on all occasions with courage, cheerfulness, calm-
ness and skill. He commanded the rearguard from Kalabaka
through Larissa to Domokos and later distinguished himself at
Thermopylae.[25]

Lieutenant K.T. Johnson, C Company, 2/11th Battalion:

The withdrawal then took us . . . under the olive groves in
the area of Megara. Trucks were then destroyed by draining
the oil and running the engines and you could only take what
weapons you could carry off, and although you might say, we
were a disorganised organisation, under the olive trees and not
able to move around, by word of mouth we got messages to
each other and as soon as darkness came, it was remarkable
how quickly sections, platoons and companies got themselves
together. And after we hoofed it down to the wharf we were
ferried out in varying type vessels . . . clambered up the ropes
on the side of the *Thurline Castle* which was a cargo boat, and
you dossed down wherever you could.[26]

As the exhausted soldiers of the 6th Division's 19th Brigade
clambered up their ships' scrambling nets during darkness on
Anzac Day 1941—the first of the 6th Division's troops to do
so—the Greek campaign had reached its tragic if inevitable end.
The 2/11th Battalion sustained 32 men killed in action, the
same number wounded, and 37 taken as prisoners of war.[27]

Ahead lay a campaign that would signal the 2/11th Australian Infantry Battalion's toughest fighting, and would cast its
officers and other ranks to a sentence of either eventual escape
or doomed servitude in Germany as prisoners of war. By
2.30 am on the morning of 26 April 1941, the 2/11th Battalion
was sailing to Crete.

6

GROPERS ALBANY

The moral and material are interdependent. Weapons without courage are ineffective, but so also are the bravest troops without sufficient weapons to protect them and their morale.

Liddell Hart, December 1929[1]

While most of the 2/11th Battalion journeyed to Crete aboard the *Thurline Castle*—with a number of near misses from bombing—Captain Ralph Honner travelled in comparative luxury aboard the British destroyer *Hasty*.[2] It is interesting to record that a sloop named *Hyacinth* was also involved in the evacuation from Greece.[3] Ralph's detailed letters to Marjory continued:

> The destroyer looked after us very well. I slept in the captain's cabin, and sat down to sausages and eggs and cocoa for breakfast. Late in the morning we reached this island and marched eight miles in the afternoon up into the hills laden with weapons, ammunition and rations. That's all we carried. We had been told to take everything with us to Greece and all I left behind in Alex [Alexandria] was a small case with two pyjama suits. Everything I own has gone—even my spectacles—I wear an army pair now—my good ones are gone with all my suits, shaving gear, books, letters, photos, shoes etc. I arrived with only the clothes I wore and my battle equipment—pistol, binoculars, respirator, compass, ammunition,

about a week's rations and a Bren gun. I'm sorry to have lost those photos of you and the boys but it's no use crying over spilt milk. I suppose I was lucky to get out with a whole hide . . .

We hear that Lord Haw Haw has described us as an island of doomed men. It's a very pleasant doom so far. These mountains and hills and groves and streams form a sunlit paradise by day, loud with the song of birds. The nights are cool, but after our recent exertions we sleep well.

You are never far from my thoughts my love and I'm longing to get back to you. Just for the present be glad I am safe and healthy in pleasant surroundings, picnicking before the next push wherever that may be.

Good night—and sleep well my darling and look after those boys for me.
Ralph.
X X
Richard Brian[4]

Ralph, forever the chavalier, may well have regarded his 'doom' in a 'sunlit paradise' as being pleasant, but when the British evacuation from Greece was complete it became immediately apparent to the senior commanders on Crete that the task ahead would be a difficult one.

The 'slender and oblong'[5] island of Crete lies about 240 kilometres south of Athens and about 80 kilometres southeast of the southernmost tip of the Greek mainland. Between its widest east–west points, the island runs about 224 kilometres, while its maximum distance north–south is about 48 kilometres. A steep mountain range runs along the middle of the island and falls away to its southern coast. Most of the level ground lies on the northern section of the island which was, in 1941, used mainly for cereal, vine and olive cultivation. Three towns then dominated the rural and commercial life of the north coast—Canea, the capital, which then had a population of about 36 000; Retimo, which then had a population of about 10 000, lying about 48 kilometres east of Canea; and Heraklion, about 80 kilometres by road from Canea, which was then the largest centre and port and had a population of about 43 000.

From a military standpoint the island lacked key logistical facilities: three airfields existed, one near Canea (at Maleme), one near Retimo, and the last near Heraklion; the road system was deficient and antiquated, the only road suitable for military transport ran along the north coast; only five secondary roads existed, linking the north coast centres with the south coast; and the only reasonable port on the island was Suda Bay, which operated with only one wharf—and no crane.[6] Gavin Long, in *Greece, Crete and Syria*:

> . . . although the possibility of an evacuation from Greece had been in mind since early in March, plans and preparations to defend Crete against a major attack were not initiated until the middle of April. Much that could have been done in the meantime—reconnaissance, shipping of vehicles, improvement of roads and harbours, the equipping and training of Greek forces, and the establishment of effective liaison with them—remained undone. The responsibility rests not with the succession of local commanders, whose role was to administer a small garrison, but higher up, whence came no directions to begin effective preparation to defeat invasion.[7]

The New Zealand Division on Crete (Brigadier Puttick assumed command after 29 April when General Freyberg became GOC) was composed of only two of its three brigades and its divisional personnel, as its 6th Brigade had been ordered to Alexandria.

The Australian troops landed on Crete in late April 1941, consisting of a conglomeration of soldiers from a number of units. The 19th Brigade group comprised the 2/1st, 2/4th and 2/11th Battalions, half of the 2/8th Battalion and the 2/2nd Field Regiment. In addition to this mostly intact formation, the 2/7th Battalion, the 2/1st Machine Gun Battalion and the 2/3rd Field Regiment arrived from Greece. Numbers of the 17th Brigade were also landed, but most of that formation had been shipped from Greece to Egypt. Brigadier Vasey, in command of the Australian Crete force after General Mackay had left for the Middle East on 29 April, found himself in command of nearly an equal number of additional troops who had arrived from various formations without their weapons and basic equipment. He requested that these soldiers be returned to Alexandria, as they were an unnecessary drain on already limited supplies.[8]

The British contingent (Major-General Weston) consisted of the fresh 14th Brigade and four 'weak and improvised battalions from Rangers, Northumberland Hussars, 7th Medium Regiment,

106th Royal Horse Artillery'[9] and various coastal artillery, anti-aircraft and base units.

In addition to the British, New Zealand and Australian troops on Crete, there existed some 10 Greek troops consisting of three garrison battalions deployed at Canea, Retimo and Heraklion and a further eight recruit battalions. Those troops had experienced minimal basic training and possessed little equipment or ammunition.

On 3 May 1941, General Freyberg completed his dispositions and identified the roles of his units. Freyberg, whose headquarters was stationed in the Suda Bay sector, determined that Crete would be defended from four localities. Running from west to east, the first sector, occupied by the New Zealanders, comprised the ground west of and adjacent to Canea. This area included the vital Maleme Airfield. Suda Bay comprised the second sector, with the British units and one Greek battalion. The British were responsible for the defence of the Bay and Canea. The third sector was under the command of Brigadier Vasey, and extended in an arc from Geogioupolis to Retimo. At Geogioupolis Vasey had his headquarters, the 2/7th and 2/8th Battalions, the 2/7th Field Ambulance less an augmented company at Retimo, and service and field detachments. Near Retimo were the 2/1st Battalion (four companies and about 500 soldiers), the 2/11th Battalion (four companies and 700 men), and the 4th and 5th Greek Battalions. The final sector lay at Heraklion and was occupied by three battalions of the British 14th Brigade, the Australian 2/4th Battalion, the 7th Medium Regiment, and two Greek battalions.[10]

Apart from the poor road system, totally inadequate port facilities, a multinational force whose components varied greatly in terms of training and equipment, and a decided lack of basic stores, General Freyberg's defence of Crete was destined to operate under a number of further critical handicaps. The first, as in Greece, was lack of air power. At Maleme the RAF had 30 Squadron, 33/80 Squadron and the 805 Fleet Air Arm Squadron, which together consisted of a paltry collection of twelve Blenheims, six Hurricanes, and six Gladiators and Fulmers. At Heraklion, 112 Squadron had twelve Gladiators.[11] The Germans would therefore enjoy almost total domination of the skies over Crete.

Lack of artillery support was the second handicap. Given

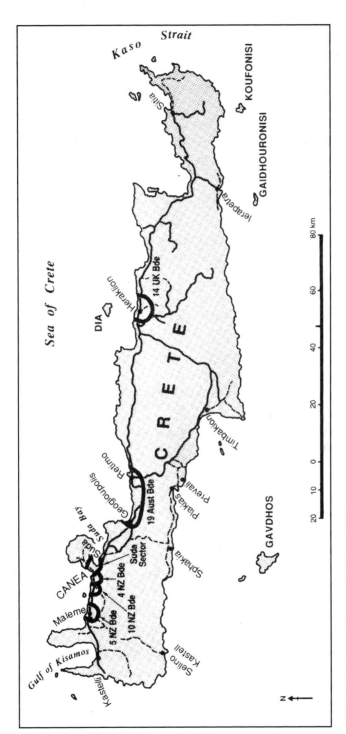

Allied Forces on Crete, 19 May 1941.

that the Australians and New Zealanders had lost their guns in
Greece and, further, that there had always been a shortage of
guns in the Middle East, little was done to ship now available
guns to Crete. The artillery personnel on that island were highly
trained and motivated but, when a force is reduced to con-
structing sights out of 'wood and chewing gum'[12] and making
'charts which enabled them to shoot without sights or instru-
ments',[13] it must be conceded that artillery support for Freyberg's
force was inadequate. And when 100 guns were later dispatched
to Crete, Freyberg noted that it was:

> Sufficient to say that many did not arrive, others came without
> their instruments, some without their sights, some without
> ammunition, and some of the ammunition without fuses.[14]

The last major problem concerned the British Navy.
Although its performance under the conditions in which it had
to operate was superb, German air domination and the primitive
port facilities, particularly at Suda Bay, meant that Freyberg's
force was inadequately supplied. By the time of the German
invasion, the rate of supply had fallen below half of Freyberg's
requirements.

While General Freyberg and his soldiers were thus engaged,
the Germans had devised a three-pronged attack for the subju-
gation of Crete. Using their captured southern Greek airfields
of Corinth, Megara, Tanagra, Topolia, Dadion, Eleusis and
Phaleron, the Germans originally envisaged simultaneous airborne attacks on Maleme, Suda Bay, Retimo and Heraklion.
The German experience in Holland the previous year, and at
Corinth during the Greek campaign, convinced them that an
airborne attack, using gliders and paratroops, was a plausible
means of capturing Crete. To support the airborne assault, it
was decided to land the equivalent of a battalion and various
heavy weapons and supplies by merchant shipping and captured
Greek vessels. However, when the German Airforce declared
that it could not guarantee satisfactory air cover for all four
venues at once, the plan was modified to allow for a staggered
assault on Suda Bay and Maleme at around 8.30 am and on
Heraklion and Retimo at around 4.30 pm on the same day.

The capture of Crete was programmed for Tuesday 20 May
1941. Gavin Long:

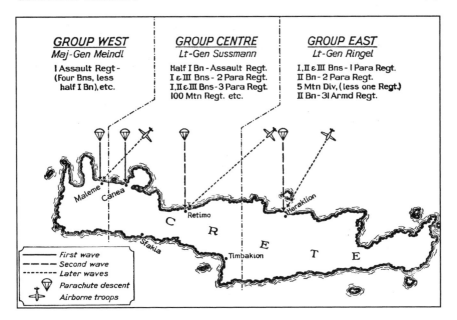

GROUP WEST	GROUP CENTRE	GROUP EAST
Maj-Gen Meindl	*Lt-Gen Sussmann*	*Lt-Gen Ringel*
I Assault Regt - (Four Bns, less half I Bn), etc.	Half I Bn - Assault Regt. I & III Bns - 2 Para Regt. I, II & III Bns - 3 Para Regt. 100 Mtn Regt. etc.	I, II & III Bns - I Para Regt. II Bn - 2 Para Regt. 5 Mtn Div, (less one Regt.) II Bn - 31 Armd Regt.

— First wave
— · — Second wave
········ Later waves
Parachute descent
Airborne troops

Crete: the German plan.

Thus, in the initial stages, 750 men would descend in gliders and 10,000 in parachutes, while 5,000 would be landed in aircraft and 7,000 from ships. The aircraft available for transport were from 70 to 80 towed gliders, and from 600 to 750 Junkers transports (Ju–52's), able to carry 5,000–6,000 men and their equipment in one lift.[15]

The German allocation of resources for the Retimo sector originally consisted of the 2nd Parachute Regiment (less one battalion). The Germans did not expect to encounter strong resistance in that area.

During the period 3–20 May 1941, Ralph Honner's 2/11th Battalion was engaged in its recovery from the Greek campaign, exercises, and establishing a perimeter in the Retimo sector. Ralph to Marjory:

On May 3 my company did a 15 mile ramble over the hills to break through the line held by the rest of the battalion—we were German paratroops. On May 4 the Catholics amongst us marched about five miles to hear mass and get home again. I went to confession and communion—it might easily have been my last . . .

At midday we started on a twenty mile march to Geogioupolis —these marches were tiring because we carried everything we possessed on our backs—greatcoats, packs, blankets, weapons, cooking gear—huge loads that made our shoulders ache.

Next morning we did another half dozen miles to take up a position to repel an invasion from the sea. As rations were short we spent all our spare time—after digging in—in visiting the surrounding villages and buying food—hares, chooks, sheep, eggs, cheese, wine, bread etc. and each day we swam in the sea . . .

On May 8 we moved on again—another 30 mile march —loaded like pack horses. We didn't start till five in the evening—and next morning we arrived beside Retimo aerodrome which we were to defend in the forthcoming blitz. The following day, Saturday May 10, I walked into Retimo and bought myself razor, strop, shaving brush and shaving cream and got back too late to go for a swim. But each day after that I went down to the beach about ¾ mile away and spent a couple of hours in and beside the sea.

It was a carefree life. Again our parties were out on the scrounge for food. Rabbits and pigs, and fruit and vegetables and goats milk were added to our diet. And down on the beach each day we sprawled on the sand after a dip and gazed out at the smoke over the sea horizon and wondered what it meant. Or looked back over the variegated carpet of wildflowers and green fields that stretched away to the curtains of green trees on the mountain sides hanging from the snowy canopy on the higher slopes. Our pleasures were simple. We dived out into the sea for stones that we threw in; we examined the catch of the few fishermen; we picked up the coloured shells piled on the beach; we played ducks and drakes with the flat pebbles that abounded.[16]

It was almost as if Honner had bedded his charger down for the night under the care of his faithful squire, and had dined freely with some mediaeval lord before accepting a joust with an honourable opponent on the morrow. Such was his epic, noble view of the life of one engaged in what he considered to be a noble quest, and in the privileged company of his troops. The 'joust' was not to be long in coming.

On 8 May, Major Sandover (Lieutenant-Colonel Louch had been evacuated on medical grounds to Alexandria) received orders to deploy the 2/11th Battalion on the left flank of the Retimo perimeter.[17] Brigadier Vasey placed Lieutenant-Colonel Campbell, CO of the 2/1st Battalion, in command of the Retimo sector.

The Retimo sector perimeter covered some 5 kilometres, starting just east of the village of Platanes and moving eastwards to a track adjacent to Hill 'A'. The 2/1st Battalion (Lieutenant-Colonel Campbell) occupied Hill 'A', which was a spur running down to within about 160 metres of the sea, and overlooking the airfield. It further occupied ground running about 2.4 kilometres to the west, which took in the airfield itself. The Wadi Bardia ran about halfway through the battalion perimeter. The 2/1st's perimeter ran parallel to and about 150 metres from the east–west coastal road. About 800 metres inland from the airfield, Campbell deployed a reserve company which was located near Hill 'D'. About 3 kilometres inland from the airfield he positioned the 5th Greek Battalion, which occupied the villages of Adhele and Pigi. Adjacent to his 2/1st westernmost flank, Campbell deployed the 4th Greek Battalion, nestled between his 2/1st and 2/11th Battalions. The Wadi Pigi separated the 2/1st and the 4th Greek Battalions.[18] Away to the west of the 2/1st perimeter stood the small village of Stavromenos, which was near an olive oil factory.

The 2/11th Battalion perimeter ran from adjacent to the southeastern outskirts of the village of Platanes eastwards to the 4th Greek Battalion perimeter. Hill 'B' lay within the 2/11th's perimeter. Ralph's C Company was stationed on the western flank of the unit perimeter, with his 13 Platoon (Lieutenant Johnson) about 'a quarter of a mile'[19] from the road, 14 Platoon (Lieutenant Stoneham) to Johnson's west, and 15 Platoon (Lieutenant Bayly) inland behind Johnson.[20] On Hill 'B' were stationed two 100-mm guns and one platoon of the 2/1st Machine Gun Battalion.

Campbell and Sandover had exercised considerable acumen with the choice of their dispositions: their troops held the high ground, with Hills 'A', 'B' and 'D' being the decisive features; their positions commanded the east–west road; the ground around the wadis in their perimeter was occupied at their decisive northern parts; the track junction to their rear near Pigi was occupied; the vitally important airfield was both occupied and covered by the high-ground features of Hills 'A' and 'D'; and, critically, in the period leading up to the German landings on 20 May 1941, Retimo Force's discipline in concealing their dispositions was first class.

The inland portion of the perimeter was under terraced vineyards which were in full leaf, while the lower reaches were terraced and under olive trees. Private Harry Johnson, C Company, 2/11th Battalion:

> That olive grove, the trees were the biggest trees I saw . . .
> you walk through Greece and the olive plantations are old
> stunted trees that looked as though they'd been pruned so
> often they're only about six feet high. And these trees were
> thirty feet high with trunks anything from a foot to eighteen
> inches, a whole grove of them . . .
>
> They used to bring the company supplies in and as soon
> as the truck went they'd go out and brush the marks out and
> scatter a bit of grass around and you couldn't tell . . .[21]

Corporal Cecil Rogers, C Company, 2/11th Battalion:

> The observation spotter used to come over every morning for
> the best part of ten days looking for us. As soon as we heard
> the noise of the aircraft we were told, or we'd been instructed
> to go to ground and remain still until the plane was gone . . .
> every morning.[22]

On 16 May Ralph was a close witness to stark evidence concerning German intelligence for his sector in Crete:

> McRobbie, Stoneham, myself and a couple of others were
> sitting in a row on the beach enjoying the sun when a German
> plane came very low along the beach straight towards us. We
> couldn't run to cover because there was none, so we sat there,
> trusting to luck, with our hearts in our mouths. When it was
> a hundred yards or so off us and we were wondering why it
> hadn't already opened fire on our naked hides—the locals don't
> swim—it turned out to sea, completed a circle and headed for
> us again. Once more we thought we were gone coons and once
> more it turned out to sea banked sharply and headed in over
> the aerodrome. Then it turned into a steep dive and we thought
> it was dive-bombing a ruined Gladiator—the only plane on the
> drome—then we saw a column of dust and smoke and flame
> soar high into the air and knew that the dive was a crash . . .
>
> Aerial photographs were rescued from the plane. They
> showed the positions of some of the troops defending the drome
> but were taken before we arrived and did not show our cunningly
> hidden posts amongst the olive groves and vineyards.[23]

Gavin Long mentioned the same episode in his official history and stated that 'only one of the defenders' positions had been located. It was forthwith altered'.[24]

At around 9 am on 20 May 1941, Ralph and his comrades stood spellbound as fourteen slow and cumbersome German troop planes were seen out to sea, seemingly heading for Retimo. This was the first wave of the German invasion, which soon wheeled to the east and headed towards the Maleme Airfield. At midday 20 troop carriers flew from west to east across their positions towards Heraklion. At 4 pm, German fighters appeared over the Retimo defences and began strafing the town and much of the Retimo sector, but their attacks, which continued for about fifteen minutes, were largely ineffective because of the Germans' poor prior intelligence. Ralph, in 'Paratroops in Crete':

Then we hurried to our fighting posts to gaze at a spectacle that might have belonged to a war between the planets. Out of the unswerving flying fleet came tumbling lines of little dolls, sprouting silken mushrooms that stayed and steadied them, and lowered them in ordered ranks into our consuming fire. And still they came, till all the fantastic sky before us was filled with futuristic snowflakes floating beneath the low black thundercloud of the processional planes—occasionally flashing into fire as if struck by lightning from the earth.

We had no armour-piercing bullets and no anti-aircraft artillery, but the frail-hulled troop carriers passing our front at close range were often on fire by the time they reached us at the end of the line. Even in disaster there was at first an air of masterly discipline about them.

The burning planes held their formation, and their troops in this tragic culmination of all their training and campaigning jumped in orderly succession, their dark shapes plummeting to earth with the last pale flames of their blazing parachutes streaming behind them. But as plane after plane, riddled by the engulfing fire from the ground, smoked and flamed and faltered, and fell out of the sky to throw back to it one more burning pyre charting the course of death, a mounting wave of confusion seemed to unsettle that arrogant armada. A few planes must have flown too high, or others too low or too fast or too close, for we saw them slicing through the cords and 'chutes of troops already dropping.

Some parachutes did not open; some that opened bore lifeless bodies, pushed out with the living. And the living, passing over our posts, did not live to reach the ground. They were sitting ducks, sitting in the air for easy shooting. One plane load dropped in perfect order into a vineyard between

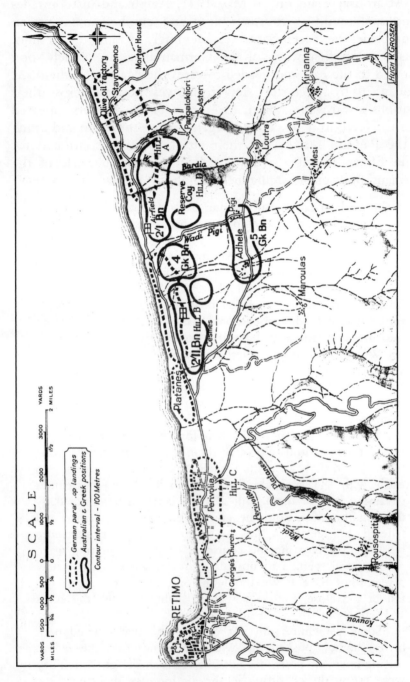

SCALE

YARDS 1500 1000 500 0 1000 2000 3000 YARDS
MILES 1 ¾ ½ ¼ 0 ½ 1 1½ 2 MILES

••••• German para¹. ᵒᵖ landings
⬭ Australian & Greek positions

Contour interval – 100 Metres

RETIMO

St Georges Church

Perivolia

Hill C

Platanes

Cestnes

2/11 Bn Hill B

4 Gk Bn

Wadi Pigi

Adhele

5 Gk Bn

Pigi

2/1 Bn

Reserve Coy

Hill D

Bardia

Hill A

Airfield

Olive oil factory

Stavromenos

Mortar House

Pangalokhiori

Asteri

Loutra

Mesi

Kirianna

Maroulas

Perivolia

Phatanes

Wadi

Rousospiti

R.

Kouvou

Retimo, evening 20 May 1941.

two of Lieutenant Arthur Stoneham's sections. I saw a party from one section rush into the vineyard and then hurriedly retire without firing a shot. Next the other section sent a patrol that peered over the vines where the Germans had landed and then ran back. So I ordered a group from company head-quarters to find and kill the enemy. They were soon back to report that the enemy were already killed—apparently shot on the way down.[25]

Honner's C Company experience near Retimo at 4 pm on 20 May 1941 was a microcosm of the fighting in the entire Retimo sector. The Germans had completely misread both the size and dispositions of the defending force. And with that error came a 35-minute slaughter along the entire perimeter that comprised little more than a human turkey shoot, where highly trained and almost defenceless paratroopers were sniped at on their way down, or shot or put to the bayonet on arrival. Small groups or individual 2/11th soldiers merely ran to the point of contact and administered the execution—only if needed, as the majority of the invaders died during their descent. On a number of occasions, Ralph described to the author the sad story of a 17- or 18-year-old German conscript who had had the misfortune to land in the middle of C Company's perimeter. As the boy landed with a leg either side of an olive tree, the defenders opened fire at all they could see—his boots.

> When he waved something white, my C.S.M., Dave Ander-son, and I went out and brought him in. We removed his tattered, blood-filled boots and saw that his feet were shot to pulp; but he had walked in on those formless stumps like a soldier. These men were hardy.[26]

Ralph recounted the incident with genuine remorse, in the sense that the shooting of these soldiers seemed almost against the spirit of war or, at least, in conflict with its more traditional values.

Private Graffin, who had rendered great service on the drome at Derna, repeatedly ran out into the vineyard from his cover at the brick shed to bayonet the invaders, before finally being shot in the head by a paratrooper who had survived his fall. Small parties or scattered individuals did find cover among the vines or olive trees and began to offer counterfire as the afternoon drew to a close.

Not long before dark Major Sandover ordered a speedy battalion advance to the northern road to prevent the enemy later forming up outside his perimeter under the cover of darkness. The battalion ran into varying strength enemy pockets, but was able to clear nearly all the ground to the road by dark. However, strong parties were seen by Ralph's C Company far away to the west—and out of machine-gun range—late in the day. He estimated their strength at about 500.

With the onset of darkness on the 20th, the initiative shifted to the Germans, as the terraced ground allowed for the 2/11th patrols to be fired on from adequate cover by the scattered and less numerous but well-concealed enemy. By 10.30 pm the West Australians had ascertained that 84 prisoners had been taken, significant numbers of weapons and ammunition had been captured, and only small pockets of Germans remained within their perimeter.

Major Sandover concluded that all must be well to his east, as Lieutenant-Colonel Campbell had not requested his (Sandover's) B Company, which had been kept as a force reserve. Apart from this theory, Sandover had absolutely no idea what had transpired at Suda Bay, Heraklion, or of the 2/1st's fate on his right flank, as he was not in radio or cable communication with any of those forces.

While events were thus unfolding in Ralph's Retimo sector, the Germans had encountered similar difficulties at the Maleme Airfield–Suda Bay area. Although their initial landings and parachute drops met fierce New Zealand and British resistance, and were largely mopped up, the Germans managed to gain two vital footholds which were destined to turn the battle for Crete to their ultimate advantage. The first was the successful landing by gliders at the dry bed of the Tavronitis River, which lay west of the Maleme Airfield. The survival of this formation against a New Zealand counterattack became the nucleus of the force which would later gain success. The second German foothold was taken southwest of Canea at a position called Prison Valley, which also then held firm against spirited counterattack. At Heraklion, on the first day, the Germans had taken heavy losses and were keeping a precarious foothold in the sector.

Three factors now worked against General Freyberg's defence of the island. The first was the decisive German air

superiority. Freyberg's British force was hampered throughout
the battle by the critical German ability to frustrate movement
during daylight. The second was his inability to create a mobile
reserve which could be deployed where needed to combat
German gains. And the overriding reason against such an acquisition was the decided lack of armour and transport. The third
debilitating factor was the appalling communications network
on the island. Radio and cipher communication was infrequent
and of poor quality, and cable supplies so poor that the Retimo
sector, for example, was unable to communicate effectively even
within its perimeter, let alone with the other sectors. General
Freyberg was thus in command of four separate battles, all of
them essentially out of communication with each other—and
with him—and, because of his lack of a mobile reserve, each
vulnerable to piecemeal elimination by the German capacity to
drive wedges between them. And once the Germans had gained
a landing foothold, they could eventually reinforce their troops
by air.

The following day was one of consolidation. Ralph, in
'Paratroops in Crete':

> On 21 May we quickly cleared the tract between our lines
> and the sea, bringing in some prisoners but suspecting that
> more of the birds had flown. Aircraft bombed us during the
> day but caused us only one casualty. At sunset, just before our
> first platoon went out for an all-night forward patrol, another
> platoon made a sudden sortie to cut off some Germans moving
> east from Platanes, between the road and the shore, probably
> in search of equipment. But they saw our platoon coming and
> escaped to the west in the dusk.[27]

Major Sandover would later write that:

> At the end of the second day our morale was still high—we
> had cleared up the area to our front—had more prisoners,
> including the Regimental Commander Col. Sturm and his
> HQ—further infiltration to the rear had been cleared up—
> Greek auxiliaries were in the area (though hard to tell whether
> they were German or not).
>   I questioned Sturm at length—we had the copy of the
> German operation order and Sturm was anxious to know
> which officer had brought it with him. He was still shaken by
> the attack by Bayliss' Platoon—he and his HQ had been
> sheltering at the end of Hill B. We knew that piece of dead

ground well. It was a complete surprise to him that defenders were there in any strength. One officer said, 'we do not reinforce failure' and another—'your men don't look like soldiers but, by God, they can shoot'. It was clear no further paratroops would be coming.[28]

Thus, at dusk on 21 May, the position on the Retimo sector was that the Germans had failed to secure the airfield and had been mostly annihilated or captured as they dropped into the Australian perimeter. Lieutenant-Colonel Campbell now decided to attack the two German pockets at either end of the sector on the 22nd. The first, on the eastern end, was to be eliminated by the 2/1st at the olive grove factory near Stavromenos, while the second, around the village of Perivolia to the west, was to be attacked by the 2/11th. Ralph, in 'Paratroops in Crete':

> . . . we received orders to clear Cesmes and Platanes of the enemy. We saw how two days of death under the warm sun turned blond Teutons black, and we learned what a noisome thing a very dead donkey can be. But the only life we found in Cesmes was a goat in sore need of milking, a few hungrily scratching fowls and, alone in a dingy room, a blind crone too old and helpless to move when her neighbours had fled, and now only able to whimper incoherently. We could not imagine what agonies of fear and uncertainty she had suffered as Cesmes was bombed and machine-gunned on the invasion day, then shot at by us with the Germans firing beside her, and again bombed on this third day of her lonely terror. We placed food and water beside her and milked the goat for her, and tethered it within her reach.
>
> On we moved to Platanes, to find that the Germans had left it too, apparently withdrawing their screen ahead of our advance. Beyond the village we came upon many parachutes— we were entering the area in which we had seen five hundred paratroops drop beyond the reach of our small-arms fire to march unmolested westwards to Perivolia. We had captured their signalling code and now laid folded white parachutes on the road, forming a signal calling for bombs on the Perivolia stronghold, sixteen hundred metres away; and the German aircraft, continually overhead seeking targets, promptly complied, severely bombing their exasperated comrades. A little farther on we came to the Wadi Platanes where we were fired on from a row of houses farther west, now occupied by the retiring screen. Here I received a message to report to Platanes

where the C.O. had arrived with orders for my company, now
less than a hundred strong, to advance astride the road, push
in the enemy screen, capture the Perivolia stronghold, and go
on to the wadi west of the Perivolia road junction.[29]

Unlike many linguistic scholars, Honner had had positive feed-
back concerning his 'brushing up' of foreign languages prior to
the war.

The ground over which Honner and C Company were
ordered to advance lacked cover and sloped gently downwards
to the outskirts of the village, where the Germans occupied the
stone buildings and the Church of St George (which was itself
surrounded by a stone wall). They had also dug in around the
buildings. The Germans, about 500 strong, also possessed mortars, machine guns and some light artillery. By the time Captain
Jackson's B Company had joined Honner during the late afternoon, C Company had taken two casualties—one killed and
the other wounded. In the late afternoon the Germans also
called in a number of air strikes which saw Ralph's soldiers
pinned to the shelter of the houses in Platanes. A proposed
night attack by C and B Companies was cancelled when it was
learned that the Greeks were to attempt the capture of the
Church of St George. This Greek effort must have been less
than impressive, as Ralph would later write that it 'turned out
to be a brief raid'.[30] The Official Historian referred to the Greek
attack as 'the Greeks advanced, captured some prisoners, and
withdrew'.[31] This would seem a spurious attempt to excuse the
failure of the action, as the capture of the village was its
objective. Further, the fact that the Greek attack failed either
to eliminate or dislodge the enemy was to have dire consequences for the 2/11th's C and B Companies the following day.

On 23 May Lieutenant-Colonel Campbell received two
wireless signals from General Freyberg: the first congratulating
him on his sector's sterling efforts, and the second informing
him that a company from the 1/Rangers was on its way from
Canea to help eliminate the German force in Perivolia. Ralph's
Crete letter to Marjory mentions the proposed Rangers attack
for the night of the 23rd, but that 'the Rangers left it to
the next morning, had a few wounded between Retimo and
Perivolia and decided not to attack'.[32] The Official Historian
claims that:

The officer commanding this company of the Rangers decided
that the Germans were immune to his weapons—Brens and
one 2-pdr anti-tank gun—because they were in stone houses
and a thick walled church and, having learnt from Lergessner
that the Australian force was in good shape, telephoned Freyberg's headquarters asking whether in the circumstances he
should attack. He was ordered to do so. The attack at dawn
on the 24th was a costly failure and the surviving Rangers
were embussed and returned to Canea.[33]

Gavin Long did not quote the Rangers' losses, nor did he
mention the fact that, given communication between the two
forces was non-existent, had the Rangers attacked in unison with
the 2/11th, much greater pressure—and from two opposite
fronts—might have decisively influenced the course of events.
As it transpired, both forces mounted uncoordinated assaults and
paid a severe penalty. It would seem that Ralph's comment, 'had
a few wounded . . . decided not to attack', might have been
an understandably sarcastic reference to the Rangers' inactivity
on the 23rd.

Meanwhile, by the morning of 23 May, Ralph, as senior
company commander, had deployed Lieutenant Johnson's
13 Platoon, Lieutenant Bayly's 15 Platoon, Lieutenant Darling's
three-inch mortar and a captured German mortar under patchy
cover between the houses and the sea. He further positioned
B Company and his 14 Platoon (Lieutenant Stoneham) in shallow ditches forward of his 13 and 15 Platoons. Ralph's company
HQ group was deployed 'flat on the ground beneath a row of
cabbages in Bayly's platoon area'.[34]

Early in the afternoon the inevitable German air assault
began. The partly exposed B Company suffered less of the
Germans' attention, because Ralph's covered ground to the rear
was seen by them as the Australians' forming-up area, where
most of their soldiers might be expected to be lying. B Company
took nine casualties, while Ralph's C Company lost three killed
and 27 wounded—'never have I longed more ardently for
nightfall'.[35] Ralph was to retain a vivid memory of the experience of continuous air strafing:

The furnace-odour of the hot metal of canon shells and
incendiary bullets was right under my nose all the long
afternoon; and scorched by their searing fire the green trees,
beneath which our reserve ammunition and our wounded lay,

wilted and withered, and then smouldered and sprang into flames. One of our stretcher-bearers had been killed and the other had been hit, and Dave Anderson had taken over the care of the wounded. Now, helped by the less serious casualties, he had to save the stretcher cases from burning to death, moving them from the path of the spreading fire and the choking smoke; while I rescued batches of mortar bombs and dashed out to stack them amongst the riven and uprooted cabbages.[36]

Lieutenant Ken Johnson, OC 13 Platoon, was not far to Honner's rear:

. . . regardless of who was above us we had to stand up and grab the mortar bombs and throw them out in their containers into the open and hope to Christ they weren't hit again. At least they were thrown away from the fire. And that strafing went on pretty near all of the day . . . they were that low that you could basically see the goggles on the pilots' eyes . . .

And there was nothing you could do but cling to mother earth . . . I was wounded at the same time as the mortar officer who was lying behind me, and when it got to the stage when it was getting a little darker, and a bit of a lull occurred, those that were injured had to find their own way back to the rear company headquarters. I remember one chap was badly wounded in the stomach and someone caught a donkey and they put him on that, and so, having got back to the rear company headquarters, where I was taken to the RAP, I took no further part in the action.[37]

Nearing sundown, and seeing the vast plumes of smoke in the distance, also thinking that their airforce bombing and strafing of the Australians' positions might have either destroyed or demoralised them, the Germans left the cover of their Perivolia positions and mounted a frontal attack on the Australians. But Ralph had sited his Bren gunners to the front of his most forward positions. The advancing Germans, without cover, were mown down. Privates 'Slim' Johnson and Fred Symmons were both wounded in this engagement but refused either to withdraw their Bren gun or to be relieved of it. Symmons died later that night. The combined German air and ground fire on 23 May near Perivolia cost Ralph's C Company dearly. Ralph would later write that:

In Bayly's platoon, two of the three sections had every man
a casualty . . .

The incombustible-looking house behind which the mortars
were emplaced was burning fiercely. We did not attempt to
extinguish it. It gave us light to tend our wounded, and lit a
path for the runners amongst the maze of craters, one of which,
beside the burning house, was large enough to swallow it.[38]

The 2/11th's A Company (Captain McCaskill) replaced
Honner's worn and diminished soldiers that same night, in anticipation of an attack in unison with Captain Jackson's B Company
on the arrival of the Rangers. As noted, the Rangers did not
arrive.

Major Sandover now scheduled an A and B Company assault
for 26 May with the decisive assistance of a tank, one of two
in existence on the 2/1st front, that had been moved westwards
to the 2/11th perimeter. But the tank, driven by an inexperienced carrier driver, blundered over a culvert into a creek before
the attack could begin. The attack was therefore postponed until
the next morning. The precious vehicle was successfully camouflaged against German observation from the air and recovered
next morning.

On the following morning the attack was attempted again,
but on this occasion, as the tank was advancing towards the
critical St George Church position, an enemy shell hit and
jammed the turret, resulting in the commander, Lieutenant
Greenway, returning with a head 'still singing'.[39] The attack was
again abandoned, with the loss of four killed and 26 wounded,
which included the OC of A Company, Captain McCaskill.[40]

It is at this juncture that the historian is presented with the
fundamental difference between an article written for publication
and a series of letters written to a soldier's wife for the purpose
of the accurate recording of history. In his article 'Paratroops in
Crete', Ralph merely mentioned that his C Company was called
back in for the attack for 27 May. In his letter to Marjory—and
for his future records—he provided an insight into both his own
and Sandover's thinking at that time:

George Greenway had commanded the tank but his head was
still singing so Jack Bedells [one of Ralph's former C Company
platoon commanders] took it over, and another one, commanded by an officer from the other Australian infantry bn.

in the area (2/1 Bn) now became available. Sandover decided
to attack with them the next morning. He seemed to think A
& B Coys had not been quite dashing enough (although it
would have been murder for them to try to get to close
quarters without tank support) and decided to give C Coy the
job of making the attack on the morning of the 27th.[41]

The point is that Honner was not only the senior company
commander in the battalion, but was now the only company commander with any comprehensive experience (Captain
McCaskill having been evacuated). Although C Company was
severely understrength—down to 60[42]—he was now reinforced
by the transport section, two platoons of A Company on his
left, and the third platoon of A Company was to lead the Greeks
'into the scrap once the attack had been driven home'.[43] Clearly,
Sandover was relying solely on his most experienced commander
and the remnants of his most prized company. What then
transpired is a classic illustration of the futility of brave troops
mounting a frontal assault over relatively open ground without
satisfactory support or communication. The battle at Perivolia
was to prove both Ralph's and his company's most tragic battle.

Ralph climbed Hill C on 26 May and surveyed the approach.
He decided to move his troops forward during the evening to
the ditch where B Company had taken its casualties during the
German aerial bombardment of the 23rd. Later that night Ralph
moved his soldiers further on again until, amazingly, they were
in occupation of a ditch within only 120 metres of the German
trenches. In the process, Captain Gook, now OC A Company,
sent Lieutenant Fred Roberts' platoon, keeping an eye on Ralph's
men, and following them to the extreme southern section of the
same ditch. Ralph to Marjory:

> At first light came the tanks. Jack Bedells . . . had just crossed
> our ditch and gone about thirty yards when a mortar bomb
> detracked the tank and left it immobile. Another knocked the
> turret lid open and Jack grabbed the lid to shut it. He
> succeeded but not before another bomb had time to take
> his fingers off just as he was closing the lid. On the side the
> tank on the left of the road was destroyed by an anti-tank gun
> . . . and was burnt out. We saw no sign of A Coy on our
> left, and without tank aid I decided attack was useless. We
> knew the Huns had something like a machine gun per yard
> of trench, and although we were only 75 yards away I could

see no reasonable chance of success. It was still hardly light when I sent away a message reporting what had happened. Then Wally Gook appeared. Leaving his reserve platoon behind he wormed his way forward with his runner and reported that he couldn't find Fred Roberts. I told him he must find him. Away he went again and came back to say Fred must have got into the Hun line. I thought it highly improbable but as there was a hell of a lot of fire going on, it was just possible, so I told Wally to make certain. He came back, said he had searched everywhere and found no sign of Fred's men and was certain they had got through on the left. That left me with only one thing to do—attack, to help Fred out of trouble or to complete the success he had started. I knew I'd have to lose men, but I couldn't lose time.

The first section—nine men—had to get to a low stone wall 50 yards ahead round a well 25 yards from the German line to cover with machine gun fire our attack across the open. They bolted flat out along the line of cover to the well. The section leader Tom Willoughby was just about there before he was killed. The man carrying the Bren went down, someone else following him picked it up, and went on till he was killed, and so the gun was relayed through till it reached the well in the hands of the last man, and he too was killed as he went down with it. Only one of the nine was saved—he was stunned and knocked back into the ditch by a bullet in his tin hat just as he started. And the last man to go through, past his fallen mates was Charlie Brown, whose widow you met at Boans. Then we tried the other side. Col Bayly headed a party down the ditch leading forward to the Hun trench to get shelter from the cross fire but he was the only one not hit. Blue Pauley was wounded there, so was young Fitzsimons, one of the 24 wounded on the 23rd—he had got away from the RAP to rejoin us but was well stopped with three hits—one in the leg, one in the arm, one in the chest. Wally Gook's runner was also hit here and then Wally came along the ditch from the left to say that Fred Roberts's platoon was lying doggo along the far end of it. I felt very annoyed . . .[44]

And with good cause. Ralph had sent a number of brave soldiers to their deaths doing what had to be done—attempting to support an apparent brave action that simply had to be supported and, in the process, attempting to conform to his orders. Twice he had ordered his A Company commander to be sure of Roberts' position, and twice he had been assured that that commander had gone forward. The whole episode is a damning indictment of poor communication in battle, communication that could have and should have occurred.

Honner hurriedly wrote a report of the situation and determined that a smoke barrage was needed—none existed at or near the front—to allow the stretcher-bearers to recover the wounded. Ralph to Marjory:

> It was impossible to show a finger above our ditch without a hail of lead flying at it. We just had to take quick peeps in turn to keep the enemy under observation and even then one corporal was sniped between the eyes as he looked. Snipers filled the houses facing us and it seemed that it would be difficult to leave the ditch but safe to stay all day (to protect Jack in the tank) as we were too close to the enemy line for aircraft to attack us. Everyone leaving the ditch since daylight had been hit . . .
>
> It was very open ground, flat stubble, going back, and half a mile to the comparative safety of AA [the next trench back]. I decided to do the job myself as there was no need for me to stay forward after calling off the attack. So I tied my message round my wrist watch and called for two volunteers to follow me at 5 minute intervals & see that the message got through. I selected the first two offering, Alex Donaldson and Dave Anderson, and away I went. I crawled, wriggled, ran, jumped, zigzagged, rested for awhile in C and B ditches and went on chased by a hundred well aimed shots a minute round me. Three times I pretended to be dead as a Hun reccy plane came down within twenty feet of me to have a good look. He wouldn't fire anyway at one man but he still scared me. While I drew the fire one way Alex Donaldson cut across the other way near the finish and was hit in the arm. Dave Anderson, the third man, was shot through the thigh. I got through unscathed, found that no smoke was nearer than 3 miles away.[45]

But the RMO, the much-admired 'Killer Ryan', came to the rescue. Once again, as he had done the day before, Ryan went out across that bare killing ground with a Red Cross flag in an attempt to bring in the wounded. Ralph was 'doubtful if the Huns would let him so close as the casualties were'.[46] Ryan's brave journey took him and his stretcher-bearers over a kilometre of open ground in full view of the Germans. Ralph recorded that:

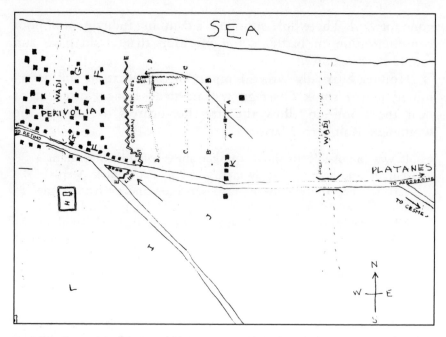

Ralph's map, Perivolia.

> The Huns ceased firing . . . he found that all those brave
> fellows who had rushed for the well were dead—riddled like
> sieves; looked into the German trench and saw it bristling with
> machine guns as they waved him away; and brought back our
> wounded—all who would come—picking up Dave Anderson
> on the way.[47]

This was not the first time Ralph had assumed the role of a
brave platoon commander or an equally brave runner. His
devotion to duty, the respect gained among his soldiers for never
requesting a task to be done that he was not prepared to do
himself, or could not do himself, was all very impressive, but
the fact remains that company commanders should not under-
take such tasks.

The events of 27 May now convinced Campbell and
Sandover that successful attacks on Perivolia during daylight
hours were unlikely. Apart from the strong German defence of
the village, the 2/11th was now devoid of satisfactory support,
as the two tanks had been lost and there was a shortage of
artillery ammunition. The problem was compounded by the fact
that the battalion had exhausted its supply of mortar ammuni-

tion, and many within its ranks were using captured German arms. That afternoon, Ralph oversaw the administration of the 2/11th's dispositions, while Major Sandover journeyed east to confer with Lieutenant-Colonel Campbell.[48] At that meeting, Campbell ordered Sandover to launch another night attack on Perivolia.

The plan envisaged B Company (Captain Jackson) and D Company (Captain Wood) attacking along the southeast road: B Company was ordered to capture the crossroads and then exploit to the sea; D Company was to capture the houses east of the road junction; Lieutenant Royce's A Company platoon was to follow up D Company and protect its left flank; the Greeks were yet again to attack St Georges Church; Lieutenant Roberts' A Company platoon was to move forward and capture the next German trench and the corner houses; and C and the remainder of A Company were to engage the Germans in the trenches opposite them.

The attack went in at 3.20 am on 28 May. B Company had travelled about 600 metres when the Greeks opened fire on St Georges Church, which drew steady and intense fire on Jackson's men (the Greeks had been ordered not to fire during B Company's advance). Despite that fire, B Company reached the crossroads and moved along the wadi towards the sea. D Company also advanced and made its ground—the houses in the main road. Gavin Long:

> At 4.33 Lieutenant Scott, the only unwounded officer, on the orders of Wood, who lay mortally wounded, fired two green Very lights—the signal that the company was withdrawing, and repeated the signal a few minutes later.[49]

The 2/11th Unit Diary—written from, at the time, recent memory by Lieutenant Dowling, the Adjutant—records a different interpretation of the Very light signals:

> Capt WOOD was killed and Lieuts. BAYLISS and LEE and CSM wounded. The remainder of the Coy reached their objective and at this stage a 'Success' signal should have been fired—2 green flares; but owing to some misunderstanding only one flare which signified 'Unable to attain objective' was fired and the Coy withdrew. Had the proper signal been fired C Coy would have pushed forward from the front and B from the rear and the success of the attack was assured [sic].[50]

The events on the B and D Company fronts are clouded in mystery. To add to the conjecture mentioned above, Gavin Long further asserted that:

> Some of Jackson's men told him that the signal to withdraw had been fired, but neither he nor any of his officers had seen it and he decided not to act on the reports, thinking that perhaps a German signal had been seen.[51]

Had the orders prior to the attack been clearly assimilated by all concerned parties, there could not have been any confusion—surely Jackson and his officers could have trusted their other ranks to recognise both the colour and number of any given flare? Further, in that relatively flat, barren terrain it seems unlikely that B Company's officers missed one or two flares, and a repeat signal. In the event, D Company withdrew and B Company remained in the village.

All but Jackson's B Company withdrew before dawn. After an amazing trek to the beach, followed by a western movement to escape the former front, where he knew his company would sustain heavy losses, Jackson eventually led his company back inland and across to the battalion lines. For this brave and astute effort, Captain Jackson was awarded a Military Cross. Ralph, in 'Paratroops in Crete':

> The idea of capturing Perivolia was now abandoned but the battalion maintained an 'observation' company near the roadside houses. The next day, 29 May, the C.O. told me my company would not be called on for duty there again. It was already afternoon, but this was our first assurance of rest for ten days, so we all washed our clothes. Then a sad C.O. came back. The Greek battalions had withdrawn from the war, and he now asked if 'C' Company could take over the 'observation' role as the military situation was becoming grave. The Germans seemed to be winning the main battle in the west, the battalion was moving east to the airfield to replace the departing Greeks, and the 'observation' company would become a fighting outpost to hold up a German advance three miles forward of the nearest help.
>
> 'We're ready any time you say,' was my reply. We put on our still wet clothes, to dry them with the warmth of our march and movement. Then just before we left we learnt, through the Greeks, that three hundred armed motor-cycle outfits had joined the Perivolia force—which actually was

reinforced that night by a motor-cycle battalion, several detachments of artillery, a mountain reconnaissance detachment and some tanks. I asked what my orders were if we should be attacked in force. The answer was, 'withdraw'.[52]

Again, there is a deal of difference between an article written for *Stand To* and a far more detailed, confidential letter written near the time to one's wife. The decision by Sandover to request C Company to take over the post was one that did not amuse Honner. In his letter to Marjory, Ralph stated that:

Wally Gook had never been quite happy since he took command of A Coy from McCaskill who was wounded on the 26th and now he asked to be relieved of his watching job at AA [the now front trench facing the Germans] because A Coy was worn out. They weren't really, they were the freshest of the lot and that's why they were there—in case something happened.[53]

Ralph further mentioned that Sandover had previously decided that HQ Company would replace A Company, but that this company did not now possess enough men for the task. When Ralph stated 'we're ready any time you say' to Sandover in the *Stand To* version, he had deleted the words 'was all I could say'[54] from his letter. While the chivalrous soldier could not deny his commander a request, he was not amused by the sheer injustice of it—C Company and its commander had borne more than their fair share of the fighting, and were severely down in numbers and physical condition. The less chivalrous elements of the company—the ex-Kalgoorlie miners for example—may have had a different view.

From a British perspective, events on Crete on 29 May 1941 were deteriorating quickly. As Ralph deployed his C Company remnants, a message was dropped on the Retimo sector. Only Australians could have hoped to understand its contents. Gavin Long:

The message was: 'Waratahs Bulli Puckapunyals St Kilda Gropers Albany Bogin Hopit.' Waratahs would be understood to mean New South Welshmen, Puckapunyals Victorians and Gropers West Australians. Bulli, St Kilda and Albany are all seaside towns south of the capital cities of their states. 'Bogin Hopit' may be translated 'Fight your way out; get moving'.[55]

In his Crete letter to Marjory, Ralph then recorded the dramatic
break up of the 2/11th's perimeter and his dash for freedom:

> In the morning at 6 a.m. we could see activity in Perivolia
> and could hear motor cycles and tanks being warmed up and
> assembled. I rang through to Bn. and told Len Dowling an
> attack looked likely and asked if there were any change in
> orders. There was none. I had just started cutting up a loaf of
> bread for our breakfast when the attack suddenly developed.
> The enemy had been bombarding us for an hour and now
> they swooped round from behind L, I, and J [see Ralph's map]
> and the tanks came straight up the road to K. The handful of
> men there let them get close and then gave them a hail of fire
> hoping to get something through the slits, and the tanks were
> driven off the road and ran across J. They were moving troops
> down to the Wadi that side of the road and looked as if they
> would cut us off, so I ordered a withdrawal, sent runners with
> the order to 14 and 15 Pls and told 13 Pl to fight their way
> back to 14 and 15 while I took my HQ men and the AA
> Platoon out near the sea. Keith Dundas, commanding the
> AA people was with me so he went to one section while I
> went to the other to tell them to pull out. I had to leave poor
> old Sailor Brown [who had dismissed himself from the RAP
> to be with C Company] behind because he couldn't run. I
> could see 13 Pl leap-frogging back in magnificent style—
> perfect copy-book tactics—one half bowled over the Huns
> while the other streaked back past them to the next clump of
> shrubbery, repeating the process till they reached the Wadi and
> carried on with the rapid withdrawal.
>
> Going along the open beach at the head of the last party
> out I had a hot time but the whole area north of the road
> and east of the AA line was now so plastered with artillery
> fire mortar fire machine gun fire and tank fire that it was a
> nightmare of noise and smoke and dust in which the enemy
> couldn't see us but hoped to wipe us out by sheer weight of
> fire. Their smoke and dust screen saved us. We just had to
> race through it and trust to luck, and can your husband run!
> I soon hit the front, but reaching the mouth of the wadi sent
> the others on and turned up the Wadi to see if my platoons
> had got clear. They had that Wadi taped with mortar fire and
> were pounding every inch of it. I was bowled over by blast
> a couple of times and was about to give up the attempt to
> make contact as hopeless when through a lifting pall of smoke
> I saw what must have been the last section moving back

through Platanes. I yelled to them to get away from the road—don't know if they heard me, but they seemed to be doing alright—and galloped back after my little band, passing them one by one until we'd done our three miles sprint to the aerodrome. We had outstripped the tanks etc., because the spirited opposition put up by C Coy's withdrawing handful had forced the enemy to spread out and go more wearily . . .

I took the lead of my small party just before we reached our own new lines at the aerodrome, met Pat Shanahan, told him what was happening, and got to new Bn H.Q. to find a conference of Coy Comds. discussing the decision of the force commander to surrender.[56]

Major Sandover was able to tell his officers that Campbell proposed to surrender, but that he had informed Campbell that he intended offering the 2/11th the alternative of surrender or of destroying their weapons and taking to the hills. In his letter to Marjory, Ralph recorded that Lieutenants Stoneham and Bayly had already taken to the hills when they had first heard talk of surrender. Before leaving, Ralph set himself one final task. He knew that Lieutenants Johnson and Beddells were lost causes, as both had sustained wounds that forbade any escape attempt. But Lieutenant McRobbie, Ralph's C Company 2/IC, was to the best of Ralph's knowledge fit and well and somewhere near. McRobbie had been ordered to find a new location for his rear echelon. No-one could tell Honner where McRobbie was, and after a brief but intense search of the area Ralph had to leave.

When news of the imminent German capture of the position had reached him, Lieutenant Arthur McRobbie had rushed off along an inland road. When a German armoured vehicle rounded a bend and came on McRobbie and a number of other soldiers, McRobbie, caught in a culvert, could do little other than lean against that parapet earth wall and raise his hands.[57] Lieutenant Ken (Katy) Johnson remembered the tragic end to his 2/11th service:

In no time German troops appeared on the scene including medical officers, and they checked the advanced dressing station over, made pretty prompt arrangements to evacuate the Germans . . . and arranged subsequently for us . . . and that was it.[58]

The 2/11th's brave campaigning from Bardia to Crete had come to a tragic end. During that campaign, the battalion sustained 53 killed in action, 126 wounded, and 423 prisoners of war. The 2/1st Battalion, which had also performed magnificently during its Retimo sector fighting, had 43 men killed in action, 64 wounded, and 511 soldiers (including Lieutenant-Colonel Campbell) taken prisoner. The 2/11th suffered higher casualties than any other Australian unit on the island.[59] In his article 'Paratroopers in Crete', Ralph wrote his tribute to C Company:

> 'C' Company as a fighting force had ceased to exist. Here in Crete, where so many of the bravest of the brave had fallen, it could vaunt no victory; but to the end of its last battle its devoted remnants had borne themselves manfully, the strong sustaining the weak and the weak not faltering; in the blackest moment of disaster there had been no sign of panic, no selfish action nor a bitter word. Their arms had been defeated, but the slings and arrows of outrageous fortune could not shake their sturdy spirit.[60]

The 549 2/11th Battalion POWs from the fighting in Crete were destined to spend some four years in confinement in Germany.

While those events had been unfolding in the Retimo sector on 30 May 1941, the British evacuation from the Maleme–Canea–Suda Bay area was well underway—approximately 10 000 troops were rescued by the British navy between the nights of 29 May and 1 June from the south-coast village of Sphakia. Brigadier Vasey was among them. A further evacuation of about 6000 troops took place from Heraklion on the night of 28/29 May. Ralph to Marjory:

> We had some exciting moments but no more hits. I had with me the three men who were wounded that morning, and we were joined by Shreeves who had jumped out of hospital in spite of his wounded arm to join his old company when the Huns started walking into it. We soon caught up the main body. I was the only one in the battalion still fully equipped with maps, and we had a conference as to where we should go—deciding in favour of Ay Galini on the south coast. Bayly had gone ahead with Fitzhardinge, and the troops after a midday halt split into two halves—one led by Sandover and

one by myself. The others went first and then we made off
by a different route.[61]

Before parting, Major Sandover distributed 'most of the
money'[62] and a few packets of biscuits he had picked up. He
ordered the men to pay 'wherever possible'[63] for food given
them by the Cretans. Ay Galini had been chosen as their
south-coast destination as it was considered the most likely place
to beg, borrow or steal a vessel for a possible sea trip to the
North African coast.

The hike to Ay Galini by Ralph's group was undertaken in
a state of exhaustion over rough country. At one point on
31 May they encountered an advance guard of Greeks, marching a large force of Italians north to Retimo and eventual
freedom. Ralph to Marjory:

> With a few rests we had been on the move carrying equipment
> etc for over twenty four hours. The first three miles had been
> in a running (and fast running) fight, by day and in the evening
> we had traversed difficult country, the night on the road was
> easy going but I made the pace hot and before the Italians
> were met the rear part of my column under Pud Scott and
> consisting of oldish blokes from HQ Coy were so exhausted
> they left the road. It took them another two days to get as far
> as we did on the following or same morning. We were well
> down the Platys River above Agea Galini [sic] and I didn't
> want to reach that port in daylight in case there were Huns
> there so we stripped off washed our clothes, and ourselves, in
> the river and hung the lot out to dry. At 5 p.m. we moved
> on to Agea Galini and found about 300 English troops there
> who had been landed some ten days earlier to go to the relief
> of Heraklion but hadn't gone with the rest of the force—
> mostly Argylls with a sprinkling of Black Watch and a few
> RAF and SAAF. Later in the evening Sandover's party turned
> up . . .
>   Our plans at Agea Galini were to fix up what boats we
> could but otherwise disperse inland by day and come down
> to the beach by night hoping to be taken off. We now heard
> of the evacuation of other troops, from Sphakia and Heraklion.
> At night we signalled to our aircraft and got replies, but
> nothing came for us. We patched up one motor landing craft
> and, to get batteries, Fitzhardinge, Tom Bedells, and Bill
> Mortimer (ex-Hale) took a boat along to Timbakion, but were

fired on, and that was where Tom was hit in the hand, foot
and chin . . .

About June 2 or 3 the MLC got away with Tom Bedells
and Killer Ryan on board and about 50 or 70 others—I've
forgotten the numbers. You've probably read the account of
how it was intercepted by an Italian submarine which took
the officers—but not Tom who couldn't swim—and turned
the MLC back for Crete. When the sub dived the Australians
insisted on turning again for Africa, and when they were some
miles off shore Bill Mortimer swam ashore to see if it was
friendly territory. It was—near Mersa Matruh . . .

Carroll, not of C Coy, but one of our battalion signallers
sailed in a little tub by himself some time later and when his
boat went down in a storm after many days at sea, swam a
couple of miles to Africa with his water tin on his back. He
got an M.M.[64]

The stories of the escapes from Crete by numerous small
parties—and individuals—after the two large-scale evacuations
from Sphakia and Heraklion are too numerous to mention and
not relevant to this work, but Carroll's remarkable exit from
Crete had a direct bearing on Ralph's plight. When Carroll
arrived in Egypt he gave information that small groups of British
and Australian troops were still awaiting escape in the Ay Galini
area. Ralph to Marjory:

. . . Friday following I got my various section leaders to take
tracings of my maps, advised them on routes, and districts,
food & water and boat possibilities, sea-routes and winds. At
midday the English CO received German envoys with a white
flag. All the week Stoneham and I had gone a couple of miles
up-river each day to a swimming pool where we swam,
washed, cooked our own meals and slept or went foraging for
more food. One day we invited Ted Royce and Jock Murray
up and they decided to join us daily. And then on the Friday
we invited Sandover and Pud Scott up. Pud and I however
stayed behind to buy some cheeses and were still there when
the envoys of the Huns arrived.

We headed up-river and broke the sad news to the others.
In the evening the six of us decided to investigate. We found
no troops in the accustomed night gathering places. We stole
on towards the town. A section in military formation marched
along the beach away from the town. We guessed they were
Germans. Sandover and I then had an argument. I wanted to

go on till I heard Germans talking because I would recognise their speech as German. Sandover wanted to go because he would not only recognise German but would understand it. We compromised by both going, leaving Royce, Murray, Scott and Stoneham to await our return. We were joined by a boy and were creeping along past the hospital when we saw a man—apparently a sentry. I was in the lead and melted into the shadow. Sandover followed suit. The boy off to the side was seen by the sentry and challenged. But the sentry was a Greek and after a talk with the boy told us the Germans were in the town. So we said good-bye to rescue from Agea Galini—and I am not at liberty to tell you what happened in the next three months—but our party stayed together, some-times with additions until we left Crete.[65]

Ralph's extraordinary letters to Marjory then ended. To his family's knowledge, he either failed to write again during his varied future campaigning or such letters were not preserved. Given his sense of history, the latter seems most likely.

The story of Honner's three-month survival on Crete is vitally interwoven with that of one Costas Folakis. This English-speaking Greek took Sandover and Honner's party to a cave near his village of Apodoulou, where he and his friends were able to provide the party with regular food supplies. The foothills around Apodoulou contained numerous caves, which allowed some measure of safety and constant changes of 'address'. But the danger of detection and capture was still acute, and the corresponding danger of capture and execution of the Cretans was high. Major Sandover would later write that:

> On one occasion Gus [Folakis] took me to see Major Ford of the Welsh Regiment who also had walked over the mountains from Retimo. He and a few others were in a cave on the south east side of Mt Ida. We slept in Gus' village and reached a point about half an hour's climb from Ford's cave when we heard shots. Through glasses I watched the little groups being rounded up by a German patrol. Thanking heavens we weren't half an hour earlier—we retired rapidly.[66]

Late in July, the fortunes of the party took a decisive turn for the better. A local Cretan gave Sandover an intriguing message:

The monastery at Prevali.

> To the English Major.
> Do you remember the young lady who swam naked to the
> Elaphonesos Islands? The man who entertained you then is
> waiting to greet you now. Follow this guide he can be
> trusted.[67]

Apart from the nature of the message—which seemed utter
nonsense to Sandover—he was immediately concerned by the
fact that the message was dated '7 July', showing the numeral
seven with a stroke through it which was a European, and most
certainly a German, custom. Newly outfitted with a new but
undersized pair of boots to replace his disintegrated former pair,
Sandover set out on a donkey for the meeting, which was
conducted in a small hut about two-thirds of the way back to
Retimo.

Sandover was greeted by Lieutenant-Commander Poole,
who had been landed by submarine (HMS *Thrasher*). He was
delighted to learn that a group of 2/11th soldiers was in hiding
near the monastery at Prevali. This group included Jackson,
Wild, Dowling, Shanahan, Greenway and Bayley. Poole had
mistaken Sandover for the well-known archaeologist Pendlebury, and had therefore related the story of the naked female
swimmer as a means of communicating with Pendlebury rather

Ralph and Sandover's evacuation point.

than Sandover. No matter, the almost unbelievable news was that Sandover and his party were to report to Brother Dionysius at the monastery on 18 August. Major Sandover:

> We moved by night (two nights march) to the monastery at Prevali . . .
>
> On arrival at the monastery we were told to take orders from certain people only. It was a great strain when some other locals told us that a submarine had arrived and we had better hurry. In fact H.M.S Torbay came in two nights running. When we received instructions from the right people to go to the beach there was a crowd of troops—Commandos, New Zealanders, Cypriots, Aussies, and many Greeks already there.
>
> Having discovered I was the senior and that there were 120 troops I divided them into three parties and drew lots for priority. We were the last group. Staring out to sea, knowing that there were Germans about a mile away on each flank I had little hope of being amongst the lucky ones. Suddenly the submarine loomed up in the darkness. She looked huge. I swam out to the Folboat canoe that came in. The naval officer asked 'How many?' and then said 'Keep them quiet or we'll go away'. He said he could take 120 but no Greeks. He had a rope and men had to go out with non-swimmers between swimmers. At this stage a Greek sailor who had swum

out and been refused was dragged ashore unconscious. There was some angry muttering. I tried without success to bring him round, but fortunately I spotted Scott who had done surf life saving—he did things the right way.[68]

On a number of occasions Ralph told the author of those last moments on the beach: of giving his tattered boots to a Cretan, which seemed such little reward for the help and compassion they had given him; of the almost carnival atmosphere and noise on the beach, which Ralph felt sure would cause their capture ('everyone in Crete knew where we were and what we were doing except the Germans'); and, finally, the sadness at the disintegration and loss of a magnificent company he had raised, trained and led in battle.

When HMS *Torbay* left Crete on the night of 19/20 August 1941, it performed one trial dive to ascertain whether it was capable of doing so if required, and then sped for Alexandria. Major Sandover:

> In a dirty pair of shorts I was invited on to the bridge of H.M.S. Torbay as we sailed into Alexandria harbour, a marvellous experience . . .
>
> After the war those of us who were so wonderfully cared for in the mountains were able to send a substantial amount of clothing etc. to the Greek Red Cross as a small token of our gratitude. One sentence sticks in my mind: one of the Greek helpers said:
>
> 'Major, my greatest wish is that you will take a glass of wine in my house with my wife the day we are free. That is all I wish to live for'—wonderful people.[69]

7

SOME UNTIDY THINGS

Richard Honner was five years of age, and his brother Brian three, when Marjory opened the door to face the telegram that told her that 'her Ralphie' was 'missing in action believed killed'. The resulting 'weeping and wailing and gathering of neighbours and relatives'[1] was burnt into the boys' memories, despite the fact that their father was more a photo on the mantelpiece in their lounge in Nedlands than a real, touchable person.

That 'weeping and wailing' was tragically duplicated across various suburbs in Perth, through the Great Southern farming belt, in country towns such as Bunbury and Kalgoorlie, as 53 sets of parents mourned the loss of their sons killed on Crete and a further 549 wondered what care their sons would receive as prisoners of war.

That sense of loss was also keenly felt by the newly promoted Major Ralph Honner when, after a brief period of leave in Cairo, he returned to his battalion and his C Company in Palestine. It was a company in title only as Ralph supervised the gradual build-up of reinforcements around a sparse nucleus of escapees from Crete. The end of that campaign also saw the end of Lieutenant-Colonel Tom Louch's association with the 2/11th Battalion. Brigadier Vasey, in a letter to his wife on 24 June 1941, wrote that:

Two of my problems have been solved. Mitchell and Louch, of the WA battalion, have been recalled for duty in Australia. This is a new technique which has been invented for disposing of some who are too old; but of course that's not publicly announced . . .[2]

And on 21 September:

As a matter of fact recommendations after Greece and Crete were very difficult. Mitchell did no good, Louch did nothing and neither of their seconds-in-command did as well as I had hoped. Consequently I could recommend none.[3]

Vasey's assertions do not bear fair examination.

It is not the purpose of this work to evaluate the command performance of Lieutenant-Colonel Mitchell of the 2/8th Battalion. But an assessment of Louch and his 2/IC, Major Sandover, is pertinent.

Lieutenant-Colonel Louch's North African campaigning had been impressive, as the record of the 2/11th Battalion clearly shows. In Greece he had sustained an injury that might have inhibited any CO's continued participation in the campaign. During a number of conversations with the author, Ralph spoke highly of Louch—of his military knowledge, his tactical decisions, his relationship with his men and his drive and energy.[4]

Vasey's assessment of Major Sandover and of Major Key (2/8th Battalion) on Crete was quite simply baseless and ignorant—ignorant, because he was in no possible position to judge them. He had been out of touch with the proceedings on the 2/1st and 2/11th's Retimo front. That operation had been commanded by Lieutenant-Colonel Campbell. An appalling communications system on Crete must also have severely prejudiced any reliable information as to events at that locality. Further, it is worth recording that the Retimo sector had held its ground longer than had the others. The fact that General Freyberg had sent his personal congratulations to Campbell for both his and Sandover's efforts during the battle is ample testimony to the point.

This work has chronicled in some measure Major Sandover's Crete performance and the circumstances of his and Ralph's escape from that island. As with Louch, it is hard to question Sandover's battle record. The superb 2/11th performance during the Greece and Crete campaigns should surely reflect on its commander.

Vasey was also critical of the 2/8th's performance at Vevi in Greece. Gavin Long would later write that:

> When he made these generalisations Vasey probably knew little of what was happening to the 2/8th in the late afternoon after its communications (which went through the Rangers' position) had been overrun. Later, in Crete, he talked about the engagement to Major A.S. Key, the second-in-command of the battalion at Vevi and its commander in Crete, with two company commanders, and left them with the impression that for the first time he had the battalion's story correctly.[5]

Nor did Vasey have any clear perception of the operation undertaken by Key's 2/8th Battalion on Crete, as this unit was taken from his operational command, and sent to Canea under the British. In fact, the historian is entitled to ask what it was that Brigadier Vasey did do during the Battle for Crete—his command of some Australian units was only restored just prior to the withdrawal, and he was therefore in no position to make clear assessments of Sandover and Key.[6] Ralph maintained that the performance of both of his battalion commanders, Louch and Sandover, had been exemplary.[7]

Major Arthur Key was destined to command the 2/14th Battalion and fight alongside Ralph at a little-known Kokoda Trail village named Isurava.

While various commanders received varied reputations in the Libyan, Greece and Crete campaigns, Major Ralph Honner's stocks were high. He had been recommended for a Military Cross at Derna and had finally been awarded one for his campaigning in Greece. Given a modest comparison between his Greece and Crete efforts, it is of interest to contemplate why he was not rewarded for his sternest and most prolonged test thus far—surely Crete. The plausible answer perhaps lies with the same ignorance on the part of Vasey as had applied to Sandover and Key.

In a letter dated 17 May 1956 to a Mr Bazley, presumably a staff member of the Australian War Memorial, Ralph described his last weeks with the 2/11th:

> Dear Mr Bazley,
> I'm sorry you think it necessary to have more detail about myself but I shall endeavour to supply you with what you want . . .

In late September or early October [1941] 2/11 Bn moved
to Syria where we started to prepare a defensive line to hold
up any invasion from the North. I had not been there long
when I was called to Corps HQ at Aley in Lebanon to act as
prosecutor in a series of courts-martial. Thence I was recalled
to my unit to be informed I had been given command of 19
Trg Bn.[8]

At that time, each AIF brigade had a correspondingly numbered
training battalion which consisted of three companies, each
manned by reinforcements for one of the three battalions.
Command of the training battalion went on battalion rotation.[9]
It must have been around this time—while Ralph was training
his training battalion—that Marjory received a further telegram
which caused a party to be staged in Nedlands. Ralph's papers
do not provide a date, but his eldest child Richard remembered
the party involving relatives, friends and neighbours.[10] In March
1942, Ralph recorded that he:

> Left the M.E. in a ship whose name ended in 'ic', White Star
> Line—changed at Bombay to 'Holbrook'—thence to Colombo,
> Mombasa, Durban (dodging Japs), arriving at Fremantle in May
> 1942.[11]

Ralph and Marjory Honner had seven priceless days together
at Nedlands. But if the temporary resumption of marital bliss
seemed perfectly normal to wife and husband, it constituted a
strange experience for sons Richard and Brian. Who was this
man? When Brian went to kindergarten at the local convent
soon after his father's return, he informed the nuns, 'there's a
strange man cuddling Mummy in the bedroom!'[12] The Loreto
Sisters must have been in the know, as years later Brian
was told, 'I apparently had the Nuns in stitches'.[13] Ralph to
Mr Bazley:

> With my staff of 19 Trg Bn (less some Eastern States personnel)
> I took over the training of some recruits in Northam Camp.
> Then I was posted as tactical adviser (and exercise umpire) to
> a brigade from Victoria located near Geraldton. I lived with
> 38 Bn and I think one of the other battalions in the brigade
> was 14 Bn, but I wouldn't bank on that.[14]

In January 1942, seven weeks to the day after the Japanese
attack on the American Pacific Fleet at Pearl Harbour, and while

Richard and Brian Honner during the war.

Marjory Honner with Richard at Nedlands, Perth.

still stationed in the Middle East, Ralph wrote a letter to his cousin in Sydney. A portion of that letter was indeed prophetic:

> And now as we look round for our next fight the threat of war looms over Australia—I fervently hope it never becomes worse than a threat because I have seen some untidy things happen to peaceful towns and harmless citizens.[15]

There had been a number of 'untidy things' occurring both in Australia and its mandated territory of Papua New Guinea, leading up to and after Ralph's return to his homeland. And those events were to have a profound influence on Ralph Honner's destiny.

While Ralph had been campaigning in Libya, Greece and Crete, immense political and military change had occurred in Australia during 1941. In February, the Chiefs of Staff provided the government with an appreciation of possible Japanese ambitions and military options, and of how Australia might best react to the apprehended threats. To respond to the needs of a South-East Asian and home defence, the forces in Australia at this time consisted of the AIF 8th Division and the militia, which comprised the 1st and 2nd Cavalry Divisions, four infantry divisions and parts of a fifth division and corps troops. In theory this seemed a formidable force, but due to the priority given to the AIF 6th, 7th and 9th Divisions in terms of training, equipment and leadership—almost a world away in the Middle East—the home forces were critically vulnerable.

If their lack of training and leadership and equipment was inhibiting enough, the militia served under a further handicap— the slur of being branded as 'chocos' (chocolate soldiers) by the AIF. The term 'choco' is hardly one of endearment, and was used by the AIF to describe the militia from the onset of the war. The AIF maintained that the militia, whose rates of pay were initially higher than those of the AIF, possessed all the 'trappings' of soldiers but, because of the conscription law of service for the militia in Australia and her territories only, were not going to fight. For their part, the militia often perceived the AIF to be arrogant in their dealings with them. Because of this ill-feeling between the two forces, many militiamen refused outright to join the AIF during the Papuan campaign.

As a result of the February preliminary appreciation, it was decided to raise a militia battalion to garrison Port Moresby. The role was allotted to the 49th Battalion from Queensland. The battalion arrived in Port Moresby in early March 1941. Until the outbreak of war with Japan nine months later, the degree of effort given to the training, equipping and morale of the 49th was a disgrace, and was to place it at a severe disadvantage when it was later to be committed to battle.

Towards the latter part of 1941, as war clouds loomed larger over the South-East Asian horizon, it was decided to boost the Port Moresby garrison to brigade strength; the 53rd Battalion from New South Wales and the 39th Battalion from Victoria were chosen to implement that decision. The raising and deployment of the 53rd Battalion bore little, if any, resemblance to the earlier raising of AIF battalions—it is a tragic and damning story.

Originally raised for service in Darwin, the 53rd came into being around 1 November 1941, after eighteen militia battalions were each ordered to supply a quota of 62 men for the new unit. To bring the battalion to full strength, an additional 100 personnel were recruited in a manner that reflects the appalling staff work of the time. Sergeant Keith Irwin, 53rd Battalion:

Even at this stage we received a draft of soldiers, mostly eighteen years of age. These poor devils had no idea what was happening to them. They had not been told where they were going, what unit they were destined for, or any information at all. They had received no final leave, were given no chance to let their families know what was happening to them. They were just taken down to the *Aquitania* and put on board. Most of them had never seen or handled a rifle. This was a disgrace because many of these youngsters, who had literally been shanghaied, later paid the supreme sacrifice during the battles in the mountains and at Sanananda. Once the *Aquitania* put to sea, we were told that we would be heading for Port Moresby, not Darwin. A training program was implemented so that we NCOs could give the new recruits some elementary training in the use and handling of the .303 rifle.[16]

This battalion, under the command of Lieutenant-Colonel Ward, had obviously no chance in its initial training to build an *esprit de corps*, so vital to any unit's morale; rather, because of the conditions of its formation, it was to develop a bitterness and anger within its ranks that would work directly against the very qualities needed for success.

The 39th Battalion was raised in Victoria in October 1941 from elements of the 3rd and 4th Infantry Divisions, and the 2nd Cavalry Division. The circumstances of its formation were far less trying than those of the 53rd's. Its original commander was Lieutenant-Colonel Conran, a veteran of the first AIF. Although 52 years of age, and later destined to suffer a decline in health from the demands of tropical service, Conran, along with some of his officers, can be given high praise for the *esprit de corps* instilled into their new battalion. In their role as a garrison brigade the 39th, 49th and 53rd Battalions had the 13th Field Regiment and the 23rd Heavy Anti-Aircraft Battery as support. Major-General Basil Morris, who had assumed command of the 8th Military District on 26 May 1941, could also look to assistance from two other sources. The Papuan Infantry Battalion (PIB) consisted of Papuan natives led by Australian officers and NCOs. Emphasis was placed on having in its ranks men with a knowledge of local conditions and, above all, of the terrain. The second territorial unit was the New Guinea Volunteer Rifles. This force was predominantly manned by returned soldiers settled in New Guinea and their enthusiastic neighbours.

Barely six weeks after the arrival of the 39th and 53rd Battalions to complete the strength of the 30th Brigade, the Japanese had attacked and captured Rabaul, bombed Port Moresby, and captured Singapore (15 February 1942). Further, before the end of the month they had landed on Timor and invaded Java. From that time on, the utter vulnerability of the Australian mainland could not be concealed from an Asian conqueror exploiting his success.

In mid-April 1942 Major-General Vasey, now Deputy Chief of the General Staff—and having arrived back in Australia on 1 January 1942—wrote to subordinate army commanders requesting monthly reports concerning the combat efficiency of brigades in the army. There were six guidelines or ratings:

A   Efficient and experienced for mobile operations.
B   Efficient as a formation for mobile operations, but not experienced.
C   Individual brigades are efficient for mobile operations, but higher training is needed.
D   Individual brigades are efficient in a static role. Additional brigade and higher training is required.
E   Units have completed training. A considerable amount of brigade training and higher training is required.
F   Unit training is not yet complete.[17]

Only five weeks before the 39th Battalion was committed to action in the Owen Stanley Range the grading given it by Brigadier Porter was an F: that is, the 39th, 49th and 53rd Battalions were given the lowest possible rating while being deployed in the most threatened area.[18]

In late June 1942 the 30th Brigade was decisively reinforced by 30 officers from the 7th Division, at that time stationed in Australia and graded at A—the highest rating. It is of significance to record that the 39th applied for, and was granted, fifteen of those young officers: one major, six captains and eight lieutenants. Combined with the young and competent and keen remaining militia officers, this injection of experience was to give the battalion excellent junior leadership.[19] Further, on 7 July Lieutenant-Colonel Owen— an escapee from Rabaul— replaced Lieutenant-Colonel Conran as the CO of the 39th Battalion.

The Battle of the Coral Sea (5–8 May 1942) was a temporary reprieve for the beleaguered garrison of Port Moresby, while the decisive Battle of Midway (6–8 June 1942) proved to be the Japanese Navy's nemesis in the Pacific War. The enemy did not, in the foreseeable future, have the necessary naval capacity to mount a major seaborne invasion of Port Moresby. Thus, in order to capture that base and port, and thereby further isolate Australia, the Japanese were now committed to a two-pronged attack—one over the Owen Stanley Range via the Kokoda Trail, the other by an invasion of Milne Bay. The area Gona–Sanananda–Buna, on the northeastern coast of Papua New Guinea, was to be used as a beachhead base for the Kokoda Trail offensive.

The American Commander-in-Chief South-West Pacific Area, General Douglas MacArthur, who had arrived in Australia in March 1942 after his campaigning in the Philippines, perceived that it might be time to change from the defensive to the offensive, and he turned his attention to the north coast of Papua. Reconnaissance of that region revealed that an area northeast of Dobodura was an ideal venue for the construction of an advanced air base from where the Allied airforces could attack Rabaul as a prelude to future invasion.

As a consequence of such thinking, General Blamey, now Commander-in-Chief Australian Military Forces, instructed Major-General Morris on 29 June 1942 to secure Kokoda, a small Papuan Administration Post which lay across the Owen Stanley Range and constituted the inland gateway to Port Moresby—the Kokoda Trail. Kokoda was of immense tactical importance, as it possessed the only airfield in the area.

To comply with Blamey's orders, Captain Sam Templeton and his B Company 39th Battalion were ordered to cross the Kokoda Trail. Templeton's young soldiers—the average age of one of his sections was eighteen years[20]—walked into a green nightmare. There were no maps of the Kokoda Trail; distance was measured in hours spent marching, not by yards or miles; supply was by native porters, the now legendary 'Fuzzy Wuzzy Angels', and later by plane drops (and never at an adequate level); the wounded and sick were destined to face a seven-day tortuous climb back over the Trail to Port Moresby before they could receive decent medical attention; communication was by a humble signal cable that was to stretch over that inhospitable terrain; and, worst of all, they and their sister companies were to be deployed in an environment completely unknown to them.

On 21 July the Japanese gained the initiative by a landing at Gona. The enemy force was an advance party, sent to ascertain the feasibility of the Kokoda Trail as a military route to Port Moresby. It consisted of approximately 1500–2000 troops. Templeton's B Company was forced to conduct a fighting withdrawal from the bank of the Kumusi River back to Kokoda. During the course of that fighting Templeton was killed. Lieutenant-Colonel Owen and one platoon were landed at Kokoda by air while the battalion's A, C, D (two platoons) and E Companies now began the laborious task of climbing the Kokoda Trail to reach Kokoda, as further flights to that village were cancelled because of the close proximity of the enemy.

At around 2.30 am on 28 July 1942 the Japanese launched an all-out attack up the steep slope at the northern end of the 39th's Kokoda perimeter. Lieutenant Gough 'Judy' Garland was among the defenders:

> When Owen came over to us we were on the perimeter of Kokoda . . . He was another one similar to Sam Templeton, that wanted to show his leadership, and he walked around the top of the perimeter where we were all lying down; naturally you would . . . And I said, 'Sir, I think you're taking an unnecessary risk walking around among the troops like that.' 'Well' he said, 'I've got to do it.' I suppose a half an hour later he got shot right through the forehead.[21]

Unable to hold Kokoda, B Company withdrew to Deniki. The 39th Battalion concentrated at Deniki between 1–5 August 1942. Major Allan Cameron, the Brigade Major of the 30th Brigade, arrived at Deniki on 4 August to assume command of the battalion. His arrival was recorded in Warrant Officer John Wilkinson's diary:

> 4/8/42. Changed to A Company. Major Cameron arrived later and took charge of all troops. Very bitter towards men. Says they are cowards. Must have met up with the few who shot through.[22]

The soldiers referred to were some of the youngsters of B Company who had 'gone bush' during that company's baptism of fire at Oivi and Kokoda. Cameron refused to acknowledge these men, and considered that the company had lost its good name; he considered it adequate for no more than a reserve role in the future. These young men had suffered the full brunt of the Japanese advance to Kokoda, and had lost Templeton and Owen in the process. Sleepless, wet and ill-fed, they had encountered the best jungle soldiers in the world at that time. Further, Cameron's slur did not fairly apply to the whole company but merely a small number who had become horribly disoriented in that jungle environment.

Cameron decided to mount a three-pronged attack to retake Kokoda. Captain Symington's A Company was to move on that village by the use of an 'unknown' track; Captain Bidstrup's D Company was to venture east to cut off the inevitable Japanese attempt to reinforce their Kokoda troops once the attack had begun; and Captain Dean's C Company was to advance along the main track into Kokoda.

The attack to retake Kokoda was reliant on A Company firing a Very light signal after having secured the village and New Guinea Force HQ then landing reinforcements by air at Kokoda. The attack was a dismal failure, as Symington's flare was not seen and New Guinea Force did not have the capability to land even one battalion—the 49th—by air. Further, the three companies were all out of contact with each other and with HQ at Deniki. The 39th Battalion expended much in energy and resources (both material and human) on a mission that was based more on wishful thinking than on military prudence.[23] After a series of attacks on the 39th at Deniki, the Japanese forced another withdrawal to the next village back along the Kokoda Trail—a village named Isurava.

On 1 August 1942, three days after Lieutenant-Colonel Owen's death at Kokoda, Major Ralph Honner was near 'the Midland junction',[24] still with the 38th Battalion, when he received orders to return to Perth. On arrival he was informed of his promotion to Lieutenant-Colonel and ordered to report to Port Moresby and assume command of the 39th Australian Infantry Battalion. Ralph would most likely have never heard of the Kokoda Trail; he would never have heard of Isurava; and, most likely, he would have been unaware of the existence of the 39th Militia Battalion.

After one day with Marjory, Ralph flew from Perth to Ceduna, thence to Parafield near Adelaide, Melbourne, Sydney,

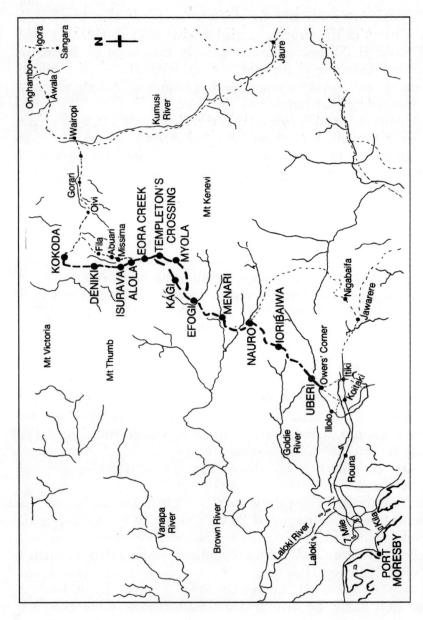

The Kokoda Trail.

Brisbane, Townsville, and, finally, by Catalina Flying Boat to Port Moresby.[25] Arriving in Port Moresby, Ralph was given orders to relieve Major Cameron and assume command of the 39th Battalion and Maroubra Force. He was further ordered to hold the Japanese on the northern ramparts of the Owen Stanley Range until reinforced.

At that primitive village, in August 1942, a ragged, exhausted, but defiant young band of warriors were to confront a tenfold enemy and then, when all seemed lost, were to be decisively reinforced by an elite battalion of AIF veterans, who together were to write a critical chapter in the Australian story.

8

A SOLDIER'S CALVARY

Creative intelligence is and always has been the supreme
requirement in the commander—coupled with moral courage.

Liddell Hart, 1936[1]

The 39th Battalion Unit Diary records that Ralph arrived at
Isurava at 1.30 pm on 16 August 1942.[2] The battle situation
forbade a battalion parade or a formal gathering of all the
officers, or even an exchange of orders. Lieutenant-Colonel
Ralph Honner's entrance at Isurava was therefore very much in
the mould of the man—quiet and businesslike. His adjutant,
Lieutenant Keith Lovett, remembered the moment:

> Well, first of all, we had no prior notice that he was coming
> up, we didn't know what was happening. At that stage Major
> Cameron was the CO and we thought he was going to be
> our CO. It was a surprise then that this person . . . walked
> up to a group of us standing around at Isurava. I walked over
> to him, I saw he was an officer, and I said, 'Can I help you
> in any way?' He said, 'Yes, I'm Colonel Honner, I'm your
> new CO.' And he said, 'Who are you?' And I told him who
> I was. He said, 'Well, I'd like you to take me around and
> introduce me to the company commanders and we'll settle
> down and start our business.' He looked a perfectly fit speci-
> men, neatly dressed and presented himself very well. He told

The adjutant of 39th Battalion,
Lieutenant (later Captain)
Keith Lovett.

me briefly about his history and what he'd done, and I thought,
'Well, that's good enough for me, let's go!'[3]

What Ralph then witnessed during his tour of the 39th's
positions must surely have appalled him. Years later he wrote:

> Physically the pathetically young warriors of the 39th were in
> poor shape. Worn out by strenuous fighting and exhausting
> movement, and weakened by lack of food and sleep and
> shelter, many of them had literally come to a standstill. Prac-
> tically every day torrential rains fell all through the afternoon
> and night, cascading into their cheerless weapon-pits and
> soaking the clothes they wore—the only ones they had. In
> these they shivered through the long chill vigil of the lonely
> nights when they were required to stand awake and alert but
> still and silent. Only the morning brought a gleam of com-
> fort—a turn at sleeping and forgetting, a chance perhaps, to
> lie and dry in the warmth of the glowing day.[4]

Captain Blue Steward, RMO 2/16th Battalion, saw the soldiers
of the 39th only days later:

> . . . gaunt spectres with gaping boots and rotting tatters of
> uniform hanging around them like scarecrows. Their faces had
> no expression, their eyes sunk back into their sockets. They
> were drained by malaria, dysentery and near starvation . . .[5]

Those soldiers were not in their mid-to-late twenties and therefore in the prime of youth; they were not the hand-picked, worldly Kalgoorlie miners, nor the farmers from the Great Southern; they had not experienced detailed training in their home state, followed by relatively extensive training overseas; nor had they experienced the public adulation and perceived prestige associated with membership of the AIF; they were, as Honner termed them, 'just growing boys'.[6] And a fifth of them carried a stigma—the worst possible military stigma: B Company had been branded as cowards by Major Cameron, who had then suggested to Honner that they be broken up and scattered within the remaining companies as reinforcements.

Few, if any, commanders in Australian military history could have contemplated walking into such a state of affairs, where the stakes were as high and the resources so seemingly meagre.

It was at this point that Ralph displayed Liddell Hart's 'moral courage'.[7] Honner held a company commanders conference late on 16 August. At that meeting and after consultation with those officers—Captains Symington A Company, Jacob C Company, Bidstrup D Company and Merritt E Company—Ralph appointed Lieutenant Bevan French, a militia officer, to command B Company. He told him that B Company's perimeter was the most likely place of attack, the post of honour. In an interview with the author in 1986, Ralph stated that:

> They were the only troops I had. I had to make them as good as possible. They wouldn't have been too well received in the companies they were sent to, coming with that reputation. I thought that I couldn't afford to lose a company. I went there with the job of holding the Japs, and this is what I had to hold them with; they were my troops and we were going to do the best we could.[8]

Such a decision inspires not only the 'victims' but those around them. Sergeant Jack Sim, Signals 39th Battalion:

> I think the battalion's spirit may have been inspired, it was certainly exemplified, by Ralph Honner the leader. That decision . . . that rather than wreck them completely, he'd let them stay with the unit that they'd helped to make . . . it was a wonderful decision, and that spirit was shown again and again by B Company.[9]

From the moment Ralph Honner arrived at Isurava, he was engaged in the creation of the Kokoda myth—not a fable, or mere story, but the making of a legend. And when he cast his experienced military eye over those 'growing boys', he most definitely did not see a jungle miniature of defeat and exhaustion and hopelessness but the lofty, ageless nobility of the eternal soldier. In his foreword to the author's *Those Ragged Bloody Heroes*, Honner wrote:

> That glory is not of the exultation of war but of the exaltation of man, the nobility of man sublimated in the fiery crucible of war, shining faithfulness and fortitude and gentleness and compassion elevated from all dross.[10]

In Ralph's epic view of life and war, Isurava was not merely a battle on the Kokoda Trail but Australia's Agincourt. Given his knowledge of Shakespeare, it is little wonder that Ralph saw Isurava in those terms: at Agincourt King Harry and his liegemen were also outnumbered by about five to one; the driving rain and mud and savage marching to Agincourt had its parallel at Isurava; and the slaughter of the English boys by the French would have its parallel at Isurava, and at other points along the Kokoda Trail. Ralph's repeated reference to the Battle of Agincourt and the nobility of the soldier in his foreword to the author's *Those Ragged Bloody Heroes* demonstrates the point. Thus, for Ralph to have disgraced B Company by removing them from the line was an anathema to everything he believed in—you did the opposite by deploying them at the post of honour.

On 17 August 1942, Ralph's thirty-eighth birthday, he made adjustments to his company dispositions on the basis of his appreciation of the previous day. He perceived that Isurava provided a reasonably good delaying position. Its northern and southern extremities allowed for some view over the eastward-flowing creeks, which provided obstacles, if narrow ones, for the enemy. Although thick scrub ran virtually up to both the front and rear creeks, there were cleared patches of ground on each side of the track in the central area. Isurava village lay on a flat clearing to the east of the track and south of the front creek. Through the village a steep descending track ran eastwards to Asigari, situated on the other side of the Eora Valley. The western flank was dominated by timber and extremely thick jungle beyond. A track from Naro ridge ran eastwards through an overgrown native garden to join the main Isurava–Deniki track just north of the front creek.

Its track command and its tactical advantages made Isurava an acceptable defensive proposition, but it was far from impregnable and it was woefully undermanned.

The Japanese had three alternatives for their attack on Isurava. The first was an advance along the eastern side of Eora Valley to bypass Isurava. The second alternative was an attack along the higher ground to the west from Naro to Alola. A direct attack on the 39th Battalion at Isurava was the last—it had the advantage of securing the main track for movement, communication and supply without having to move far afield and over severe gradients. The element of time made the last option the most attractive. If the Japanese were to choose either of the first two, they must cut the track near Alola and then move north to deal with the 39th Battalion from the rear.

Ralph deployed his companies to meet the expected attacks. The area bounded by his B, D and E Companies and the main track contained open, overgrown gardens, with some high grass and a sugar cane plantation. The only real killing ground—low grass with good fields of fire—lay west of B Company's main positions towards the edge of the timber. The enemy should avoid it. But, because they could swing from the Deniki track to the Naro track and cross the creek to come in from the high ground, through sparse jungle and rather open woodland opposite B Company, to assemble in large numbers near the timber edge for the short rush across the killing ground, they might be tempted to try it.

Ralph therefore ordered B Company to dig in, in deep, narrow weapon pits, with forward posts in the timber edge in front of them and reserve positions behind them for their support—or their retirement in the event of a limited withdrawal. And despite the fact that the 39th's soldiers did not possess entrenching tools, but had dug in with bully-beef tins and bayonets, Honner's orders were explicit concerning the depth of the pits. When touring his perimeter he had noticed far too many shallow pits, and sometimes shallow depressions rather than pits.

Very dense jungle between D Company's gentle ridge and the hidden rear creek made an attack from the south unlikely.

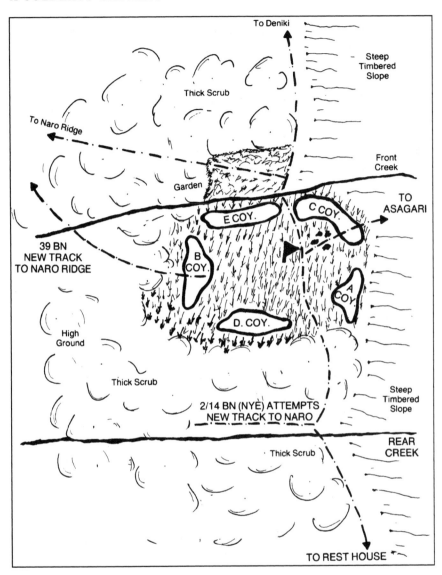

Isurava before the attack, 27 August 1942.

Therefore, D Company was held available to support B Company's left and prevent the enemy from slipping past. To the east, difficulty of access, lack of an assembly area and the prospect of a very steep climb up a jungled slope made a major organised attack extremely unlikely.

On the north, the shallow creek was crossable. It did not provide a great killing ground to the defenders, whose requirement of cover for survival minimised the effectiveness of what fields of fire were available. This would be the enemy's prime target. Ample assembly areas were available north of the creek opposite E Company and south of the creek opposite B Company, with easy access to E Company by slipping past B Company's right flank. Above all, there were covered approaches, day or night, into the heart of E Company's stronghold.[11]

Ralph knew that the 39th could hold its open left flank while its B Company commanded its killing ground. But once the enemy penetrated E Company's locality they could pour in in sufficient numbers to achieve the conquest of Isurava; and the enemy had the numbers and the capability to concentrate a large force. For the entire struggle for Isurava, this position was the prime piece of Australian military real estate.

Late on the afternoon of 17 August Ralph journeyed out to the 39th's standing patrol, which was deployed about 45 minutes' march forward of Isurava. D Company had provided this two-platoon strength patrol since the evacuation from Deniki. During his reconnaissance, Ralph determined that the patrol should be reduced from two platoons to one, as there was an acute shortage of fit men inside the Isurava perimeter. The battalion unit diary described Ralph's use of the standing patrol and its procedures:

> Patrols lightly equipped for 24 hrs tour of duty were now changed during the first hour of light when morning mist made visibility bad and the enemy, owing to difficulty of night movement, were unlikely to attack so far forward of Deniki base. Role of the patrols was to deny the enemy use of the track and thus delay enemy reconnaissance of our main positions at Isurava. To give defence in depth and a ready reserve at the time when an enemy attack was most likely (mid-morning), each patrol, when relieved, moved back to the next delaying position about 200 yards to the rear and remained there until 1130 hrs, then returned to Isurava. The platoon next for duty stood ready equipped for instant action for 24 hrs before taking over the standing patrol, ready to move to the support of the forward patrol if needed.[12]

This forward-standing patrol is an illustration of the 'creative intelligence' of the Isurava commander. In an interview with the author in September 1986, Ralph stated that:

There wasn't much I could do in the way of an attack except hold the enemy at arm's length as long as possible to prevent them from finding out how weak we were and how small indeed was our garrison. Had they known how small we were they should have gone around us and cut us off from our supplies and annihilated us. We had to buy time and buy distance as long as possible and as far as possible.[13]

Within 36 hours, Ralph had stamped himself on events. And his style of command and quick feel for the situation did not go unnoticed by his adjutant:

First of all, he was always a perfect gentleman, no matter what the situation. He didn't lose his temper, he didn't show disgust. If I approached him with certain things that I was unhappy about he'd try and smooth it over. He had a strong personality about him. He could get around something . . . he'd get around it in some way and we'd solve the problem and it'd work out very well. A very easy man to work with. You could rely on what he said was going to happen . . . and he'd give you confidence to go on and do it. He went to give himself a bit of time to work everything out, instead of just taking over what was there. He made the war his war. He didn't bounce things off me, he was the commander and he had a plan in his mind . . . as CO he did most of the reconnaissance himself . . . he wouldn't communicate what he was thinking or what he was proposing to do until he'd worked out his plan . . . he knew what he wanted.[14]

It is interesting to note that this brief period of Honner's command constituted the first time that the 39th Battalion had been together as a battalion during its Kokoda Trail campaigning. They now perceived their platoons and companies as a vital part of a whole battalion scheme, where plans for mutual support and counterattack were in place and, further, they were fortified by the return of hitherto lost or cut-off groups from their recent fighting at Deniki. And on 21 August came the news that they could expect relief—'all the news seemed good news, and courage feeds on hope'.[15]

The 39th's anticipated relief was a result of a number of dramatic changes to both the command and formation structure in Port Moresby in early August 1942.

It will be recalled that the Japanese had landed at Gona on 21 July 1942. With the imminent threat of invasion to Australia

having passed some weeks earlier, as a result of the Battle of
Midway, General Headquarters South-West Pacific Area issued
embarkation orders from Queensland for the 7th Division on
3 August. The intentions of the Japanese at that time must have
been unclear to General MacArthur. It is most likely that he
had decided to move his veteran Australian 7th Division to Port
Moresby and Milne Bay to secure his existing air bases there.
While en route the convoy split, taking the 2/9th, 2/10th and
2/12th Battalions of the 18th Brigade to Milne Bay to reinforce
its militia garrison, and the Victorian 2/14th, the Western
Australian 2/16th and the South Australian 2/27th Battalions of
the 21st Brigade to Port Moresby. The third brigade of the 7th
Division, the 25th, was held in Queensland pending further
events in Papua.

On 11 August Lieutenant-General Syd Rowell, who had
commanded I Corps since April, arrived in Port Moresby.
Accompanying him was Major-General Allen, commander of
the 7th Division (Allen had been the distinguished commander
of the 16th Brigade in North Africa and Greece, which Ralph
had referred to as 'the Push Brigade'). As a result of the arrival
of Rowell, Major-General Morris assumed the command of
ANGAU (the Australian New Guinea Administrative Unit). The
commander of the 21st Australian Infantry Brigade, Brigadier
Arnold Potts, had arrived at Port Moresby by Sunderland Flying
Boat in advance of his troops on 7 August 1942.

Potts was a grazier from Kojonup in Western Australia and
had served with the original 16th Battalion in France during
the Great War, rising to the rank of captain. By the end of the
war he had won a Military Cross and had been mentioned in
despatches. With the outbreak of the Second World War, Potts
had joined the 2/16th Battalion in April 1940. By the conclusion of the Syrian campaign, he had added a DSO and a MID
to his awards and had become the CO of the 2/16th Battalion.
He had succeeded Brigadier Stevens as the 21st Brigade commander in May 1942 after that formation had arrived back in
Australia. It is not known whether Honner and Potts had had
much prewar contact, but it is highly likely that the two knew
of each other. Ralph Honner would later write:

> Admiration for Potts went beyond his own brigade. I served
> under some distinguished brigade commanders: Morshead,

Lieutenant-General S.F. Rowell,   *Brigadier Arnold Potts.*
GOC New Guinea Force.
(AWM 26299)

Robertson, Savige, Vasey, Porter, Eather and Dougherty—
under six of those in action. But to follow and to fight beside
in a hazardous campaign, I could not have preferred any of
them to Arnold Potts. He had a magical, yet natural, charisma
of leadership that inspired confidence and loyalty and devotion.
To me, he was the Bayard of them all—'sans peur et sans
reproache' [without fear and without reproach].[16]

On 13 August, as the 21st Brigade began arriving in Port
Moresby and while Ralph Honner was climbing the Kokoda Trail
to assume command of the 39th Battalion, Major-General Allen
and Brigadier Potts held a conference with Major-General
Morris. Their newly issued orders were quite brief, if ambitious:
21st Brigade was required to recapture Kokoda as a supply base
for further operations against Buna and Gona.

The outcomes of this conference were twofold. Morris pledged
that at least two plane loads of rations, wrapped in blankets, would
be dropped at Myola each day, pending the arrival there of the
21st Brigade, to provide a 40 000 ration dump for its offensive.
However, Morris was astounded to hear Allen and Potts inform
him that the troops would carry their own supplies to Myola.

Morris believed this to be an impossibility. He warned that the terrain would limit the weight of the troops' packs to 15 pounds. For their part, Potts and Allen knew that existing porterage capabilities were grossly inadequate to provision 21st Brigade's movement over the Owen Stanley Range. They therefore determined that the troops would indeed carry sufficient rations to enable them to reach Myola.

On the very night preceding the departure of the 2/14th Battalion, intelligence reported that a further 4000 Japanese had landed at Gona, of which some 1800 were identified as combat troops. Potts was undeterred. He believed that, provided the 2/27th was sent to him immediately—that battalion was being held in Port Moresby pending events at both Milne Bay and along the Kokoda Trail—and the promised supplies were awaiting him at Myola, all would be well. He could look to his command of Maroubra Force consisting of five battalions: the 39th, 53rd, 2/14th, 2/16th and 2/27th. He had an advanced drop zone at Myola for his supplies and, in addition, native carriers. On information available to him, his enemy would be of comparable numerical size. But unbeknown to Potts, four critical factors worked against him.

The first was the fact that his Port Moresby-based intelligence concerning the size of the Japanese force was woeful. Dudley McCarthy, the Official Historian:

> . . . Horii got the main body of his *South Seas Force* away from Rabaul on 17th August. He then had with him his own headquarters, the remaining two battalions of the *144th Regiment* with their guns, signals and ammunition detachments, the balance of the *55th Mountain Artillery* and *47th Field Anti-Aircraft Artillery*, a company of the *55th Cavalry* with an anti-tank role, lesser ancillary detachments, more of the *5th Sasebo*, 700 Rabaul natives and 170 horses. Hard behind these came the bulk of the *Yazawa Force*. On 21st August two battalions of the *41st Regiment* landed at Buna with strong supporting arms (including a regimental gun unit, a mountain battery, a quick firing gun detachment), about 100 of the *5th Sasebo*, 175 Rabaul boys, and 230 horses . . .
>
> About 13,500 troops had been landed in Papua of whom some 10,000 formed a well-balanced fighting group. The rear echelon of the *South Seas Force* and one of Yazawa's battalions was still to come.[17]

Therefore, the intelligence estimate furnished to Potts prior to his departure for Myola was inaccurate—by some 7500 troops.[18]

The second factor was supply. At approximately ten o'clock on the morning of 17 August, the Japanese bombed the 7-mile airfield near Port Moresby and destroyed two Dakota transport planes and three Flying Fortresses. In addition, five Dakota transports and five Flying Fortresses were damaged. The Dakota transports were the 'biscuit bombers' on which Maroubra Force was so heavily reliant.

The third factor that worked against Potts was the continued decision to keep his 2/27th Battalion in Port Moresby in the face of his repeated and, indeed, desperate requests that it be sent to him. It should be recognised that not only was Potts destined to be critically outnumbered and outgunned, but he commanded only two of his three battalions in action until the Brigade Hill battle.

The last inhibiting factor Potts faced was the inability of the 53rd Battalion to perform at a satisfactory level of competence. This issue will be examined later.

Thus, when the 2/14th Battalion began its climb of the Kokoda Trail on 16 August 1942 (the very day that Ralph assumed command of Maroubra Force and the 39th Battalion), the Japanese were busily engaged in concentrating a massive force near Isurava to attack him, and Brigadier Potts was in the process of being despatched to relieve him.

On the morning of 26 August 1942, the Japanese struck. At around midday Lieutenant Simonson's E Company standing patrol 45 minutes forward of Isurava was attacked. The platoon standing by, D Company's platoon under the command of Lieutenant Sword, immediately marched out and reinforced Simonson, while Lieutenant Clarke's C Company stood by at Isurava as the next for patrol duty. Ralph, in 'The 39th at Isurava':

> When the reinforced forward patrol had beaten off the main attack Simonson pushed the enemy back and advanced 200 yards along the track towards Deniki in an attempt to locate and destroy their guns. But he decided that they were at least another 300 yards ahead and, unable to make further progress against increasing resistance, he returned to the security of his patrol position.
>
> While the main Japanese thrust was contained by Simonson, other enemy forces moved up into the more difficult high

ground to the west and advanced southwards through it, keeping clear of the apparent perils of the track.[19]

The Japanese attacks were assisted by a mountain-gun bombardment of the battalion perimeter. Lieutenant Lovett, adjutant 39th Battalion, remembered Ralph's brave and yet pragmatic reaction to that shelling:

> We were standing out in the open Ralph Honner and I. I don't know who else was there, probably an officer or two, and we were talking about what we were going to do. And a mountain gun . . . they were ranging onto us. When the first shot landed we all looked around to see what Ralph was going to do. You could hear the preliminary shot fired from the gun and you knew that a shell would land . . . within say, five seconds . . . he was looking at us. And the bloody thing landed fairly close to us and he said, 'Look, there's no point in us just standing around here when a bombardment's going on'. He said, 'We're only going to get ourselves hurt here. What I'm going to do when we hear the preliminary shot fired, I'm going to ground, and I think you'll serve me well if you go to ground with me'. So we were waiting for a move from him, because we didn't want to let him think we were bloody frightened! We all laughed, and it brought us back onto an equal level.[20]

During the afternoon, Lieutenant Clarke led his stand-by C Company platoon section leaders and seconds-in-command out along the track to reconnoitre the forward positions. While returning at around 5 pm, he clashed with the infiltrating Japanese in the garden forward of the front creek. This small but aggressive 39th Battalion 'force' drove the Japanese through the garden and into the high grass to the north. Clarke's men then stalked their enemy to the point where eight of the invaders were slain, and only darkness and the resulting deepening gloom of the jungle forced their withdrawal to their battalion perimeter.

During that action-packed afternoon, Captain Dickenson's C Company, 2/14th Battalion, arrived at Isurava and immediately began to relieve C Company of the 39th. That relief was the result of Brigadier Potts finally receiving the build-up of promised supplies at Myola.

On the night of 26/27 August the Japanese again attacked Lieutenants Simonson and Sword's forward-standing patrol. Norm Downey was one of Simonson's men:

That night two Japs broke through our perimeter and in the shooting that followed Lieutenant Simonson and two men from Lieutenant Sword's platoon were wounded besides Norm Whitehead who got a bayonet through the shoulder. One of the Japs managed to get away, but the other copped a bullet 'up the Kyber' and lay moaning in the jungle all night. When this clash was reported to BHQ via our phone hook-up, the CO instructed Don Simonson to return to Isurava with the wounded if they could make it in the pitch dark. There was a possibility that the track in between was occupied by the Japs, but they decided to take the risk and got through safely.[21]

Although Simonson and his wounded comrades heard noises and movement along their perilous path to Isurava, Lieutenant Clarke's sweep through the garden the previous day had temporarily cleared the track. The enemy were still at 'arm's length', but time was rapidly running out for both the standing patrol and the defenders of Isurava.

At daybreak on 27 August the position was that Ralph had had his C Company reinforced by Dickenson's C Company 2/14th Battalion, and had a standing patrol towards Deniki consisting of Sword and Simonson's platoons—less Simonson and the wounded. That morning Brigadier Potts ordered a platoon from the 39th to occupy Naro (on the Naro ridge away to the west), to block any Japanese outflanking movement towards Alola from that western flank. Given that C Company had been relieved the previous day, Ralph selected Lieutenant Pentland from C Company for the task, as he considered Lieutenant Clarke had earnt a rest after his exploits in the front garden the previous day. The Naro track through the garden facing E Company was already in enemy hands again, so Pentland led his soldiers west from B Company's perimeter, cutting through the timber and crossing the creek to the Naro track higher up, beyond the enemy infiltration, to reach Naro unopposed.

On 27 August, the Battle for Isurava erupted in an awesome fury, such as had not previously been witnessed during the Kokoda Campaign, as General Horii committed his superior numbers and firepower against Ralph's desperate defenders. Horii also launched an attempt to outflank the Australians by an eastward outflanking movement to Alola via the Kaile–Missima track. This was an astute tactic, as the western flank was far too densely timbered and steep.

The stage was set and the defining hour had come—the hot, rain-soaked and steamy days and the dark, chilling nights at Isurava were now to be the decisive setting for a battle that would produce appalling slaughter in the wake of wave upon wave of attacking Japanese, breaking against the spirited and determined Australian resistance. By early morning, the Japanese had moved through the front creek garden and had also penetrated the thick jungle on the Naro flank, and were soon testing B and E Companies' positions.

That same morning, Ralph ordered Sword's two platoons— now cut off, as Clarke's stand-by platoon could not journey out along the main Deniki Track—to delay the Japanese as long as possible and then fall back to the 39th's perimeter when the position should become untenable. As the intensity of the battle increased, Honner determined that Sword's two-platoon force was far too invaluable to lose and must be recalled, but when he sought to implement that decision it was discovered that the enemy had cut the signal cable. Sword was on his own. Norm Downey, still with Sword, remembered the ensuing events:

> Lieutenant Sword was now in command, and he and the two platoon sergeants decided we should withdraw to the next delaying position about two hundred yards further back. When we got there we tried to contact BHQ by phone but the line was dead. Albert Grace was sent to report to battalion but he never got there and was never seen again. Soon after Albert left, Jimmy Woods was given permission to return to Isurava (he was shaking with fever) but he had only been gone a little while when we heard gunfire and Jimmy came pelting back to our perimeter. When he got his breath he said: 'The bastards are just down the track and had a go at me'. (Perhaps the fact that Jimmy was tall and very thin saved him, but there wasn't much of his haversack left!) We knew then that we were cut off and that our only chance was to head up the ridge above the track and try to circle round the Japs back to Isurava.[22]

Brigadier Potts envisaged a complete relief of the 39th Battalion on 28 August. He therefore required the recovery of Lieutenant Pentland's Naro patrol to allow Ralph's battalion to withdraw intact, and he ordered him to replace that patrol with a platoon from the 2/14th's C Company. Captain Dickenson assigned Lieutenant Arthur Davis' platoon the task.

When Davis and his patrol, guided by the 39th Battalion

Intelligence Sergeant, Buchecker, set out to follow Pentland's Naro route they found, on crossing the front creek, the jungle alive with Japanese. In the ensuing fight Davis lost a man killed and was then seriously wounded himself. Despite his wound, he fought a single-handed rearguard action, sacrificing his life to enable a successful withdrawal of his platoon. Buchecker was wounded in the leg, suffering a shattered thigh. Chaplain Earl and Captain Shera, the RMO, marched out through the enemy-infested jungle and carried Buchecker back to safety.

With Pentland as well as Sword now cut off, Ralph was without his fittest soldiers from three of his five companies. To replace E Company's missing personnel, Sergeant Kerslake, with the remainder of C Company after Pentland's Naro patrol had gone, was posted in the reserve platoon position with a counterpenetration role. At the same time Sergeant Murray's platoon from A Company became the battalion reserve, ready to dash wherever it might be needed.

Each day Ralph and as many of the men as possible walked down to the rear creek—out of the battalion perimeter to the only available water supply—to wash and shave. On the 27th, with the battle situation apparently well under control, Ralph and about twelve men were engaged in this daily ritual when an exhausted runner brought him a message. Ralph, in 'The 39th at Isurava':

> . . . the enemy had broken into 'E' Company's position. I looked over at the unsuspecting Merritt. It seemed a pity to disturb him. 'Captain Merritt', I said. 'When you've finished your shave will you go to your company. The Japs have broken through your perimeter'. Merritt didn't appreciate the Drake touch. An astonished look hung for an instant on his half-shaved face; then it lifted like a starter's barrier and he was off like a racehorse.[23]

Lieutenant Keith Lovett recalled the incident well and also remembered Ralph's demeanour under the intense pressure of 27 August 1942:

> Oh god, he was strong! He'd have a smile on his face. He'd always have a little bit of a grin. He was trying to relax himself I guess. With the episode having a shave down at the river . . . he had a smile on his face when he told Captain Merritt . . . he always called them by their rank. He was very settled

Captain John Shera, RMO   *Captain Max Bidstrup, OC*
39th Battalion.   *D Company, 39th Battalion.*

in every way. He could have been scared like hell inside but he didn't show it on the outside.[24]

Honner's daily Isurava routine consisted of constant contact with his signallers (who were maintaining contact with Potts at Alola), his company runners, and the 39th's padre and RMO. When the battle circumstances permitted, Ralph constantly toured his company perimeters and consulted with those commanders. Covering ground at Isurava was not difficult, as the company perimeters were all within 100–150 metres of the village.[25]

Most human beings seek some form of friendship or companionship during testing times. It would appear that Padre Norbett 'Nobby' Earl and the RMO Captain Shera fulfilled that need for Ralph. In Earl's case their Catholicism may have been a factor. In an interview in January 1986, Captain Max Bidstrup, OC D Company, gave the author an impression of 'Nobby' Earl:

> Father Earl, Nobby to us heretics, and whom he liked to be called by us who were not of his faith; never have I met a man who has made such an impression on me by his absolute, simple faith; and if I was asked to say what my definition of

a thoroughly happy man was I would say Nobby Earl. He owned nothing and yet he owned the world.[26]

Lovett remembered he, Honner, Earl and Shera 'sharing' sleeping arrangements at Isurava—a fragile four-poled shelter with a thatched roof which had been constructed by the natives. And, critically, when circumstances permitted, Ralph slept well (one groundsheet per two men in the shelter was laid on the ground, and one covered the pair sleeping back to back).[27]

When Captain Merritt returned to his E Company perimeter he found his soldiers under enormous pressure. Although the E and B Company fronts possessed open killing grounds which enabled the young soldiers of the 39th to take a heavy toll of the Japanese, the enemy mountain-gun, mortar, machine-gun and small-arms fire was so intense, and the repeated weight of numbers of infantry so frequent, that E Company's line began to yield.

An early Japanese gain was soon driven back by Kerslake's counterpenetration platoon and Sergeant Murray's mobile reserve. Having temporarily failed on this front, the enemy now turned to B Company's perimeter. Ralph, in 'The 39th at Isurava':

> For the rest of the day B Company bore the brunt of the enemy's attacks.
>
> Its forward platoons had occupied advanced positions near the timber edge to obtain some cover from it and to force the infiltrating Japanese deeper into the denser forest; but the violence of the enemy onset pressed them back to a better line prepared slightly to the rear to give them more open killing space on an occasion such as this. There they held, fighting magnificently, while the enemy came on in reckless waves, regardless of the casualties that soon cluttered that short stretch of open ground.
>
> These incessant assaults were slowly sapping 'B' Company's strength—and at the end of the day, when the heaviest attack of all rolled in over French's men their endurance was stretched to breaking point. Lieutenant Garland, their second-in-command, reported that they were unlikely to hold much longer unless reinforced. I gave him a message for French that he would have to hold—there was only battalion headquarters behind him. But in the light of the enemy's obviously superior strength I recognised that it would be only a matter of time

before our small garrison was overrun—in the evening, the night, or next morning. There was only one source of quick reinforcement to forestall disaster.[28]

That 'source of quick reinforcement' was Captain Claude Nye and his B Company 2/14th Battalion.

During mid-afternoon on the 27th, Nye and his men had arrived at Isurava, the second 2/14th company to do so. But Ralph had to 'watch with considerable misgiving'[29] as Nye's soldiers, obeying Potts' orders, attempted to hack a jungle path to relieve Pentland at Naro. As the fury of the Japanese attacks on his B Company intensified during the late afternoon, Ralph decided 'to recall Nye if he could be reached'.[30] But Nye's jungle path had really constituted little more than a jungle wall—during two hours of slashing, the main column had moved little more than 300 metres off the track. The entrance of Nye's soldiers to the Battle of Isurava made a profound impression on Ralph:

> . . . I do not remember anything more heartening than the sight of their confident deployment. Their splendid physique and bearing, and their cool efficiency—even the assembly line touch as two platoon mortar-men stepped on either side of the track to pluck bombs from the haversacks of the riflemen filing past them without checking their pace—made a lasting impression on me. And they were to prove even better than they looked.[31]

Ralph immediately sent one of Nye's platoons to strengthen E Company's left; another to bolster D Company's right to 'close the pincers from either flank on the enemy still endangering B Company';[32] and the third to fortify French's embattled B Company.

On the morning of 28 August 1942, Captain Cameron and his D Company, 2/14th Battalion, took over E Company's positions, which in turn allowed Nye's three platoons to congregate under his command and assume control of his opposite number's 39th Battalion positions. Captain Merritt's two E Company platoons and Lieutenant French's soldiers now occupied gaps in the lines to the rear that had been created by Sword and Pentland's missing patrols.

The dogged resistance offered by the 39th Battalion at Isurava, pending their reinforcement by the 2/14th Battalion, was of paramount importance not only to the four-day battle of Isurava, but also to the resounding success of the Maroubra Force fighting withdrawal to Ioribaiwa. Had Ralph's soldiers broken, Isurava would have fallen with awesome consequences. The 39th Battalion had held the Japanese beyond arm's length to conceal their fundamental paucity of both numbers and material, and by doing so they had pugnaciously held ground that for them was really unholdable; they had prepared definite and trusted plans for counterattack—necessarily at the risky expense of defensible gaps elsewhere; and, critically, they had found a faith and a trust to accept, come what may, the odds against them and not to flinch or falter or panic.

In simple terms, the saga of the 39th Australian Infantry Battalion's Kokoda campaigning is a classic illustration of what egalitarian Australia has always rejoiced in—the seemingly impossible triumph of the underdog against all conceivable odds. If the battle of Isurava constituted his battalion's finest hour, then history should record that it may well also have been Lieutenant-Colonel Ralph Honner's defining moment. Here was the culmination of the painstaking acquisition of, and the interplay between, what Liddell Hart called the 'moral courage' and the 'creative intellect' of the competent commander.

If the situation had improved dramatically at Isurava, then events on the western Kaile–Missima–Abuari flank had deterio-rated on 27 August. On the previous day the 53rd Battalion had lost Missima and had fallen back towards Abuari. Brigadier Potts ordered the 53rd to retake Missima on 27 August. Lieutenant-Colonel Ward sent his B and D Companies to accomplish this task. The *Report into Operations*, 21st Brigade, recorded those tragic circumstances:

> As far as could be ascertained later, B Company did no more than make contact with the enemy but broke and scattered, while it is doubtful if D Company did more than make contact with the enemy. At 1620 hours a runner from 53rd Battalion informed Brigade that the Japs had come around the waterfall and were making towards the river crossing and Alola. 53rd Battalion were ordered to hold Abuari Village, waterfall and river crossing with the remaining companies pending the arrival of 2/16th Battalion. At nightfall the position on the right flank was as follows: B and D Companies, 53rd Battalion, out of contact with Brigade and reported to have pressed on to Missima. Jap patrols thought to be in occupation of Abuari

Village. In addition seventy of 53rd Battalion on patrols NOT reported in and subsequently found to have taken to the bush.[33]

Brigadier Arnold Potts must have been deeply concerned at this train of events. In the process of relieving the 39th with his 2/14th Battalion at Isurava, he stood to lose both units should the enemy cut the track near or at Alola.

From a Japanese perspective, Horii forfeited a priceless opportunity to rout the Australians on 27 August. By failing to exploit the 53rd Battalion's failure on that day—by simply occupying Abuari and pushing out patrols—he lost the chance to cut off the two Australian battalions at Isurava. On numerous occasions in discussion with the author, Ralph marvelled at Horii's error. And further, the judgement was not one made with the advantage of hindsight—he made the point that at that time he fully expected to be cut off and bypassed at Isurava.

At around midday on 28 August 1942, having been preceded by his A Company and parts of his Headquarter Company, the 2/14th Battalion's CO, Lieutenant-Colonel Arthur Key, arrived at Isurava and assumed command of the battle.

Key had been an original member of the Victorian 2/8th Battalion—part of the 19th Brigade as was Ralph's 2/11th Battalion—and had therefore taken part in the battles at Bardia, Tobruk, Derna, Greece and Crete. It is highly likely, therefore, that Key and Honner would have had some contact with each other before Isurava. Sergeant John Gwillim, 2/14th Battalion:

> I was rather disappointed when Lieutenant-Colonel Key was introduced to us as our new C.O. when Lt Col Cannon was transferred in January 1942, as he had a rather fragile appearance and did not at all fit my picture of an infantry commander. He did not project an 'I would follow you through hell or high water' air, but rather an 'I need your assistance' air. It was therefore more of a shock to find that he was indeed of very tough moral fibre and had obviously learned to handle hard types during his service with the 6th Australian Division. He was nevertheless a very quiet man who did not have to raise his voice to get things done, and he made no attempt to court popularity with the troops . . . He was a very sound soldier who spared himself in no way, and was in evidence to the forward fighting troops to inspire their performance.[34]

When Ralph met Key at Isurava he immediately suggested that they together convince Brigadier Potts that the 39th should not be relieved:

> I told Key I considered the holding of Isurava against the strength the enemy had shown the previous day would need more than one battalion, and I would not leave him in the lurch.[35]

Potts took their advice. Honner's men were now used to bolster the gaps in the southern part of the perimeter.

The story of the Battle for Isurava now became chiefly concerned with the 2/14th Battalion's magnificent fighting. It is not the purpose of this work to tell that story in detail, but it is necessary to provide a brief overview.[36]

It should be appreciated that of all the battalions involved in the Kokoda campaign—during both the withdrawal and pursuit phases—the 2/14th Australian Infantry Battalion sustained the highest losses, and arguably fought the toughest and most critical fight. From 27 to 30 August 1942, the Japanese unleashed an awesome volume of mountain-gun, mortar and machine-gun fire on the 2/14th. And with that fire came wave upon wave of infantry attacks that brought with them savage close-quarters fighting and numerous acts of incredible bravery. When Ralph described Nye and his men's arrival at Isurava— 'Their splendid physique and bearing, and their cool efficiency . . . And they were to prove even better than they looked'—he was not engaging in superfluous praise. The fact that the 2/14th could have made that sort of impression on a soldier of Ralph's experience is high praise indeed. Lieutenant Keith Lovett's recollection of the arrival and confidence of the 2/14th is succinct:

> They handled the walk over the Kokoda Trail very well. They weren't dragging the chain when they got to us. When you're lying in the mud and you see these blokes walk up and they're fit and they all look big and confident . . . and they said, 'Well, we'll fix this mob up!' We just told them, 'You're welcome! We're glad you've arrived, we desperately need help!' And they said, 'We'll give it to you.' And they did.[37]

A stirring example of the 2/14th's Isurava story is that of Private Bruce Kingsbury. On 29 August, the Japanese staged repeated attacks across the 2/14th's front. The Official Historian Dudley McCarthy recorded that:

> Sergeant Thompson led a forward party from Captain Rhoden's Headquarter's Company which had arrived during the morning. Corporal Bear and Privates Avery and Kingsbury of Cox's broken platoon insisted on attaching themselves to Thompson and fought with him. Soon after midday the break through was menacing the whole battalion position. Clements drove in a counter-attack leading a composite group of his own men, Thompson's men and what had been Cox's platoon. As the counter-attack moved Kingsbury rushed forward firing his Bren gun from the hip through terrific machine-gun fire and succeeded in clearing a path through the enemy. Continuing to sweep on them, Private Kingsbury was then seen to fall to the ground shot dead by a bullet from a sniper in the wood.
>
> Mainly as a result of Kingsbury's action the position was restored.[38]

If events at Isurava were thus delicately poised, proceedings on the right flank of the Alola–Abuari–Missima axis were also cause for grave concern.

On 29 August, the 2/16th Battalion was committed to that right flank to stabilise the position and, if possible, push on to Missima. The Commanding Officer of the 2/16th was Lieutenant-Colonel Albert Caro. Captain F.H. Sublet, 2/16th Battalion:

> Lieutenant-Colonel Albert Caro was a courageous officer who displayed plenty of military knowledge. To me he seemed a little too forgiving and his compassion was pronounced. I held him in the highest esteem as a commanding officer, and as a man of great goodness.[39]

In order to execute Potts' directive, Caro despatched his A Company under the command of Captain McGee and his B Company under the command of Captain Sublet, who recalls:

> All was quiet around Abuari when I reached there and almost immediately I made a reconnaissance with a couple of men along the track to Missima. About one hundred metres down this track we came across the bodies of Lieutenant-Colonel Ward, C.O. of the 53rd Battalion and his adjutant or Intelligence Officer. I concluded they had been ambushed, and firing on my right rear told me that A Company had contacted the

enemy. Soon afterwards I received orders to take command of both A and B Companies, and I did so. When A Coy scouts discovered the enemy in position above Abuari Village, the Company Commander ordered 7th and 9th Platoons to attack, and they went in with gusto and continued to press the Japanese all afternoon. 9th Platoon killed about fifty of the enemy and captured several light machine guns while 7th Platoon continued their assault. In accordance with Colonel Caro's wishes, I had handed over B Coy to Captain George Wright when I assumed command of the two-company force and I decided that B Coy should move and attack the enemy's right flank while A Coy continued their frontal attack. I judged that at least one hundred Japanese were holding well prepared positions covering the partially cleared area of the village and the Missima track where it emerged from the cover provided by a thirty foot cliff at the top of a sidling track up which we had travelled from the deep gorge below Alola. In view of the threat of Japanese reinforcements from Missima, B Coy was to post a strong standing patrol to secure their left flank.[40]

By mid-afternoon it was clear to Sublet that if he was to push on to Missima he must mount an attack using his A Company in a frontal assault, his B Company on his left flank, and a fresh third force along his right flank to fall on the Japanese rear. He requested that a 53rd Battalion company come forward to accomplish this last task.

The initial 2/16th Battalion action had been executed with standard 21st Brigade confidence and skill. Captain Sublet:

All day I had heard the shattering noise of the other battle taking place about two miles away on the other side of the Eora Creek gorge but received no definite news as to the likely outcome . . .[41]

By nightfall on 29 August, the situation at Isurava was becoming desperate. Although the 2/14th Battalion had inflicted over 500 casualties on their enemy and had held their ground magnificently against odds of five to one, the Japanese had penetrated the battalion area and still held the high ground to the west. Key had committed his reserves to the battle that day—he needed reinforcement. As a response to this request, Brigadier Potts ordered C Company from the 53rd Battalion to move from Alola to Isurava. That company was to prove an abject failure—it simply camped by the track at the Isurava Rest House while others performed its role.

But Key was indeed destined to have his much-needed reserve that day. It was by no means of the size needed and it came from a most unexpected quarter. The 2/14th, in its inspiring performance in the leading role during the last days at Isurava, was supported by the depleted and exhausted 39th Battalion, still committed to battle after declining orders to leave the front line. That reinforcement came from two extraordinary quarters. Ralph would later proudly write:

Into Alola, along the track from Naro, marched a scarecrow crew of haggard, hungry men. Simonson's and Sword's platoons had been out for four days. After a long day and a night and another day of battle, with the enemy cutting them off from Isurava and their telephone line severed, they had fought their way up the mountain-side, across the path of the advancing Japanese, to join Pentland's platoon on the Naro ridge. It was a murderous climb, the sharp scrub tearing their uniforms and their hands and hides, and the rocky outcrops cutting their boots from their lacerated feet.

Pentland's men were in not much better shape—they had been forced to cut a path through the jungle for the first part of their climb. When they had not been relieved on the second day, as arranged, or even on the third day, hunger had forced the three platoons to retire to Alola. A corporal of the 2/16th told me afterwards, 'It was enough to make a man weep to see those poor skinny bastards hobble in on their bleeding feet'. They were greeted with the news that the 39th and the 2/14th were fighting for their lives. Without a word, or a thought for the food their stomachs craved, they turned and hurried off to Isurava as fast as their crippled feet could carry them.

There were other stout hearts in frail frames at Alola. When, on the 27th, the complete relief of the 39th was ordered for the following day, I sent back, under Lt Johnson, the weakest of the battalion's sick to have them one stage ahead on the long march to Moresby—they were too feeble for the fast-flowing fighting expected at the front. But they, too, learnt of the plight of their comrades at Isurava; and all who could walk spontaneously volunteered to return to the battle . . .

Unprepared for such an apparition, I was surprised to see a grimy, bearded figure leading in a tattered line at twilight.

I did not recognise him till he saluted and announced: 'Sword, Sir, reporting in from patrol'. There was more than mere formality in my answering salute. Pentland and his gaunt gang were with him, too; and then came Johnson and the last stumbling reinforcement of the stout-hearted sick—fit for the hospital, yet worthy of Valhalla. Key had a reserve again.[42]

By 8.45 pm, Lieutenant-Colonel Key had no option but to request a withdrawal to the Isurava Rest House area. Potts concurred. To Ralph fell the task of reconnoitring the fallback position. Lieutenant Stan Bisset, the 2/14th's Intelligence Officer, accompanied him.

The withdrawal to the Rest House by the 2/14th and 39th Battalions was accomplished during the last hours of 29 August 1942. It was a grim, deathly quiet and backbreaking struggle, as the sleepless and exhausted soldiers of the two units, assisting—and in some cases carrying—their wounded, made their way back to the positions Ralph had selected. The 39th now numbered 150.[43] By 2 am on 30 August both battalions were in occupation of their perimeters and awaited the renewed enemy assaults.[44]

On 30 August the Australian position deteriorated further. There were three reasons for that deterioration: the first was the fact that General Horii had again been reinforced by two battalions of the 41st Infantry Regiment Group (Yazawa Force), giving him both fit and fresh additional troops; he could also bring his supplies forward rapidly, as he had a substantial dump of materials at his beachhead and could move those supplies rapidly forward because of his relatively short line of communication; lastly, he could maintain the impetus of his offensive because of his superiority in numbers, which inhibited Potts' ability to do anything other than deploy his companies and platoons piecemeal. The 39th Unit Diary, 30 August 1942:

At midday most of the unfit of 39 Bn were detailed to go to the rear en route for Myola. This left the 39 Bn with 150 fit fighting men. Shortly afterwards, the enemy moving round to the high ground to the west attacked our left rear. B Coy, then 13 strong, took the first shock of the attack. With nothing on their flanks the forward posts were overrun, but the enemy were then held by the remainder of the Coy and A Coy which had been hurriedly called up to strengthen the position. 2/14 Bn now took a hand to hold the enemy.[45]

On the right flank—the Alola–Abuari–Missima axis—Captain Sublet's attack went in without the 53rd Battalion's company assistance on 30 August. The role of this attack transpired to be a vital one, as it frustrated the Japanese attempt to cut the Kokoda Trail at Alola. For the 2/14th and 39th Battalions, the consequences of the success of that attempt would have been catastrophic.

At 3 pm, Brigadier Potts ordered a substantial withdrawal, from both his eastern and western flanks, to Eora Creek. His decision was a sound one—he could not contemplate Alola as his next defensive perimeter as it was a totally unsuitable position. Ralph was given the task of reconnoitring holding positions for the 2/14th and 2/16th Battalions at Eora Creek and dispositions for the 39th and 53rd Battalions to cover the final withdrawal to those positions. He left with his D Company and the wounded at 4 pm.[46]

Ralph travelled with a small 39th headquarter group and with characteristic energy outstripped most of the traffic to Eora Creek. The heart-rending scenes he witnessed along that tragic path became what was now to be a Kokoda Trail routine. John Dawes, 39th Battalion, described his passage out from the Isurava Rest House:

> . . . we all made our way back through some native gardens below the track. I remember Lieutenant Mortimore carrying a wounded bloke out on his back.
>
> Towards dark, Hedley Norman and I caught up with a 2/14th chap. He'd been shot in both arms which were tied to his chest and he was having a lot of trouble getting along. As soon as Hedley saw him he handed me his rifle and helped the 2/14th bloke along. At that stage, going along the side of a very steep ridge, the poor bloke slipped from Hedley's grasp and rolled down the slope into some prickly bushes. Hedley didn't hesitate—he dived after him and dragged him back up to the track. This bloke's main grievance was that he'd been hit five times with 'Tommy' gun slugs and hadn't even seen a Jap!
>
> And it was about this time that Captain Jacob [OC C Company 39th Battalion] was accidentally killed. He was carrying the rifles and other gear of some of the chaps who were too weak and sick to carry them themselves. One of the rifles must have been cocked with the safety catch off.[47]

When Ralph arrived at Eora Creek the 53rd Battalion had not arrived. In view of recent events, he then established his plan for the holding position purely as a 39th Battalion operation, until the 2/14th and 2/16th Battalions—now engaging the enemy in the fighting withdrawal—could reach him. While Ralph had been thus occupied, the 2/14th Battalion was in the process of completing its triumphant yet tragic Isurava fighting.

Late on 30 August, to facilitate an unimpeded withdrawal from his Isurava Rest House perimeter, Lieutenant-Colonel Key ordered Dickenson and Cameron to clear the enemy from the timbered slopes above the battalion positions. Just before five o'clock C and D Companies swept into a wide attack along the covered hillside and a brisk fire-fight developed there at the same time as a strong attack came along the lower track-side ground against the rearguard A and B Companies. Key and his headquarters group, assembled on the track ready to move, suddenly came under the most intense fire from the opposite slopes that forced them over the edge of the precipitous descent to Eora Creek.

Lieutenant-Colonel Arthur Key was captured some ten days later by the Japanese and subsequently executed. His intelligence officer, Lieutenant Stan Bisset, and a handful of companions regained the battalion lines five days later. Some of the remaining headquarters soldiers were missing for a number of weeks. Key's long and distinguished campaigning had come to an end—Bardia, Tobruk, Derna, Greece, Crete and now Isurava. Throughout the critically important and climactic battle for Isurava, he had led his 2/14th Battalion with sound, decisive, professional judgement and cool resolution.

When the 2/14th arrived at Isurava on 28 August 1942, it had numbered 542 troops. After 'stand to' on the morning of 31 August it mustered 160—30 in HQ and A Company, 54 in B Company, 42 in C Company and 34 in D Company—little more than a full-strength company. Ralph Honner's tremendous respect—and feeling for—the Victorian 2/14th Battalion was born out of the desperate struggle for Isurava. Later circumstances were to cause that association to become even stronger.

At Eora Creek, Ralph formed his 39th Battalion into two composite companies: Number 1 (A, B and C Companies) under the command of Captain Merritt, and Number 2 (D and E) under the command of Captain Bidstrup. He deployed

Number 1 Company, with a 3-inch mortar, on the high ground astride the track to Templeton's Crossing to block, or at least contest, any Japanese attempt to bypass the forward Australians and then venture up the eastern side of the Eora Valley. His second company took up positions on the edge of the village covering the creek approaches from the direction of Alola. He further sent his rear echelon and the sick on to Myola.[48]

At 10 am on 1 September 1942, Brigadier Potts ordered Ralph to deploy the 39th at Kagi. He did so with good reason. The Japanese, as they had done at a similar loop in the track near Isurava, were in a position where they could advance from Eora Creek to Efogi either via Templeton's Crossing–Myola or Templeton's Crossing–Kagi. Should the enemy advance through Kagi to Efogi faster than the Australians could withdraw and evacuate their wounded through Myola (where Potts' main supply dump was situated), Maroubra Force would be cut off from their line of communication and supply.

Those of the 39th able to travel were despatched from Myola and reached Kagi at about 5.30 pm, while the two 39th composite companies reached a position about 3 kilometres east of Kagi by nightfall. At daybreak on 2 September, Captain Bidstrup's company occupied Kagi and Captain Merritt's stayed in ambush positions. On 3 September the 39th Battalion Kagi remnant was rewarded for its prolonged Kokoda Trail campaigning with a dive-bombing by four American Airocobras.

The first two companies of the South Australian 2/27th Battalion arrived from Port Moresby at Kagi on 4 September. However, the battle situation had further deteriorated, and Potts then ordered a Maroubra Force withdrawal to Mission Ridge– Brigade Hill, just south of the village of Efogi. Yet again, Ralph was ordered to reconnoitre positions, this time on Mission Ridge. The 39th Battalion Unit Diary, 5 September 1942:

> At about 1530 hrs, 2/27th Bn commenced taking over 39 Bn positions with all automatic weapons, grenades, rations, blankets, signal stores and medical supplies. In the afternoon 39 Bn marched to Menari.[49]

While Ralph and Key and their soldiers had been fighting at Isurava—and the 2/16th at Abuari—two Australian reporters and a cameraman had arrived at Eora Creek—the reporters were Chester Wilmot (ABC) and Osmar White (Melbourne *Sun* and

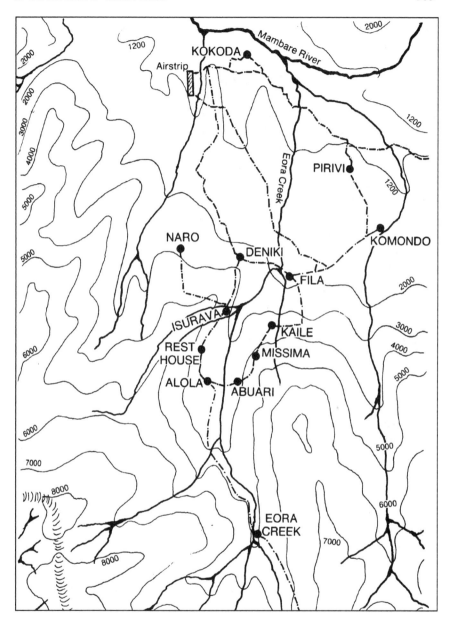

The Kokoda Trail: Kokoda to Eora Creek.

Daily Telegraph), and the cameraman Damien Parer (Australian Department of Information). It will be recalled that Parer and Ralph had met at Derna, where the former had asked the latter to use his soldiers to re-enact a desert charge. During the

skylarking that followed, Damien had also taken an informal
still of Honner.

Along the Kokoda Trail during September 1942, Parer
captured some of the most dramatic film footage of the Second
World War. And he and Ralph's 'meeting' at the village of
Menari was destined to provide its crowning climax.

When White, Wilmot and Parer arrived at Eora Creek,
Osmar White described the scene:

> Hundreds of men were standing about in mud up to their
> shins. The whole village built of pandanus and grass looked as
> if it were about to flounder in the sea of mud. The huts leaned
> drunkenly. There were piles of broken-out ration boxes half
> submerged. The men were slimed from head to foot, for weeks
> unshaven, their skins bloodless under their filth.
>
> Lines of exhausted carriers were squatting on the fringes
> of this congregation eating muddy rice off muddy banana
> leaves. Their woolly hair was plastered with rain and muck.
> Their eyes were rolling and bloodshot with the strain of long
> carrying. Some of them were still panting.[50]

Damien Parer's Eora Creek film is the only footage shot on
the Kokoda Trail that comprehensively depicts the scale and
magnitude of Maroubra Force's fighting withdrawal—the congestion in villages that were built to house and supply small
groups of Papuans, not battalions of modern-day soldiers;
the severe gradients and jungle conditions, of which the average
Australian knew nothing; and the general debilitation of the
troops. While Wilmot and White went forward—and encountered the early stages of the withdrawal—Parer kept filming at
Eora Creek.

With Kokoda now clearly lost and news that Milne Bay had
been attacked by the Japanese, Wilmot and White made the
decision to return with their stories to Port Moresby. Neil
McDonald, in *War Cameraman: The story of Damien Parer*:

> Parer's position was now desperate. He was too sick and tired
> to carry the tripod and cameras as well as the cans of exposed
> film stock that he was trying to protect from the mould and
> damp. In a weak moment at Eora Creek he had asked 'Smokey'
> Howson of the 39th Battalion if he might give him a hand
> with the camera gear. 'You can go and get fucked, I have
> enough of my own to carry,' Howson told him.[51]

Eora Creek village. (AWM 013257)

Congestion at Eora Creek: the withdrawal is now in full swing.
(AWM 013260)

Laurie 'Smokey' Howson later remembered his walk from
Mission Ridge to Menari, which makes his comment to Parer
understandable:

> At Mission Ridge we were relieved and handed over our
> automatic weapons and other stores to the 2/27th, but I kept
> four grenades. I was at the RAP when the order came to
> move out. Walking along the track I was half-crazy with
> pain—no rifle or automatic weapon, just four grenades, two
> in pouches and two hanging from my webbing ready to
> rip off.[52]

Not long after, Captain Max Bidstrup saw Parer throwing
some of his cans of film into Eora Creek. When he offered
assistance Parer refused it.[53] Rather than impose on the soldiers,
Parer began to discard his 'excess' weight—all his personal
gear went first, including his socks; next went 'the leather case
and accessories for the Newman camera';[54] next his tripod;
finally, he jettisoned his prized Graflex still camera. Neil
McDonald:

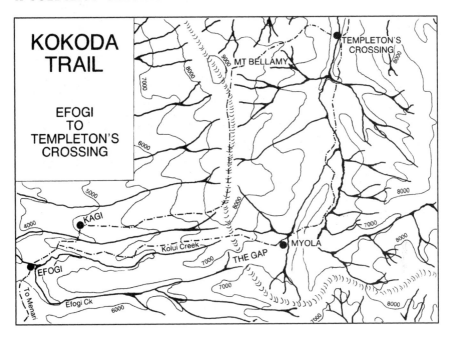

When the correspondents reached the hills above Templeton's Crossing, Parer received a message that 1,500 feet of film stock had been dropped with supplies at Myola. He decided at once to continue filming . . . Rather apologetically, he asked White and Wilmot if they would leave him a spare shirt, a pair of socks and some quinine. The last the two reporters saw of Parer, he was standing in the rain, clutching his Newman in one hand and his tins of exposed film in the other.[55]

As Damien Parer followed the withdrawal along the Kokoda Trail through Myola to Menari, he shot graphic film of the stretcher cases, the heart-rending care of the wounded by the legendary 'Fuzzy-Wuzzy Angels', and the inhospitable terrain— and all this while suffering acute dysentery and coping with that affliction: 'somehow he got hold of a tube and a bottle and inserted the tube in his anus and ran it down his trouser leg into the container which he shoved into his sock'.[56]

On 6 September 1942 at Menari, Ralph issued an order to his adjutant:

. . . I want you to put the battalion on parade for me, I want to talk to them. I haven't met a lot of them, I don't know them, I don't know them by name. They should be very proud of their performance and I'd like them to know that I think

*The 39th Battalion at Menari. Lieutenant Johnson is in front.
(AWM 013289)*

they're some of the best soldiers that I've had anything to do
with and they've got no fears about being able to hold their
heads up.[57]

This was a unique gathering. Few battalion parades in Australian
history could have consisted of only about 50 unregimentally
dressed, exhausted young men, waxen-faced and many carrying
not rifles but the common Kokoda Trail stick. As the soldiers
lined up and then snapped to attention, Parer began to move
along the lines of men, his 'eye fixed to the eyepiece of the
box-like Newman camera'.[58]

As Ralph passed on Brigadier Arnold Potts' commenda-
tion—Potts later wrote, 'their efforts represented gallantry,
courage and fortitude of the highest order, and their fighting
prowess was an inspiration to all who saw it'[59]—Parer also
captured Lieutenant-Colonel Ralph Honner's proud and digni-
fied bearing. Immersed in the moment, Ralph, like most of his
men, was unaware that Parer was filming. Sergeant Jack Sim
was at the parade:

He stood in front of those men and he gave us in Australianese
that great Henry the Fifth oration, and he paid us that
compliment of telling us we were heroes, in his own way.

Lieutenant-Colonel Ralph Honner addresses the 39th Battalion at Menari. The adjutant, Lieutenant Keith Lovett, is behind him. (AWM FO1212)

> I think I knew that it was a moment when history was in the making or had been made. I did know that here was a man that knew it . . .[60]

Honner made a further remarkable reference at the Menari parade. Jack Sim:

> I can't remember his exact words; I can't quote him verbatim, but I'll always remember what he meant and what he implied when he said: 'You're all Australians and some things you've just been through you must forget. Some of the men that were with you you feel have let you down [Ralph was referring to the 53rd Battalion]. But they didn't. Given different circumstances they'd be just the same as you. The fact that their leaders may have failed them, and yours didn't, doesn't mean they're any worse than you.[61]

Damien Parer's historical perspective, unlike Ralph's, did not perceive an Australian Agincourt, but in his diary he referred to the Menari parade as 'almost like the roll call on Anzac'.[62]

Both Honner and Parer saw not only the historical significance of the campaign but the nobility of the young soldiers who participated in it—and both made such perceptions through Catholic eyes. Honner would later write:

> But Kokoda came to signify much more than an outpost and its airstrip. The Kokoda Track, up from the northern beaches and over the Owen Stanley Range, was chosen by the Japanese South Seas Force for its push to Port Moresby, the final stepping-stone for the invasion of Australia. That primitive path was to become a soldier's Calvary; and, along that grim Golgotha, the decisive action was not some valiant, fruitless venture at Kokoda but the grinding four-day Battle of Isurava.[63]

Neil McDonald, in *War Cameraman: The story of Damien Parer*:

> Ron Williams believes that Parer was portraying redemption emerging out of suffering in these sequences [Parer's shots of the stretcher bearers]. While Damien's notes give no indication of any such intention, one particular shot does have a religious undertone. It shows Salvation Army Major Albert Moore on the far right of the frame lighting a cigarette for a wounded soldier. This is carefully balanced by a group of soldiers on the other side. Parer's composition is similar to a mediaeval or Renaissance painting showing as its centrepiece Christ being taken down from the cross. The religious analogy is strengthened by the fact that the soldier is naked, covered from the waist down by an army blanket.[64]

The 39th Battalion now continued its journey through Nauro, Ioribaiwa, Uberi, Owers Corner (the beginning of the Kokoda Trail), and thence 8 more kilometres to the Koitaki camp—approximately 30 kilometres from Port Moresby. A sample of the participants' recollections best describes the ordeal. 'Bluey' Jardine:

> I was running a temperature at Menari, my boots were busted and in the heap of boots the only ones fit to wear [at Myola as some 39th members passed through, the others having travelled via Kagi] were a size 8 and size 7 . . . Les Burnett of the 2/16th went crawling past (he had been shot in both calves and had walked and crawled all the way from Abuari).
>
> When we reached Nauro that evening my head was

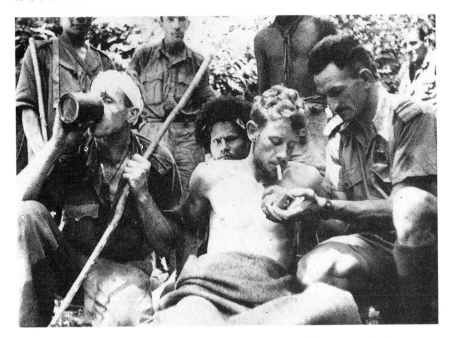

Lieutenant V.G. Gardner, 2/14th Battalion and Albert Moore.
(AWM 013287)

throbbing and I was sweating freely. Next day, as we reached
Ioribaiwa, I flaked out. Keith McKinnis and Jim Cashmore
brought a meal to me because I couldn't stand up. But the
next morning I was on my feet heading for Uberi—the
thought of getting back was spurring us all on.

It was raining galore when we arrived at Uberi. My mates
got a meal for me and fixed me up with a bed. Next day it
took me the whole day to walk to the ADS [Advanced
Dressing Station] at Owers Corner. 'Sparrow' McIntosh helped
me along the track. When we got there we both collapsed.
From there an ambulance took both of us to 2/9th AGH
[Advanced General Hospital].[65]

Allan Smith:

I finally made it to Uberi and on to Ilolo. I had scrub typhus
(90% fatal then), hookworm, both malarias and weighed 5
stone.[66]

The 39th Battalion lost 54 men killed in action, four died of
wounds, and 125 wounded during its Kokoda Trail fighting.[67]
If Ralph Honner and Damien Parer saw the Australian

Kokoda Trail soldier in romantic and noble terms—one helping to create a Kokoda myth while the other filmed it—then their perceptions were most certainly not shared by the powers that be in Australia.

9

ENERGISING THE
SITUATION

September 1942 was a critical month, both in Papua and Canberra, for the Australian nation. It will be remembered that the final arrival at Mission Ridge–Brigade Hill of the third 21st Brigade battalion—the 2/27th—had facilitated the relief of the 39th Battalion.

The main feature of the Mission Ridge–Brigade Hill battle was the recurring effort by Brigadier Potts to delay the Japanese passage to Port Moresby, while inflicting the greatest possible casualties and thus taxing the enemy's lengthening line of communication and supply. In doing so, given that the Japanese outnumbered Maroubra Force by approximately five to one, he could expect the usual Japanese response of heavy frontal attacks in unison with a determined and speedy outflanking movement. The tactical aim was therefore to hold until the position was untenable and then withdraw in good order. This had been done repeatedly with great military finesse and determination from Isurava to Mission Ridge. To withdraw too early meant a premature acquisition of ground for the Japanese; to withdraw too late was an invitation to the enemy to either surround and annihilate their foe or cut them off from the Kokoda Trail—the one and only tactical lifeline.

But by the time the Japanese had gathered outside Efogi, facing Mission Ridge, they too had refined their drill. General Horii's assault on the Australian force was this time characterised

by a superbly synchronised frontal assault on the fresh 2/27th
at the forward Mission Ridge, and a concentrated attack on
Brigade Hill to the rear. The result was that the 2/27th Battalion
held its embattled territory but was later cut off, while the
2/14th and 2/16th Battalions, after a desperate and bloodied
attempt to clear the track between Potts and the bulk of the
two battalions, were forced to regain the main track by way of
a circuitous jungle route to Menari.[1]

By mid-September the Australians had reinforced the
exhausted and diminished 2/14th and 2/16th near Ioribaiwa—
now organised into a composite battalion—with the 3rd Militia
Battalion, and soon after with the 25th Brigade.[2] But the
Japanese who were soon to swarm over the Ioribaiwa feature
were grievously debilitated. Their mission had fallen far behind
their ambitious timetable; they were receiving an Allied air
harassment of their line of communication and supply; they
were soon to be confronted by a fresh Australian force of two
experienced AIF formations (the 25th and 16th Brigades); they
had suffered crippling battle and sickness casualties; and their
lengthened line of advance imposed on them the same supply
difficulties with which Maroubra Force had originally had to
contend.

Given the resounding Australian victory at Milne Bay and
the intense battle against the American Marines at Guadalcanal,
the Japanese now had little alternative but to withdraw to their
north-coast Papuan beachhead at Gona–Sanananda–Buna, pending a favourable result at Guadalcanal.

Although Brigadier Potts and Maroubra Force had accomplished arguably the most critical fighting withdrawal in
Australian military history, their sterling efforts were not being
seen in a favourable light in Australia. Believing that the
Australians had been of comparable numerical strength to the
Japanese, and further believing early in the campaign that
the Japanese operation on the Owen Stanley Range had been
little more than an incursion to protect their beachhead and air
bases, General MacArthur and the Australian government began
to panic during late August and early September 1942.

After the 1940 federal election the then Prime Minister,
Mr Menzies, had founded the Advisory War Council, composed
of members of all political parties in the parliament, to debate
and formulate advice with regard to the Australian war effort.

As a direct reaction to the events at Isurava and Myola and, critically, Mission Ridge–Brigade Hill, and to the continuing withdrawal of Maroubra Force, the Advisory War Council thought it desirable that the Commander-in-Chief of the Australian Military Forces (General Blamey) journey to Port Moresby to examine the military situation there and report back to the Council. General Blamey duly flew to Port Moresby, satisfied himself as to the Allied conduct of operations, and returned to report to the nation on 16 September by means of a radio broadcast and to the Advisory War Council on 17 September. Blamey's report to the Council contains some noteworthy points:

> On the 17th of August the Japanese made a heavy air raid on Port Moresby and destroyed Allied land transport aircraft. This disorganised our forward supply arrangements, with the result that supplies could only be made available for 1500 men in the forward area.
>
> The 53rd Militia Battalion was infiltrated by the Japanese, and the 39th Militia Battalion was attacked. The Commander, 21st Brigade, A.I.F., was unable to deploy his Brigade to make a fight, as he had to extricate the Militia Battalions . . .[3]

The fact that the Commander-in-Chief of the Australian Military Forces could have been so grossly misinformed is striking testimony to both his own and the nation's total ignorance of the military operation in the Owen Stanley Range. Further, the report is but one of many noted in the Advisory War Council minutes, wherein General Blamey chose to disparage the militia as a means of providing answers to questions as to the higher command's conduct of the Owen Stanley campaign. The fact is that the 39th Battalion was a vital part of Potts' force at Isurava. Far from prohibiting his deployment of the 21st Brigade at Isurava, it had facilitated it. And there is further evidence of Blamey's ignorance of the fighting along the Kokoda Trail during August 1942.

The main body of the 39th reached Koitaki on 9 September 1942. The following day clean clothing, parcel mail and Comforts Fund material was issued, including tobacco, soap and razor blades. On 11 September, only two days after his return, Ralph was ordered to report to New Guinea Force Headquarters. When Ralph arrived in Port Moresby—on 12 September, the very day that Blamey arrived—he reported to General Rowell, Commander of New Guinea Force:

> . . . and he said, 'Blamey's here. I'll arrange for you to see him tomorrow morning because he'll want to know what's going on up in the mountains and what the fighting is like and what the position is'. And I said, 'Good, I'll be glad to give him the information'. So the next morning I saw that I was properly attired and went to Blamey's tent and waited while my name was carried in and I was invited in and he said, 'Oh good morning, you've just arrived in Port Moresby have you?' I said, 'No Sir, I have been here for some time in Papua'. But no reference was made in our interview to the war whatever, we just passed a few pleasantries and he said, 'Good morning Honner', and away I went.[4]

As a consequence of the Japanese advance from Brigade Hill towards Ioribaiwa, General Rowell had been faced with the problem of the Japanese potential to infiltrate into the Port Moresby region via the Brown, Goldie and Laloki Rivers. Ralph was given command of a new, ambitious mission. The creation of 'Honner Force' was designed to check the possibility of a Japanese movement down the Goldie River. If the enemy were not encountered, Honner Force was to proceed by way of that river to cut the Japanese line of communication on the Kokoda Trail between Nauro and Menari.

Honner Force numbered about 500 soldiers, consisting of a company each from the 36th, 49th and 55th Militia Battalions and elements of the 2/6th Independent Company.[5] Ralph took Captain Lovett as his force adjutant (Ralph had promoted this officer straight after the Kokoda Campaign) and the 39th's Lieutenant McNamara as his Intelligence Officer.[6]

By mid-September 1942, the position was that the 25th Brigade had arrived from Australia and had been sent along the Kokoda Trail (with the 3rd Militia Battalion attached) to reinforce the now diminished and exhausted remnants of the 21st Brigade. This force had the task of halting the Japanese advance and then pushing back to Kokoda. While this operation was in progress, patrolling was to continue to the east to inhibit any enemy likelihood of infiltration via Nigabaifa–Jawarere, and, with most of the 2/6th Independent Company disposed at Laloki to prevent a similar Japanese infiltration from the west via the Laloki River, Honner Force was to cut off the enemy line of communication between Nauro and Menari.

Little is known of Ralph's subsequent mission: the Official Historian mentioned the operation on four separate pages and in few lines; according to the adjutant, there was no unit diary or report written after the campaign; and, understandably, the 39th Battalion Unit History mentions it only in passing.[7] Dudley McCarthy:

> It constituted an interesting experiment, and represented recognition of the fact that, in the form of warfare which had developed in the mountains, an enemy could and should be struck along his vital supply and communication lines. Unfortunately plans to maintain Honner by means of horse transport and air drops could not be realised for lack of enough horses and lack of suitable dropping grounds. Honner was told, therefore, that he was not to go beyond the limits of the rations which he carried and, about the 17th, he was approaching that limit without having encountered Japanese.[8]

Dudley McCarthy, the Official Historian, was in fact towing the official line. The truth is that both the concept and the allocation of resources for Honner Force were severely flawed. It is crass stupidity to plan a mission on the basis of horse and air supply and then determine, after the force has been despatched, that such resources are unavailable; no provision was made for the evacuation of potential wounded; and, critically, such a venture requires well-trained, fit and highly motivated troops. Captain Lovett:

> After we'd been marching about three or four days . . . and we were dragging along these troops that they gave us . . . who had not had service before and had not been trained . . . and they were most reluctant to push on, and Ralph was setting a pretty high standard of movement, he wanted to get them there quickly. They were dropping out, between ten and fifteen each day. And I said to Ralph, 'What are we going to do about these? We've got to call the roll each day'. He said, 'Well, if they're missing and haven't reported in, missing believed deserted!'
>
> One night we were in a native village and Ralph was in the hut and I was down below, and I was trying to get some of the troops settled down . . . no one seemed to be willing to cooperate with us, and I started to point out to the sergeant

there that he ought to be ashamed of himself. Well, did he
go crook at me! Ralph Honner heard the conversation up
stairs and when I got up into the native hut I said, 'Did you
hear what went on down below?' He said, 'When you use
language like that Lovett, you've got to expect it!' But he said,
'I think they got the message all the same'.[9]

Ralph, Lovett and McNamara returned to the 39th Battalion
on 1 October. The author can vividly remember a comment
from Ralph concerning Honner Force: 'It was a bloody stupid
idea'.[10] When Ralph returned to the 39th Battalion, much had
happened both in Port Moresby and within his unit.

As Ralph was moving to report to Port Moresby on 11 September, the battalion was moved to a campsite near the Laloki
Pumping Station, where it was to be refitted, rested and
retrained. On 14 September, as a result of the 39th being placed
on AIF establishment, the battalion's E Company was disbanded,
and some of its personnel were allocated to its rifle companies
and the remainder to other units. The following day, 100 former
members of the much-maligned 53rd Battalion were taken on
strength.[11]

On 17 September 300 reinforcements from Australia were
taken on strength and the battalion was moved to the base area,
where it was assigned the role of patrolling the Bisiatabu–
Hombrom Bluff–Eilogo region to counter any Japanese infiltration
from the north. When Ralph returned to the unit it was stationed
at Hombrom Bluff.[12]

If a number of changes had occurred within the 39th
Battalion during Ralph's absence, then the controversy and
change within New Guinea Force and its units during the period
22 September to 9 November were monumental.

After General Blamey had made his first visit to Port Moresby
on 12 September, had broadcast his confidence in Rowell and
his troops on radio in Australia and had further reinforced that
confidence to the Advisory War Council, the question of the
conduct of operations in New Guinea should have been resolved.
It should be stated, on balance, that at this juncture General
Blamey's conduct and loyalty had been commendable. But when
Brigadier Eather's first action at Ioribaiwa had come unstuck and
he had quite rightly withdrawn to Imita Ridge, panic stations
were declared in Australia. On the evening of 17 September,

Generals MacArthur and Blamey visit the end of the motorised section of the approach to the Kokoda Trail. (AWM 013424)

General MacArthur contacted Prime Minister Curtin and suggested that General Blamey proceed immediately to Port Moresby to take personal command of operations there—that he should 'energise the situation'. MacArthur claimed during this conversation that the Australians greatly outnumbered the Japanese and had withdrawn to Imita Ridge because of a 'lack of efficiency'. David Horner, in *Crisis of Command*:

> When Blamey journeyed to New Guinea [the second time] to assume command he was, in essence, fighting for his military life. He was a pragmatic politician. He was jealous of his own position and believed that he was the best man for the job. Indeed he had grave doubts about the suitability of some of the possible successors, like Laverack and Bennett. A ruthless man when his own interests were at stake, it was not likely that Blamey would tolerate opposition to his plans.[13]

This most astute statement could be taken further. Blamey was not only prepared not to tolerate 'opposition to his plans' but was fully prepared to remove anyone from power—regardless of the truth—if such action gave the appearance that he was taking a firm grip of the situation and was therefore being seen to be decisive. He arrived in Port Moresby on 24 September 1942.[14]

Rowell was first to go. Just when the tide had turned at Imita Ridge and the enemy had made his decision to withdraw, so Blamey was perceived to have taken over the reins (at nightfall on 27 September the 25th Brigade was again near Ioribaiwa and on 28 September found that the enemy had withdrawn). Although a number of other issues entered into Blamey and Rowell's relationship, the fact remains that Blamey could have, and indeed should have, shown loyalty to his subordinate by standing up to MacArthur and Curtin. On 28 September, after a number of heated exchanges between the two men, Blamey informed Rowell that he had relieved him of his command of New Guinea Force and had sent an adverse report on him to Curtin and MacArthur. Blamey's pursuit of Rowell's further demise continued with an unnecessary passion, urging his retirement, or demotion to the rank of Colonel.

Brigadier Arnold Potts was the second. On 22 October Blamey sacked Potts from his command of the 21st Brigade. It is staggering to contemplate that an Australian brigade commander could be thrust into a campaign with such a damning inadequacy of military intelligence, support and equipment and yet conduct a near-flawless fighting withdrawal, where both the military and political stakes were so terribly important, and could then be sacked from his command as a reward.[15]

Major-General Allen was the third to go. When the pursuit phase of the Kokoda Trail fighting began, Allen had journeyed forward to command his 25th and 16th Brigades fighting their way back to Kokoda. After a constant stream of signals from Blamey to Allen ordering faster progress, Allen was relieved by Blamey. General Vasey was sent to assume command of the 7th Division and took over on 28 October. Kokoda was re-entered on 2 November.[16]

General Blamey's last act of ignorance, disloyalty and self-service was not one of removal from command but one of degradation—of dishonour. On 9 November 1942, at Koitaki, Blamey accused the 21st Brigade of defeat and lack of endeavour.[17] Who better than his ADC and staunch supporter, Lieutenant-

Colonel Norman Carlyon, to have witnessed the authenticity of Blamey's remarks:

> I was there when those fine soldiers formed up, not far from what had been the start-line for their thrust against the enemy. New Guinea's stormy temperatures being what they are, it may seem absurd for me to say that I was in a cold sweat. Standing beside the small platform from which Blamey was to address the troops, I realised that he was in a most aggressive mood. He was soon expressing this in harsh words.
>
> He told the men that they had been defeated, that he had been defeated, and Australia had been defeated. He said that this was simply not good enough. Every soldier here had to remember that he was worth three Japanese. In future he expected no more retirement, but advance at all costs. He concluded with a remark which I think was particularly ill-chosen and unfair. 'Remember' he said, 'it is not the man with the gun that gets shot; it's the rabbit that is running away'. It amazed me that Blamey should deal so insensitively with the men of such a well-proven brigade.[18]

After finishing his diatribe to the troops, Blamey addressed the officers separately. He made it clear that he considered that some of the brigade's officers had failed to perform adequately during the campaign. Captain Harry Katekar, Adjutant, 2/27th Battalion:

> He was displeased with the performance of at least some of our officers [21st Brigade]. He felt that they hadn't led their men properly; in other words 'you've got to pull your socks up!' Which officers was he referring to, and what knowledge did he have of any officers who hadn't? Blamey's inference left us dumbfounded, as it was so distant from the truth.[19]

But the really damning consequence of General Blamey's words was not the collective slur against the innocent—that has been done before and will no doubt be done again—but more the tragic and lingering influence that those words had on the conduct of operations at the ensuing beachhead battle at Gona.

Three critical factors worked in favour of Lieutenant-Colonel Ralph Honner's military career—and worked just as critically against certain other officers' careers—at this ·time.

The first was the Battle of Isurava. That the little-known and poorly trained 39th Militia Battalion had been pushed back to Kokoda and thence to Isurava was one thing; that a crack AIF brigade was forced to withdraw from Isurava after its brigadier had been ordered to advance beyond it to retake Kokoda was unfathomable to higher authority. Blamey knew nothing of Ralph's role in that battle, nor of the performance of his magnificent troops (as demonstrated by his interview with Honner in Port Moresby and his report to the Advisory War Council). But the point is that Ralph Honner bore none of the carping criticism given the other commanders or their units— other than the 53rd Battalion—as a result of the Isurava battle.

Mission Ridge–Brigade Hill was the second. New Guinea Force Headquarters and General Headquarters could not appreciate why or how 21st Brigade Headquarters could have been in grave danger of annihilation; how three AIF battalions could be cut off from their line of communication; and, above all, how one of those battalions could have been lost from the battlefield after only a few days of fighting. Ralph Honner and his 39th Battalion had missed participation in this battle, and therefore avoided the consequent criticism.

The third factor concerned the new commander of the 21st Brigade. After Brigadier Potts had been removed from his command of that formation, Brigadier Ivan Dougherty was flown from Darwin to assume command. Dougherty brought with him a distinguished record of service in the Middle East. He had originally journeyed to war with the 6th Division and had fought in Cyrenaica, Greece and Crete. Dougherty had commanded the 2/4th Battalion of the 19th Brigade—the very same brigade that also contained the 2/11th Battalion, in which Captain and later Major Ralph Honner had served.

Thus, none of the controversy of the Owen Stanley campaign hung over Ralph Honner's head, and, unlike his fellow Maroubra Force officers, Brigadier Dougherty could look to his first-hand knowledge of Honner's acumen as a soldier and leader. Brigadier Ivan Dougherty:

> When Potts was taken off from command of the brigade and Allen the division . . . now the only story I heard was a story Herring [Rowell's replacement as GOC New Guinea Force] told me. There was criticism within New Guinea Force and Supreme Allied Headquarters, concerning the leadership of 21st Brigade. Much of this criticism arose from that particular

withdrawal from Efogi [Mission Ridge–Brigade Hill]. And I
know at the time I was summing things up.[20]

With the debouchment of his troops from the mountain terrain
after his occupation of Kokoda on 2 November 1942, General
Vasey had gained freedom of movement both to concentrate
his forces against enemy lines and to envelop them with
strength, speed and flexibility—impossible for both him and his
predecessor, General Allen, to achieve in the confines of the
high ridges of the Owen Stanley Range.

An encircling onslaught between Oivi and Gorari, in which
Vasey committed his reserve for maximum concentration, killed
approximately 600 Japanese and ensured that no effective opposition could be offered by the enemy between the Kumusi River
and the beachhead defences. The chaotic crossing of the Kumusi
swelled the Japanese losses, many fugitives being overwhelmed
in the turbulent waters that swept their rafts away. Their most
notable casualty was Major-General Horii.

General MacArthur's objective was now to capture the
beachhead locations of Gona–Sanananda–Buna as quickly as
possible. His plans centred around a three-axis advance. The
Australians, commanded by General Vasey, were to approach
from the southwest with the 25th (the 3rd Battalion attached)
and 16th Brigades, and Chaforce. Chaforce was raised to yet
again attempt to cut the enemy line of communication behind
the front. It consisted of three companies, one each from the
2/14th, 2/16th and 2/27th Battalions, and was commanded by
Lieutenant-Colonel Hugh Challen from the 2/14th. However,
the rapid Japanese withdrawal to Templeton's Crossing prevented
Chaforce's deployment and caused it to become employed in
such tasks as the carrying of wounded and supplies. Vasey's line
of approach was through Wairopi–Awala–Popondetta–Soputa.
The approach on the second axis, coming roughly parallel to
Vasey's and about 50 kilometres from it, was to be by a battalion
of the American 126th Regiment crossing from the south coast
towards Buna. The third movement was to be the airlifting of
the 128th Regiment to Wanigela on the northeast coast, whence
it would travel overland northwest also towards Buna.

After General Vasey's 25th Brigade had crossed the Kumusi
on 15 November, it began the trek across 65 kilometres of
tropical lowland towards Gona. Allied intelligence estimated that

the Japanese were a diluted, spent and sick force. By an ironic twist of fate, the relief of the 25th Brigade and the capture of Gona were to be entrusted to the 21st Brigade, and this time the AIF veterans would be reinforced by the 39th Battalion.

Amid tragic tactical errors, a consequent slaughter of magnificent infantry and the lingering influence of the Kokoda campaign and its aftermath, Lieutenant-Colonel Ralph Honner was to dramatically stamp himself on events at Gona.

10

ONCE MORE UNTO
THE BREACH

The best hope of tilting the scales and of overcoming the
resistance inherent in conflict lies in originality—to produce
something unexpected that will paralyse the opponent's freedom of action.

Liddell Hart, 1936[1]

The Allied operations conducted during the period November 1942–January 1943 at the Gona–Sanananda–Buna
beachhead were confined to an area approximately 19 kilometres
long, from Cape Endaiadere on the northeast coast stretching
westwards to the Amboga River. The total defended ground
was approximately 38 square kilometres.

Intelligence estimates of the Japanese strength at the beachhead varied considerably among the Allies. The 7th Australian
Division's assessment was between 1500 and 2000; the 32nd
American Division's calculation was approximately a battalion
across the whole front; while General Headquarters Intelligence
determined that 4000 of the enemy occupied the area.[2]

When Major-General Horii received his order to stage a
fighting withdrawal to the beachhead, the Japanese troops stationed at Gona, formerly the picturesque site of an Anglican
mission, had nearly two months in which to prepare their
defences. The location of the Japanese Gona defences and their
consequent fire plan resulted from a masterly combination of

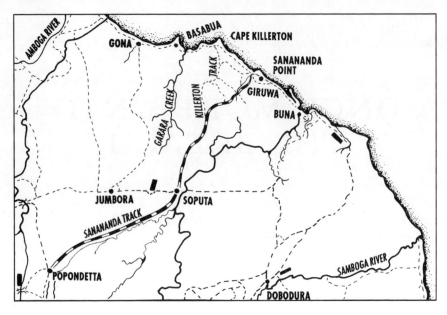

The beachhead.

the use of the military potential of the ground and the allocation
of the available defenders. Approximately 90 metres west of the
Mission lay Gona Creek, a natural feature wide enough at its
mouth, and inland to just past the Mission, to inhibit an
Australian attack across it. A substantial coconut grove, about
100 metres in depth, ran eastwards from the creek, stretching
approximately 1200 metres along the coast to a small creek
(named Small Creek by the Australians) and onwards towards
Sanananda.

Gona Mission lay about 110 metres inland from the coast,
and from it, roughly parallel to Gona Creek, the main Gona–
Jumbora track ran southwards. The ground around the Mission
was dominated by two areas of jungle and scrub. The smaller
was bordered by Gona Creek to the west, the Mission to the
north, an elongated stretch of bare ground to the south, and
the track to the east. The larger area of jungle and scrub was
to the east of the track. A large swamp split the final scrub
entrance to the Mission into two forks. The area was extensive
and ran almost 250 metres southeast from the Mission. Using
the natural features between Gona Creek and Small Creek, the
Japanese toiled long and hard on a fire plan that concentrated
their defence in three key areas.

The first position consisted of numerous machine-gun posts stretching approximately 100 metres along the eastern bank of Gona Creek to its mouth and then along the coast to Small Creek. Throughout the area, slit trenches were sited to allow infantry cover for the machine-gun posts. The slit trenches were not all occupied at any one time but were available as the nature of the fighting dictated. A double shallow trench system stretched from due west of the Mission, along the creek and coast to a position slightly northeast of the Mission.

The second position formed a semicircle around the south-eastern and eastern sides of the Mission. A network of slit trenches and a shallow trench system, often filled with water, linked the numerous machine-gun posts in the area.

The third position, at the southern edge of the smaller scrub area between the creek and the main track south from the Mission, consisted of a line of slit trenches fortified by machine-gun posts and larger strong posts.

Posts in adjacent areas and within all areas were mutually supportive; a number of kunai grass patches were levelled to establish substantial killing grounds; highly concentrated enfilading machine-gun fire was a keynote of the killing grounds; snipers abounded high up in the coconut palms, showing a profound interest in Australian Bren gunners; the protruding banyan tree roots were used as natural cover for camouflage; coconut log and sandbag bunkers were covered with dirt and fast-growing vegetation, to make strong posts and smaller machine-gun posts very hard to identify until it was too late and, above all, such posts later seemed impervious to machine-gun fire, grenade burst and artillery bombardment—only direct hits from air bombing or artillery fire seemed capable of their outright destruction.[3]

To man his defences, the commander of the Gona area, Lieutenant-Colonel Yoshinobu Tomita, had elements of the 41st and 144th Regiments as well as base personnel who had been in the area since July—a total of between 800 and 1000 desperate defenders. But there was an additional positive Japanese defensive trait at the beachhead. There can be little doubt that the Australians appreciated the uncompromising and ruthless nature of their enemy. However, they had not as yet encountered him in a large, complex, static defensive position—many of the enemy were debilitated before the campaign began, but were

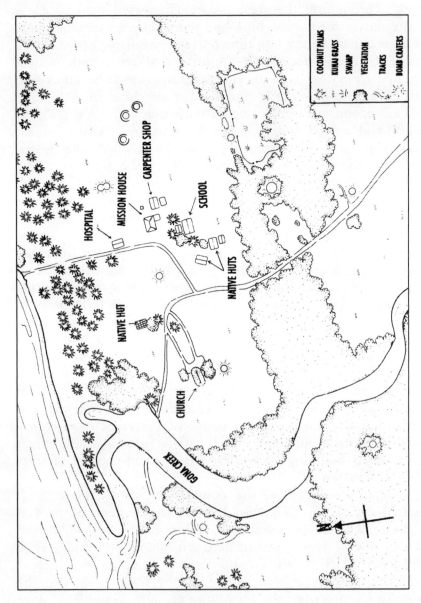

Gona Mission, 1942.

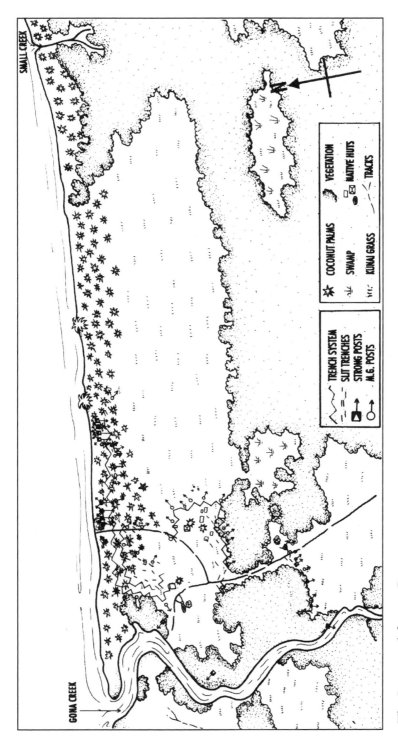

The Japanese defences, Gona.

still prepared to use their strong post or slit trench as a latrine, rice larder and charnel-house. Denied movement as the closeness and intensity of battle increased, their politico-military code of behaviour enhanced their resolve to fight on and die in circumstances that the Australian soldier could not have contemplated, let alone endured.

After the crossing of the Kumusi River in mid-November, General Vasey decided to commit Brigadier Eather's 25th Brigade and 3rd Militia Battalion to the capture of Gona and Brigadier Lloyd's 16th Brigade to the capture of Sanananda.[4] By employing this two-pronged tactic, General Vasey severely prejudiced his potential to concentrate his available force at either of his two objectives. Despite the fact that he was operating under the disadvantage of poor intelligence, the forces under his command were brigade forces in name only.

Immediately prior to crossing the Kumusi, Vasey's force had lost 53 officers and 900 other ranks as battle casualties in addition to a very substantial evacuation of the sick. Eather's attacking force of four gravely depleted battalions, even with the addition of Chaforce, still only approximately equalled in number the well-prepared defenders of Gona.

Between 21 and 26 November, the 25th Brigade made a number of attacks from the south and southeast. In addition, Eather positioned Lieutenant Haddy's Chaforce Company to the west of Gona Creek, with the role of harassing the enemy from that flank and also of providing a standing patrol to the west of Gona to block any attempt by the Japanese to bolster their strength from that direction.

By 26 November it was painfully clear that the Japanese were successfully contesting the Allied advance on the beachhead and inflicting telling casualties. The 16th Brigade had ground to a bloodied halt on the Sanananda Track; the inexperienced and often poorly led Americans had been turned back near Buna in tragic disarray, and the brave 25th Brigade at Gona, riddled with disease and stunned by horrendous casualties, was basically burnt out. Including his diminished 3rd Militia Battalion and his Chaforce contingent, Brigadier Eather's total malaria-ridden force now numbered little more than 1000 men.

On 23 November Vasey requested that his New Guinea Force Commander, Lieutenant-General Herring, despatch the 21st Brigade to Popondetta forthwith.

If the prevailing mood at the front was grim, it was perhaps even more so at Port Moresby. A blunt discussion was held between General Blamey and General MacArthur. The main topic under discussion was the choice of reinforcement formations for the Gona–Sanananda–Buna area. Four alternatives were offered: the 128th American Regiment, the 41st American Division, the 21st AIF Brigade, and the 30th Militia Brigade (the 39th, 49th and 55/53rd Battalions).

General Blamey had long been harbouring a resentment towards General MacArthur's criticism of the Australian performance on the Kokoda Trail and at Milne Bay. He plainly and firmly advocated that the two Australian brigades be sent to the front, as he said he knew they would fight.

The story of the 21st Brigade's subsequent fighting at Gona is one of a wanton waste of an already diminished force. After its Kokoda Trail campaigning, the brigade flew to Gona with a combined total of 63 officers and 874 other ranks—the approximate strength of one battalion. In five short days, between 29 November and 3 December, the 21st Brigade lost 340 men out of a total of 874, while being repeatedly committed at the wrong place and with paltry artillery and air support. The adjutant of the 2/27th Battalion, Captain Harry Katekar, best summed up this sorry state of affairs:

> All those involved at command and staff level in a properly conducted operation, first of all have an appreciation of the situation; from the enemy's point of view and our troops' point of view. That wasn't done at Gona. We were thrown in with scant information about the enemy; no aerial photographs, nothing to go on. I don't recall ever seeing a proper plan of the area showing where 25th Brigade was at that time when we were supposed to go in, or in fact, what the 2/14th were doing on our right. The whole thing was rushed and therefore one can expect there to be what actually transpired—a slaughter of good men! The correct way to get information was to send in recce patrols. That's always the way you do it, because you get the enemy to disclose where he is. You don't go in with a full company rushing in against something you know nothing about.[5]

As the first 21st Brigade attack went in on Sunday 29 November at Gona, the 39th Battalion, near Port Moresby, received a movement warning order. The 39th's Unit Diary:

Throughout the night packing and re-equipment proceeded. All ranks were issued with green clothing and American-style gaiters, and deficiencies in all equipment were rectified. The amount of gear which higher formations ordered to be carried by each man was far in excess of what was found to be necessary or practicable in the Bn's previous experience of mobile jungle warfare. This included extra set of shirt and trousers, mosquito nets, felt hats and packs.[6]

The following day, the advance party consisting of Lieutenant-Colonel Ralph Honner, Lieutenant McNamara (the Intelligence Officer), the RMO, Captain Shera, and elements of C and D Companies emplaned for Popondetta. From Popondetta, the battalion faced a hot, stifling 13-kilometre march to Soputa. Keith Crisp, 39th Battalion:

> After unloading our stores we moved off on foot. Somewhere near Soputa darkness fell and we decided to stop for the night. It began to rain heavily, too wet to light a fire, so we ate a couple of 'dog biscuits' each and set up our groundsheets to keep off some of the water which poured all over us—it rained all night, we got soaked . . . Next morning we got something to eat and then continued on towards the front. Along each side of the track there were little wooden crosses made from Kraft Cheese boxes, the crossbar secured to the upright with a twist of 'sig wire', and on the crossbar a name and number written in bright purple indelible pencil. At the foot of some of the crosses was a 'tin hat'.[7]

At around midday on 2 December, General Vasey held a conference at Brigadier Eather's headquarters. In attendance were Vasey and Brigadiers Eather, Dougherty and Porter. Vasey had originally intended to relieve the 25th Brigade with the 30th Brigade; however, the unexpectedly heavy Gona casualties brought about a change in plans. He decided to send Dougherty and his 2/14th Battalion, with the 39th Battalion under command, to Sanananda to assist in its capture; and he decided to amalgamate the depleted 2/27th and 2/16th Battalions, under the command of Lieutenant-Colonel Caro, to assist Eather's 25th Brigade in a blocking or holding role at Gona.[8]

Vasey's plans were to last only a day, as the 2/14th Battalion soon discovered that the mapped 'track' along the coast was interrupted by very thick scrub and large areas of swamp and was, therefore, not a suitable infantry route to Sanananda. As

General George Vasey.
(AWM 52620)

Brigadier Ivan Dougherty,
Commander 21st Brigade.

the 39th Battalion paused behind the 2/14th while progress was
halted by the terrain, misfortune struck. Jim Hardie, A Company, 39th Battalion:

> The whole battalion was . . . on this little beach and there
> was a clearing that went back about thirty yards before the
> jungle began. Further up the coast some Beaufighters were
> strafing the beaches. They were making a half-circle out to
> sea and on their way in again they were strafing a sunken Jap
> transport which was suspected of being used at night as an
> off-loading point for supplies that they'd bring into shore in
> barges. And I remember saying to someone: 'I hope those
> RAAF blokes know we're on this beach'. Just then one of the
> Beaufighters finished its half-circle and straightened up to
> sweep along the beaches again. We were watching him, and
> it didn't look too good at all. And the next minute, flame
> from the front of him—he'd opened up with his machine-guns
> and strafed virtually the whole battalion! To this day I can't
> understand how we got out of it so lightly . . .
>   And out of it all A Company had only one chap hit. And
> the rest of the battalion only had four other wounded besides
> a couple of native carriers.[9]

If the futile trek towards Sanananda made no great impression
on Ralph, then his observations of the Gona battleground—and
particularly those of the 21st Brigade along the coastal coconut
belt—most certainly did:

> . . . we were able to see the kind of ground along the beach
> under the trees, but with open stretches of ground, over which
> the 21st Brigade was being thrown against at Gona Mission,
> and we didn't like the look of that ground at all . . .[10]

No competent commander could have 'liked the look of that
ground'. It was at this juncture that Ralph and his battalion
were given a critical piece of good fortune. Ralph Honner, in
'The 39th at Gona':

> On the opposite side [from 21st Brigade's positions on the
> coast] the enemy were protected by a creek; our western
> company occupied its left bank but could not attack across it.
> The rest of the battalion was on the southern front which was
> divided into two sectors by a track running north to the
> mission and parallel to the creek. In the sector between the
> road and the creek was a broad belt of low kunai grass; and
> a long stretch of this grass in front of the timber line that
> marked the enemy's position had been cut off at ground level.
> To the right of the road there were covered approaches right
> into the enemy lines; this was obviously the best area from
> which to launch an attack.[11]

Ralph's allotted ground was therefore in two parts: the left flank,
between Gona Creek and the main track leading into Gona
from the south; and the right flank, a covered approach of scrub,
jungle and some swamp that led into the heart of the enemy
defences. It is at this juncture that two issues of controversy
arise. The first concerns the jungle and scrub approach. Ralph
would later write:

> Strangely enough its possibilities seem to have been overlooked
> while bloody losses were sustained in reckless attacks elsewhere.
> Brigadier Eather had told me that in this area the 3rd Battalion
> posts were so close to those of the Japanese that the favourite
> pastime of both forces was the throwing of grenades at one
> another. I relayed this information to Captain Joe Gilmore but
> when his A Company took over from the 3rd Battalion he
> immediately obtained my permission to move his company

forward to make contact with the enemy and dig in there, not yet within grenade range but in what had been no-man's land.[12]

On 1 December, the 3rd Battalion was to have offered critical fire support to an attack by the 2/16th–2/27th on Gona Mission. Brigadier Ivan Dougherty:

> And he [Lieutenant-Colonel Cameron, whom Ralph had met at Isurava] was to liaise with them on the left flank . . . the crux of the thing is he didn't do that, and when O'Neill's company got into Gona, instead of him going forward, he hadn't gone forward . . . and I don't think he was ever forward where he said he was.[13]

The reason that the covered approach through the jungle and scrub sector had been 'strangely overlooked' was that Cameron's masterly inactivity in the area, his false reports as to his position, and his 'grenade throwing jousts with the enemy' had masked the potential of his front. It should also be stated that had maps and aerial photographs of Gona been made available to the forward commanders—and such photographs did exist—and sensible, measured reconnaissance been undertaken, then the potential of the area would surely have been realised.[14] Thus, Ralph was allotted two areas at Gona—one militarily useless (the bare killing ground between the creek and the track), and the other priceless (the jungle and scrub approach to the east of the track).

The second issue constitutes Lieutenant-Colonel Ralph Honner's greatest military regret. On 5 December 1942 Ralph received orders from Brigadier Dougherty to attack the Japanese through his left flank. The attack was to be assisted by yet another attack by the 2/27th–2/16th Composite Battalion through the coastal coconut belt. Captain Max Bidstrup, OC D Company, 39th Battalion, was also present at the meeting. When the attack was explained to the 39th's officers Bidstrup protested in strong terms.[15] Ralph also voiced his opposition to the plan but deeply regretted not taking a firmer stand with Brigadier Dougherty.[16] The attack was to proceed.

Bidstrup's assault was to be mounted through the kunai grass and then over about 80 daunting metres of bare ground facing the enemy positions—a number of mutually supported bunkers with machine guns on fixed lines. To support the attack, a 3-inch mortar barrage was to be laid down shortly before daylight and a smoke barrage at dawn as D Company's 16 and 17 Platoons attacked.

The 39th Battalion's first Gona attack on 6 December 1942 was a costly failure. Ralph Honner:

> Our orders were to attack directly from the front. I do not know why, because I protested against the idea, but these were the orders and I take it that they must have fitted into some plan that was beyond my conception . . . the only support from another sub-unit was a section from B Company which was to provide flanking protection along the track should Don Company's attack succeed. That flanking protection which went in where the attack should have gone in, around the flank of the Japanese position, was able to go right through the jungle behind the bunkers, go on, find out what was there and get a sight of the village, but as the attack had failed, they had to come back . . .[17]

Lieutenant Doug McClean led 17 Platoon in the D Company attack:

> The Japs were in deep dugouts protected with thick logs at ground level separated by other logs just to allow the weapons to protrude . . . providing a field of fire for the one hundred and eighty degrees facing the scrub. Now our troops as they attacked were hit in the lower leg and body . . . and I later found some of my boys lying against enemy positions with unexploded grenades in their hands. They were riddled with wounds but struggled as they died to get to the enemy . . . if ever blokes had earnt a decoration . . . one lad was shot twice in the same action . . . flesh wounds . . . and the tears in his eyes when he asked for a safer spot . . . 'Sir', he said crying, 'Every time I move some bastard shoots me!' . . . he was only eighteen.[18]

The 39th Battalion's attack on 6 December 1942 cost it twelve men killed and 46 wounded—a high cost from a total force of two platoons.

Lieutenant-Colonel Caro's 2/27th–2/16th attack through the coconut belt fared no better. The leading platoon, commanded by Lieutenant Charlie White (a former student of Ralph's at Hale School in Perth), made a desperate dash towards the first Japanese post. White was wounded in the leg and while being carried out was shot again, this time mortally. A smoke barrage was laid down in order to evacuate the wounded. A patrol later recovered White's body, having found it among numerous enemy dead. This action cost the 2/16th four men killed and six wounded. Another attack was scheduled for the following day. Ralph Honner:

> . . . the scope of the attack was extended. We were this time allowed to attack on the right of the track, where we could attack through some cover . . . but we still had to attack on the left of the track where Don Company's attack had failed the previous day . . . I didn't know how to get out of this, I didn't want to disobey orders, I didn't want to have another company killed off, and I didn't know how to get out of it.[19]

The answer to Honner's conundrum came from a most unexpected quarter—his own air support. And that air support must have seemed almost comical to a soldier who had endured German Stuka strafing along the high passes of Greek mountains and in the ill-covered olive groves of Crete. The resulting 'air support' consisted of a paltry few bombs which landed behind his lines. Captain Bidstrup remembered his commanding officer's wrath:

> They fell closer to us than the Japs! And Ralph said, 'We're not going in!' And I remember Ralph standing up and saying, 'Give me a squadron of Stukas!'[20]

Ralph Honner:

> The bombing attack was to end in a wing-waggle signal to us that the bombing had finished and then we were to leap into the attack . . . I took a gamble. I cancelled the attack. I couldn't cancel it on one side and not the other and I rang up the brigade commander and told him that I had cancelled the attack because the mis-directed bombing attack had jeopardised its chances of success. This was a spurious pretext but the brigade commander accepted it and I tried to fortify it, or to bolster it, by giving an optimistic assessment that if I were allowed to attack the next day through the jungle approaches on the right of the track and abandon the attack approach on the left which had already proved disastrous, I should have a good chance of getting into Gona Mission. And this was approved.[21]

That 'this was approved' contains some noteworthy points. First, if Ralph enjoyed his superior officer's trust and support and

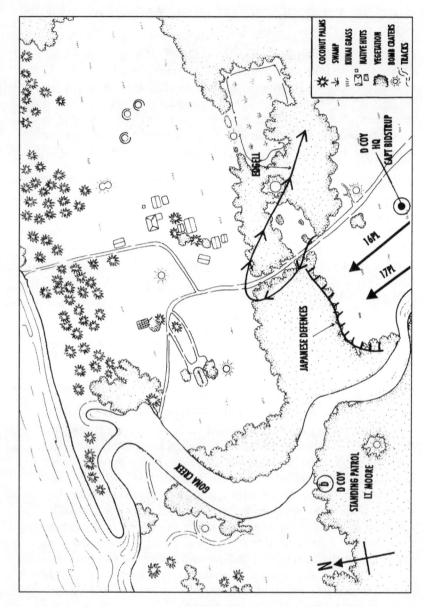

COCONUT PALMS
SWAMP
KUNAI GRASS
NATIVE HUTS
VEGETATION
BOMB CRATERS
TRACKS

EDGELL

D COY
HQ
CAPT BIDSTRUP

16PL

17PL

JAPANESE DEFENCES

GONA CREEK

D COY
STANDING PATROL,
LL. MOORE

N

The 39th Battalion's attack, Gona, 6 December 1942.

loyalty at this juncture, a similar display of those qualities was
not enjoyed by equally capable commanders less than a kilometre
away.

After being wounded at Gona on 1 December, and after
having been involved in an acrimonious discussion with Brigadier Dougherty while lying on a stretcher near HQ at Gona
concerning the tactics employed during his battalion's fighting,
Lieutenant-Colonel Cooper did not gain another battalion command—a great injustice to a soldier who had led his battalion
with such zeal and competence both at Mission Ridge and
Gona. Cooper's replacement was Major Hearman from the
2/16th Battalion. He lasted a matter of days, because he had
protested at the unjustifiable slaughter of his men and the poor
fire support afforded them during repeated futile attacks along
the beach. Hearman was replaced by Lieutenant-Colonel Caro—
by wide repute, after the Syrian and Owen Stanley campaigns,
a commanding officer of the highest order. Caro's command of
the 2/27th–2/16th Composite Battalion lasted but three days.
He, too, became very bitter about the blind slaughter of his
troops and protested at the futility of frontal attacks over open
ground into Japanese enfilading fire without adequate fire support. Caro was relieved on 7 December—the very day that
Ralph had used his 'spurious pretext' of the inept aerial bombing
support to cancel his attack. The truth is that Ralph Honner
was not Isurava and Mission Ridge and Koitaki Parade branded;
in addition, his Middle East reputation stood him in good stead
in his brigade commander's eyes.

That trust must have been strained to the limit with news
that reached Dougherty that same day. He would later write
that:

> . . . I ordered that the attack by 39 Aust Inf Bn be cancelled
> as it had insufficient support. At this time a Jap force, which
> appeared to be well equipped and fresh, was moving along the
> coast track from the AMBOGA RIVER towards GONA
> MISSION, and appeared to be a definite threat to our force
> and an attempt to relieve the Jap forces in GONA MISSION.
>
> General Vasey at this time was in favour of containing
> GONA MISSION until some other part of the front was
> captured. However, in view of the threat from the west I
> considered that it was necessary to capture GONA MISSION

on 8 December. I rang General VASEY and he agreed to my plans and allotted me 250 rounds of 25 pr ammunition . . .

I had sent Lt-Colonel CHALLEN with all the men of the 2/14th Aust Inf Bn he could muster to move to the west of GONA, reinforce the patrols already delaying the Jap, and prevent him from approaching within 1200 yards of GONA MISSION.

As I intended that the attack on 8 December would be a very strong one it was decided to drop surrender pamphlets on the Japs early on 8 December. This I feel had some influence on the Jap's morale.[22]

There are a number of interesting points contained in the above passage. The issue of the Japanese potential to reinforce their beachhead and the manner in which this affected the Australian conduct of operations, and Ralph's reaction to this subject, will be examined later.

Brigadier Dougherty did not cancel the attack on 7 December 1942—Ralph had already done that when he phoned Dougherty. Dougherty's report was written after the fall of Gona and therefore with the advantage of hindsight. Had the attack on the 8th been a dismal failure, Dougherty's report would, no doubt, have mentioned the fact that Honner had cancelled the attack. The truth is that if Dougherty had really seen fit to cancel the attack on 7 December due to 'insufficient support', then he would most certainly have cancelled earlier attacks for precisely the same reason.

The notion that the Japanese were influenced by the dropping of surrender pamphlets early on 8 December borders on the comical. There is absolutely no evidence that the enemy resolve to fight was in any way influenced by this tactic—in fact the events of 8 and 9 December 1942 at Gona suggest the opposite. One company commander at Gona has suggested that this supply of paper could have been put to far greater practical use had it been dropped on the Australian lines.[23]

But Dougherty's mention of a Japanese movement from the west to reinforce their comrades at Gona Mission was a matter of some concern. His movement of the 2/14th Battalion to the west was a response to the plight of Lieutenant Alan Haddy's Chaforce standing patrol on that western flank.

On 30 November Haddy had relieved Lieutenant Greenwood's standing patrol at a small village—to become known as

Haddy's Village—near the Amboga River and about 3 kilometres west of his own Chaforce base. Haddy had forestalled an
enemy attempt at movement eastwards, sustaining two killed
in action, and subsequently estimated that approximately 150 to
200 enemy troops were west of the Amboga River. Lieutenant
A.W. Moore, 18 Platoon, 39th Battalion, was sent with a
number of his men to relieve Haddy on 4 December. Lieutenant
A.W. 'Kanga' Moore:

> Haddy's Village was a clearing on a beach about one hundred
> and fifty yards long; probably fifty yards in depth before you
> got near the swamp; right in the centre of it there were about
> half a dozen native huts that were on high stilts . . . and further
> along towards the Amboga River there were another couple
> of huts . . . Haddy to me was the tiredest-looking man I had
> ever seen, he looked exhausted . . . malaria; he hadn't eaten
> properly; hadn't slept, because there was no sleep in this
> position . . .
>   Haddy, with a flow of rather good language, said to me,
> 'You can bloody have it!' That was during the afternoon, and
> we were left there in that position . . .
>   Now during that night a barge came in and ran up onto
> the beach right in the centre of Haddy's Village. The flap was
> lowered; some Japanese jabber went on in the barge; the flap
> was lifted and it pulled out from the beach and went off west,
> no doubt to the Japanese supply dump . . . After that night
> in the village we were relieved by Haddy . . .[24]

In the middle of the rain-soaked night of 6 December, the Japanese
converged on Haddy's position. Private Charles Bloomfield,
2/16th Chaforce Company:

> The attack came at the height of a storm. The Japs came in
> throwing grenades and in the attack one man was killed,
> presumably Stephens . . . and four were wounded, among
> them being Haddy. As our lines of communication were cut
> one man was sent back to alert the company. I think the man
> was Private Archer . . .
>   Another attack came in shortly after but was unsuccessful,
> and during the lightning flashes we could see lines of Japs
> making their way along the beach. Haddy, who was badly
> wounded . . . decided to vacate the position; he ordered me
> to take the wounded and withdraw; two of the wounded—one
> with a groin injury and the other caught a bomb blast to the

stomach—both seemed in a dazed condition and the other man
had a bad leg wound and had to be carried.

   We hadn't left the position for many minutes when sounds
of gun fire came again from where we had just left.[25]

The remaining Chaforce contingent on the western side of
Gona Creek numbered a paltry and disease-ridden fifteen soldiers. Sergeant Jones lost no time leading them back to assist
Haddy. But that small group was confronted by the advancing
enemy. Jones killed four of them, but was bayoneted by the
fourth. Command of the group fell to Corporal Murphy, who
led them with such vigour that the enemy were temporarily
forestalled.

   The 2/14th Battalion contingent sent by Brigadier Dougherty to reinforce Haddy's worn and understrength force was
led by Lieutenant Bob Dougherty (no relation to Brigadier
Dougherty). Lieutenant Dougherty and 50 men were able to
surprise the enemy about a kilometre southeast of Haddy's
Village. Along the way, Dougherty gathered in Lieutenant
Moore and approximately ten of his 18 Platoon, 39th Battalion.
Dougherty was renowned within the distinguished ranks of the
2/14th Battalion as an aggressive soldier. He decided, in spite
of the fact that the Japanese outnumbered him by about four
to one, to mount a spirited attack. Lieutenant A.W. 'Kanga'
Moore:

> I was beside him when a bullet cut a gouge about six inches
> long in his rifle butt. Dougherty was the coolest man I've ever
> seen in my life. He just sort of looked at it and said, 'Ah, look
> at that!' He put in a most remarkable attack . . . and I just
> couldn't believe that men were going in as Dougherty and his
> men were . . . he went in as if he was saving England! They
> were actually walking through bullets flying around every-
> where and not seeming to notice . . . a little fella of mine by
> the name of Reid was killed there . . .[26]

The embattled 2/14th's audacious attack under Lieutenant Dougherty temporarily checked the Japanese advance. In the evening of
7 December Lieutenant-Colonel Challen arrived with the remainder of the 2/14th Battalion to consolidate the blocking position.
But what of Haddy?

   When Haddy's Village was eventually recaptured the body
of Stephens was found at its sentry post in the command hut;

and beneath the hut's raised platform Haddy lay, still at bay, ringed by dead Japanese.

Thus, on the night of 7 December 1942 at Gona, the position was that Brigadier Dougherty's planned attack on the Mission had been cancelled by Ralph; the 21st Brigade's Composite 2/27th–2/16th Battalion was still facing the enemy in the coconut belt on the coast; the enemy had temporarily been checked on the western flank across Gona Creek; and that Ralph had assured Dougherty that, if allowed to attack through the southern area of jungle and scrub, Gona would fall the next day. The situation was thus most delicately poised.

For the final throw on 8 December, Brigadier Dougherty insisted that the attack would be undertaken on three fronts. The first was along the well-worn and useless coastal coconut belt by the 2/27th–2/16th Composite Battalion; the second was through the equally useless open area between the creek and track; and the third was through the covered jungle and scrub area to the east of the track.

After cancelling the attack on 7 December, Ralph spent the rest of that day in a reconnaissance of the ground—particularly the jungle and scrub sector to the east of the Gona track. His adjutant remembered that this reconnaissance was undertaken with his intelligence officer, Lieutenant McNamara. Ralph apparently shared his thoughts with no-one,[27] but, given that the attack was to go in the next day, he must have done some savage and rapid thinking.

Ralph Honner's plan for the capture of Gona Mission was a masterly combination of his own wide experience as a soldier, his expert adherence to the principles of war and, critically, his preparedness to take two calculated risks—one of disobeying or 'modifying' his superior's orders, and the other concerning his support. His plea to Dougherty concerning being allowed to attack via the jungle and scrub approach at Gona had a number of distinct advantages. The first was the obvious one. Ralph Honner:

> It doesn't matter what cover you have getting close to the enemy if in the last stretch he's got an unbroken field of fire where he can mow you down. But if you've got a covered approach right into the heart of his defences he's gone![28]

Ralph's second advantage concerning this avenue of attack was that success through this corridor would have two major

consequences for the Japanese. The first was that a wedge would
be driven between their right and left flanks. Such a wedge
would make the enemy's Gona Creek–Gona Track front redundant, as it would become hemmed in between the creek and
the 39th Battalion. Further, those enemy soldiers would then
be in absolutely no position to assist their comrades elsewhere.

Ralph's next consideration was concentration of force.
A Company (Captain Joe Gilmore) was in occupation of the
southernmost area of the jungle and scrub, the point through
which Honner wanted to attack Gona. After their brief but
successful probing of the Japanese defences in this sector on the
6th, they were the logical company to spearhead the attack.
Late on 7 December, Ralph moved the remnants of D Company
—decimated by the previous day's attack—behind A Company,
with the role of exploiting A Company's anticipated initial
success. And it was on this consideration of concentration of
force that Ralph disobeyed orders concerning the attack between the creek and the track:

> . . . I had made up my mind to modify the attack . . . I
> instructed C Company's commander [Captain Seward] who
> was to attack on the left, to attack with fire only; just enough
> fire, waste no ammunition, to keep his company intact, fully
> armed and ready to fight, but lose no lives.[29]

When A Company and the D Company remnant had made
their breach into the Japanese defences, Honner planned that
C Company would be rapidly moved from its fire demon-
stration on the left flank to exploit his gains through the jungle
and scrub flank. This plan relied on the D Company remnant
maintaining the momentum of the attack—however briefly,
because of their diminished numbers—until Seward could rede-
ploy his C Company.

But Ralph knew that there remained one last but significant
problem—the network of enemy bunkers and their telling
machine-gun fire. Ralph Honner:

> . . . the plan was added to by a couple of significant factors.
> I knew from experience that infantry could fight under their
> own artillery bombardment, and using their own bombardment
> they could use surprise to catch the enemy unawares. I had
> arranged with the artillery FOO, the Forward Observation
> Officer, to have the artillery barrage on the Japanese defences

use shells fused to burst eighteen inches or two feet deep in
the soft soil. If they managed to break through the roofs of
the bunkers they would damage the bunkers, if they dropped
into the soft ground alongside the bunkers, they would stun
the defenders. Now, in either case they'd distract the defenders
while our troops reached the defenders. And to capitalise on
that I arranged my timetable for our troops who would be
lining up about a hundred yards away from the Japanese
defences, to move two minutes before the barrage lifted, so
that they had one minute to get into the Japanese defences
and one minute to fight among them with the artillery shells
still dropping.[30]

It is highly likely that this decision was based on Ralph's
experiences with the Italian artillery in Libya, and the fact that
he had witnessed few casualties in relation to the number of
troops committed.

However, unbeknown to Ralph, Lieutenants Dalby and
Kelly of A Company had decided to creep with their platoons
towards the enemy positions during the barrage. And those
two enterprising officers were unaware that their commanding
officer had 'extended' the barrage with the same idea in mind.
One critical and life-saving minute right among the enemy thus
became two. Lieutenant Hugh Kelly:

> . . . they were spot on with the barrage, and actually, it didn't
> worry us all that much; the ground was a bit soggy and there
> was just a bit of a soggy thump as it hit and then the explosion.
> I suppose if it'd been on hard ground there would have been
> a hell of a lot more noise and it might have been a bit more
> dangerous too.
>
> We went in two sections forward and one section in
> reserve. When we actually stood up to move across the ground,
> this car body (across the swamp near the school) came to life
> by machine gun fire and my right hand section got into strife
> . . . that's when I yelled out to a Bren gunner in the reserve
> platoon, that was 'Darky' Wilkinson, he was within earshot of
> me, to tell him about this. In typical fashion he made a remark,
> 'What's wrong with your rifle!' . . . that's when he moved
> forward to a little peak of scrub there . . . there was an old
> fence that petered out and he stood up and put the Bren on
> a post. He quietened that and when we got to the edge of
> the Jap weapon pits we just met up with Dalby. He struck
> the heavy opposition; he had the heavy machine gunners in

Lieutenant Hugh Dalby,   *Lieutenant Hugh Kelly,*
A Company, 39th Battalion.   *A Company, 39th Battalion.*

front of him . . . I saw him once on my left; where his platoon
was there was a weapon pit, an obvious weapon pit; it was
round and raised up . . . I saw Dalby stand up in front of
it and on the off chance he chucked a grenade into it. And
a body came hurtling out of it and he just fired from the
waist with his rifle. There's no doubt about him, he was right
into it![31]

Lieutenant Hugh Dalby:

We had our bloody objective, and I think once you got
committed, and you got in among being shot at, and shooting
at . . . you just hoe in . . . it was pretty close warfare; there
wasn't the room to manoeuvre beautifully like you could in
the desert . . . unless the platoon commander and the platoon
section leaders were of a mind to charge in, well then how
do you expect the troops to? . . . and so really there was no
set formation as far as I was concerned . . . we got in a
reasonably straight line, the two forward platoons, and charged
straight in at the bloody Japs. We had to get in among them
while the artillery was firing.

. . . the Japs still had their heads down and in the pillboxes.
They didn't come out until we started shooting . . . the first gun
that I ran into, I was on top of them as the last shell exploded.

And I started shooting and the bloke on the left and the bloke on the right and everyone else got in for the bun fight![32]

In an interview with the author, Ralph proudly described the consequences of his both astute and innovative planning:

A Company's initial attack had an extraordinary success. Post after post fell to them. But there was a severe time gap between their attack and the arrival of C Company from across the other side of the track to support them. Into that time gap the reinforced D Company, including the platoon which was not engaged in the attack on the 6th of December, were thrown in straight after A Company to maintain and expand the impetus of the attack, and behind Don Company came C Company, pouring across from the other side of the track fully armed and rearing to go. The impetus of the attack carried them through the Japanese network of posts until they reached the sago swamp which was an integral part of the Japanese line of defence. There the A Company attack had to branch into two. Hugh Dalby's platoon went around the left of the swamp to clean up the network of enemy posts between the swamp and the main track into the Mission. On the right Hugh Kelly's platoon went around the right of the sago swamp up through the cover there, and turned west across the north of the sago swamp through the timbered corridor leading to the Mission school.

And so the attack continued in two prongs around the sago swamp. That attack went on through the day and at the end of the day, the 39th Battalion had captured the centre of the Japanese defensive positions right up to the Mission school; had captured all the jungle around the sago swamp on the right of the track; had isolated the unattacked Japanese bunker line on the left of the track which had been our disaster on the 6th of December and by-passed it; and as night fell, we had already taken about half of the Japanese perimeter and had hit right into the heart of the defences.[33]

The game was up. With their centre positions penetrated, the Japanese were now in possession of two isolated pockets of ground—the now redundant western bunker network between the track and the creek, and the far-distant front facing the 21st Brigade on the coast. Some time after dark on 8 December 1942, the Japanese determined that those fit enough to stage a breakout would do so at midnight, with the intention of

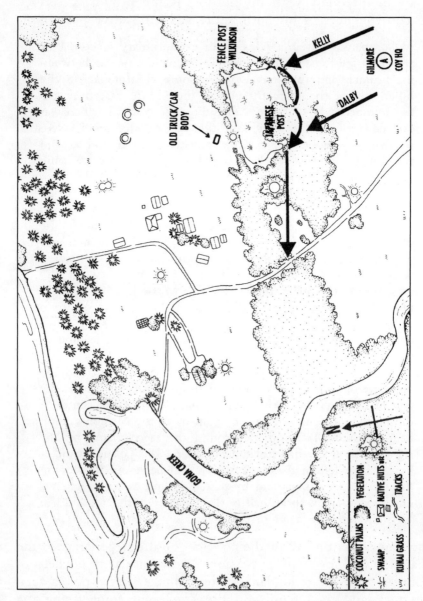

KELLY

FENCE POST
WILKINSON

GILMORE
Ⓐ
COY HQ

DALBY

JAPANESE
POST

OLD TRUCK/CAR
BODY

GOMA CREEK

N

VEGETATION

COCONUT PALMS

NATIVE HUTS etc

SWAMP

TRACKS

KUNAI GRASS

The 39th Battalion's attack, Gona Mission, 8 December 1942.

marching either along the coast or inland to Sanananda. Brigadier Dougherty:

> And at the end of the day I had to report that the attack
> was unsuccessful whereas in fact it had been successful, because
> the Japanese at midnight on the night of 8–9 December staged
> a breakout. Frank Sublet [in command of the Composite
> 2/27th–2/16th Battalion] rang me and told me that they were
> being infiltrated. And I said, 'Frank, just order your men to
> stay in their holes and just shoot anything that moves on top
> of the ground, it doesn't matter what it is, shoot it!' These
> men were the Japanese remnants of Gona, they were finished![34]

The Japanese breakout is best described by a sample of
the Australian troops who confronted it. Private B.J. O'Connor,
A Company, 2/27th Battalion:

> We were close to the beach . . . there was a group out on patrol
> . . . the next minute three or four blokes went past our post,
> and we thought, 'Ah, back early!' . . . of course they went into
> the sea further on . . . the 2/16th got most of them . . . [35]

Major Frank Sublet, CO Composite 2/27th–2/16th Battalion:

> We had a Bren-gunner sited on the beach for support. This
> machine gunner became invaluable during the night because
> quite a few Japanese came out of their bunkers and tried to
> move along the beach to Sanananda. The machine gunner got
> quite a few of them. Others went out into the kunai. Our
> chaps had positions all through the kunai and so did the 39th
> and they walked straight into our fire! And there was a lot of
> hand-to-hand fighting in the dark.[36]

Corporal Jim Hardie, A Company, 39th Battalion:

> . . . Company HQ was involved . . . on my left there was a
> section . . . one Jap got in with these blokes on the left; they
> suddenly found they had a stranger in their midst . . . some-
> body fired a Very light which lit up everything and there in
> front about twenty yards from the company HQ were these
> little groups of Japs looking for a way through. Of course they
> were all killed . . . not too many got any sleep.[37]

Lance-Corporal E.G. Pannell, 2/27th Battalion:

> . . . I had a ground sheet laid out on top of the slit trench
> with the Bren on it and a spare barrel and I got four magazines

and I had my rifle alongside it with bayonet on it . . . I was
set! We could hear all this firing out on the beach . . . Doug
was in there with me, shoulder to shoulder . . . and all of a
sudden he said, 'Look out Bill, right in front of you!' And
with that a sheet of flame went between our bloody heads . . .
I just went with the Bren and probably got rid of half a
magazine . . . everything went quiet for a couple of minutes
. . . it was still going on on the beach . . . come daylight
there was three dead there . . . one bloke had a revolver in
his hand; one of the other blokes had a sword in his hand and
a grenade with the pin still in.[38]

During the night of 8/9 December 1942 at Gona, the Australians
accounted for some 100 or more Japanese soldiers attempting
their escape. It would seem that at least a similar number of those
defenders did make good their flight.

By the early morning of 9 December the 39th Battalion held
all the jungle edge looking across the open ground to the beach,
where a few enemy posts still held out—mainly manned by the
sick and the injured who were too enfeebled to have contemplated escape.

Lieutenant Sword's A Company platoon that had cleared the
huts in the Mission area and the pits around them saw parties
from the composite battalion moving westwards along the
beach. He immediately led his platoon towards the sea, clearing
out pockets of the enemy until he reached the beach, where
he was killed in the capture of the last post to fall. When
A Company's telephone line came up to the Mission area,
Ralph approached Jack Sim, his signals sergeant:

Keith Lovett was there, and the colonel. And the colonel just
said with a wry smile, 'You'd better pass this message on Sim'.
And the message was 'Gona's Gone'. That's all he said; that's
all he needed to say.[39]

The scenes that confronted the Australians on 9 December
1942 at Gona Mission were totally repugnant to even the most
hard-nosed veterans. Lieutenant A.W. 'Kanga' Moore remembered the base area near the mouth of Gona Creek:

My enduring memory is of the beach itself, which was the
greatest shambles you've ever seen in your life . . . it had been
bombed and strafed on a number of occasions. Just back from
the beach among the coconut trees they had a lot of stores

. . . they had a bit of food there, there were quite a few bodies lying around; the stink was horrible, I don't think they'd ever had latrines or anything; Gona beach was a dirty, filthy mess.[40]

Major Frank Sublet, CO 2/27th–2/16th Composite Battalion:

Their hygiene was shocking! You see, they were pinned down so closely in their posts that they couldn't move around or out of them during daylight, so they were using them for latrines, for feeding and of course they couldn't bury their dead, because they'd get shot in the attempt. I don't know whether it was by choice or not but they stacked their dead on top of, and underneath bags of rice, to fire over them! Some of them had fought in respirators because of the stench.[41]

Ralph would later write:

We reverently buried our gallant dead and moved out as burial parties went in to dispose of the Japanese—they had buried 638 of them by the end of the next day, but many days later we still stumbled over the ones they didn't find, or momentarily stopped brushing our teeth in the lagoons as decayed bodies nudged past us. We did not envy the burial parties their task. We had seen the Japanese put on their respirators when our bombardments churned up the stench of their comrades' rotting corpses. And many of our battle hardened veterans, fighting their way forward over that polluted ground, were unable to face their food. It was sickening to breathe let alone eat.[42]

The 21st Brigade lost 34 officers and 375 other ranks as battle casualties at Gona; the 39th Battalion lost six and 115; and, between 19 November and the morning of 23 November, the 25th Brigade lost seventeen officers and 187 other ranks, with more to follow before its relief on 4 December along with the 3rd Battalion and the Chaforce companies. Thus, the incomplete battle casualties totalled 57 officers and 677 other ranks. The Japanese losses are difficult to ascertain—638 were buried by the Australians after the battle and some 200 may have been either evacuated by barge or buried. The respective losses from both sides were therefore approximately equal.

After the Australian capture of Gona Mission, the Japanese Amboga Force was considerably isolated; its nearest friendly force was now at far-distant Sanananda; the terrain to be traversed to the east was a debilitating mixture of thick scrub

Gona after the battle: 'the greatest shambles you've ever seen'.
(AWM 013878)

and jungle and swamp, except for a narrow coastal corridor
which was blocked by the 2/14th; its line of communication was under constant threat by Allied air superiority; and
approximately one-fifth (the remnant from the Owen Stanley
campaign) of the combined force was sick and fatigued. But
that enemy force was, nonetheless, of sufficient size to warrant
extermination. Brigadier Dougherty:

> We were now much more secure, and in a position to strike
> a blow on the Jap force west of 2/14th Aust Inf Bn.
>   On 10 December I sent 39 Aust Inf Bn by an inland route
> to cut the track west of the 2/14th Aust Inf Bn . . . and then

move east destroying enemy between track junction and the 2/14th Aust Inf Bn.[43]

At 8 am on 10 December 1942 the 39th left the 21st Brigade HQ with all the ammunition it could carry, six days' rations and 16 kilometres of signal cable. The battalion was guided by Lieutenant Schwind and Sergeant Iskov, who had been engaged in a 2/14th reconnaissance patrol through the scrub, jungle and swamp in the Amboga River area during 6–8 December. They had found a labyrinth of tracks that led into extensive swamps rather than crossing points for that river—and no evidence of Japanese passage through the region. Ralph Honner:

> All went well till we reached the Amboga River and turned north to surprise the Japanese garrison in the village whose strength we did not know. But unfortunately as we advanced with B Company, which had been in reserve at Gona Mission, leading the advance, three Japanese officers came down from the village [Haddy's Village or sometimes referred to as 'Gona West'] to have a swim at a creek and track junction which we had just left. There was no opportunity to jump them without someone opening fire, because they were armed with pistols and swords as well as towels.
>
> I was with the leading section because I had to know what was happening . . . and the word came back to me, 'what will we do?' I had to make a quick decision. There was no way I could maintain the surprise of silence, there had to be firing . . . so I just made arrangements for B Company to be ready to race forward as soon as we killed the Japanese officers. The two leading scouts and one of the guides killed the three Japanese officers as the rest of B Company raced forward . . . there was a swamp line in front of us, and if they could get across that swamp line into the edge of the jungle beyond, our first objective would be reached.[44]

In order to make that crossing a speedy one, and therefore gain that critical bridgehead, B Company attacked straight down the main track leading into the village, which by necessity would be the same passage into battle for a now fully alerted enemy. Ralph described the confrontation in 'The 39th at Gona':

> An enemy machine-gun opened up on them and the section-leader, Edgell . . . received two bullet wounds in his right arm. They did not slow him down; he changed his Owen gun to his left hand in full career and, blazing away with it, charged

the enemy gun, killing the three men manning it. This enabled the section to establish itself far enough ahead to allow the company to move and launch its attack from forward of the swamp which the enemy post had covered. Two of Edgell's men had also been wounded by the machine-gun fire, and he assisted in their evacuation and reported on the forward situation before going to the R.A.P. for attention to his own wounds.

The leading platoon, Plater's, carried on the attack along the main track. It struck strong resistance but pressed on, leaving a trail of enemy dead to mark its progress until it was held up by a strong post on its right. Plater stalked this post single-handed, killed the two officers and four others manning it, and captured their machine-gun and five bomb-throwers. For the next four hours he led the platoon in one attack after another on enemy posts, forcing a passage himself with grenades and Owen gun, and personally placing his sections in position when he was able to move them forward. Shortly before nightfall he was manoeuvring a section into position to strike at a machine-gun post when the section commander was wounded beside him. He was dressing the corporal's wound when he was himself shot through the shoulder-blade. However Plater took the section in hand, led it forward, and destroyed the enemy post. After consolidating his position he staggered back to report to company headquarters and had to be carried out on a litter.[45]

As soon as Plater's platoon had encountered opposition on the track, outflanking movements by Lieutenant Mortimore's platoon to the right and Lieutenant Gartner's platoon to the left were undertaken. Gartner, after four hours of persistent fighting, was able to gain a distant look at the Haddy's Village huts. But the day's progress was not without cost—Gartner's platoon was reduced to section strength and replaced by the 25 survivors of C Company's Gona Mission campaigning. Sergeant Meani led the ten remaining soldiers of Gartner's platoon as right-flank protection for Mortimore's positions, while Gartner took command of Plater's leaderless platoon.

Captain Seward's C Company encountered determined enemy opposition on the left flank and were forced to dig in. That dark, rain-driven night of 11 December brought with it a furious enemy midnight assault on the embattled ranks of C Company—one platoon position was wiped out except for a few wounded survivors, who returned the following morning.

An utterly miserable night awaited the remainder of the exhausted and malaria-ridden 39th. Ralph, in 'The 39th at Gona':

> The village was on high ground between the beach and a swamp, and was flanked by the Amboga River on the west and a creek on the east, both fordable by sand-bars at their mouths. When it rained, as it did throughout this night, not only the swamp line but all the low ground we occupied to invest the village was covered by water from a few inches to a couple of feet deep. Our only men not in the water were the wounded. For them we built table high platforms to keep them above that unpleasant tide in which floated all the refuse of the living and the dead. All through that deluged night I sat, tree-backed, on a log to lift my face above the spreading sewer. When the flood receded, latrines and new-dug graves and weapon-pits looked all alike.[46]

On 12 December, with insufficient troops to surround Haddy's Village, Ralph determined that his prime objective was to cut the enemy off from reinforcement or escape over the Amboga River sandbar. By 14 December, with his last reserve platoons of D Company accelerating the advance on the left, he had committed his entire force to his extended front line. The next day Lieutenant Moore's platoon pushed north beyond A Company and occupied a blocking position near the beach. Lieutenant A.W. 'Kanga' Moore:

> My platoon and I actually sneaked through there under some fairly heavy-duty fire which fortunately seemed to be about three feet above the ground . . . we actually got right through to the edge of the coconuts, overlooking the beach. I found a telephone line there which I cut. But I also cut everything, because this was their line of supply . . .[47]

With the Japanese hemmed in by Moore's platoon at the sandbar, Honner's remaining force stretching inland and parallel to the coast, and the 2/14th blocking the ground to the west, the fighting at Haddy's Village now became a deadly but studied war of identification and elimination carried out by the expertise, teamwork and cunning of the section leader and his men. The closeness of the fighting is graphically portrayed by Lieutenant Hugh Dalby:

> I went around to visit one of my section commanders . . . it was early in the morning, just after sun-up . . . and I was

squatting behind the section commander with my rifle across
my stomach and knees, when a shot rang out and my section
commander let out an almighty bloody yell. A bullet had hit
him in the arm, and I shot the Jap, and he wouldn't have
been any more than fifteen feet away at the most . . . and he
was camouflaged . . . his face was muddied; he had no shiny
spots on his face; his hands were the same. When he fired he
moved. And when you move at that close range it is fatal! . . .
and although I didn't kill him, I hit him, and he started to
crawl away, and I could see everything. He was crawling, he
was moving, and of course he was dead a second or two later
. . . now he was a spotter for the medium machine-gun; a
pillbox with seven or eight men in it only about another thirty
feet away . . . and we located his machine-gun post by him
being killed.[48]

Ralph Honner, in 'The 39th at Gona':

Ever since taking over Plater's platoon on the 11th, Gartner
had fought his new command forward in the teeth of the
enemy along the strongly held main track, which was continu-
ally swept by fire from a series of posts in depth. He dashed
untiringly from section to section, checking their positions,
leading them forward into new ground, and filling in odd
moments with grenade sorties on the enemy. The jungle in
front of other parts of our attacking line was too thick to
penetrate without first cutting a path, and too high and close
for grenades and mortar bombs to be thrown over it. Only
along Gartner's track was the ground open enough to permit
the bombardment of enemy posts. Each day he pounded them
with 2-inch mortar bombs and rifle grenades from some
shallow hole beside the open track. The enemy along the track
turned all their weapons on him during these sessions but he
coolly sat and fired bomb after bomb to help the other
companies forward. At nine o'clock in the morning of the
16th he was sniping at the enemy when he was hit by a burst
of machine-gun fire . . .

Forty yards his platoon pushed on through the jungle in
the next six hours, and thirty-five dead enemy on the ground
they captured showed how bitterly the Japanese had fought
to hold every yard of it. At three o'clock in the afternoon
even the lion-hearted Gartner could do no more. His left leg
was useless even for crawling, and he had to be carried from
his post.[49]

Efforts by the Japanese to pierce the steadily closing Australian net were becoming difficult—as were attempts at reinforcement from the west. About 30 enemy troops attempted a late-night passage across the Amboga sandbar with entrenching tools, grenade dischargers and other supplies, but were forced into the water by Lieutenant Moore's vigilant platoon. Fifteen beached corpses, including that of an officer, were daylight testimony to the fate of that mission.

On the morning of 17 December the enemy attempted a new approach. A fighting patrol crossed the river behind the 39th's forward positions, waded through a swamp and mounted a spirited assault on D Company HQ—all were killed and a machine gun was captured.

On the afternoon of 15 December, the 2/14th Battalion had closed in on the creek on the eastern outskirts of the village, linking up with Lieutenant Harry Mortimore's platoon. Late that day, the active remnants of the battalion came under Ralph's command. The 2/14th's officer strength now stood at four—Captains Russell and Bisset, Captain Cortis (the RMO), and Lieutenant Schwind. During 15 to 18 December the 2/14th was able to pinpoint and destroy a number of posts with a minimum of their own casualties.

On 16 December Acting-Sergeant Ted Sheldon's platoon moved across the creek and into the village. His aggression and initiative carried him into confrontation with three Japanese posts in succession and, under covering fire from his platoon, he used his Tommy gun and a liberal supply of grenades to destroy all three. And a new weapon—the No. 68 Anti-tank Grenade discharged from an EY rifle—in the menacing hands of Private Walters caused incredible carnage the next day. Acting-Sergeant Ted Sheldon, 2/14th Battalion:

> Cpl Ron Russell displayed outstanding coolness and bravery, till killed by a sniper he was trying to locate; Digger Walters moved calmly out into the open ground in the village to dispose of a troublesome 'Woodpecker' . . . and behind it all, encouraging, coordinating and inspiring numbed brains and exhausted bodies, was the quiet figure of Capt Stan Bisset (minus one eyebrow burnt off by a Jap sniper's bullet) and the very efficient planning and guidance of Captain Bill Russell, beloved by all and now in charge of the Bn, which consisted of 2 platoons, each 15 strong, and Bn HQ's. My platoon was

weakened by Bobby Baird and Blondy Nielson being sent back
with what we thought was malaria; three weeks later . . . I
discovered they both had died of scrub typhus.[50]

On 18 December 1942 the last of the Japanese posts were
assailed and the final victory won. But, yet again, the 39th had
gone into battle with a number within its ranks still militarily
unskilled. Ralph proudly recorded the end:

Shortly after midnight an enemy barge was heard off shore by
our beach posts, and later two Japanese came out of the sea
to be killed by the 2/14th.

During all this time, Corporal Andy Heraud of C Company had been busy. Twice in the night he had led a patrol
of four men among the enemy positions looking for a medium
machine-gun which was holding up his section. He spent four
hours searching for the gun without locating it . . . And at
two o'clock in the morning, Corporal Stan Ellis of A Company, who had already shown his mettle at the mission, went
out alone, wormed his way to within ten yards of another
medium machine gun, and with a shower of grenades killed
its crew . . .

On the morning of the 18th Heraud located the medium
machine-gun he had been looking for during the night. It was
a strong-post in the jungle a few yards in front of his section
but invisible through that impenetrable dark-green wall. The
section outflanked the enemy post, killed its defenders and
captured the gun. Then A and C Companies both moved
forward in the face of still heavy fire to the edge of the jungle.

From there the final assault was made. Dalby, who had
taken the first post in the capture of Gona Mission led the
attack. Again his dash carried him among the enemy ahead of
his men. And again he made a machine-gun his objective,
killing the gunner and six others. The rest of A Company
completed the destruction of the post which had been manned
by thirty men with two medium and several light machine-
guns. Then all four companies swarmed over the village
blotting out the remaining pockets of resistance. Only one
prisoner was taken . . .

As soon as the village fell, malaria-ridden troops, who had
hung on fighting till the fight was over, staggered into the
R.A.P. . . . And to my Intelligence Officer came one of our
last-minute reinforcements, asking shyly, 'Please, sir, would
you show me how this gun works? I never had one of these
before.' I glanced up to identify the strange weapon; it was

the ordinary .303 rifle that every recruit cuts his teeth on. And I looked at the lad in wonderment; he was probably the best of that batch of newcomers—the first to respond to the invitation to join the A.I.F. He had played his part with a fixed bayonet and a stout heart in all his section's battles through the jungle filth, the swamp miasma and the fetid stench, too proud to proclaim his ignorance of the functioning of a rifle bolt to these friends who had accepted him as one of themselves.[51]

When Haddy's Village fell on 18 December 1942, the battle for the Gona–Kumusi area was ended.

If Isurava had been both the 39th Battalion's and Lieutenant-Colonel Ralph Honner's defining moment, then their almost inevitable final test and ultimate triumph was Gona. The 39th Battalion's remarkable Kokoda Trail transition from a raw militia battalion thrust into a fighting withdrawal through a closed jungle environment—and against all the odds—became at Gona a resounding, professional feat of arms that would have done any unit, anywhere and at any time, proud. And central to that achievement was the performance of a commanding officer who had applied considerable military experience and sheer intellect to his craft.

If Ralph's adherence to the military principles of concentration and economy of force at Gona had been an astute component of his planning, then his decision to use delayed-action fuses for his artillery, and then send his troops in under that bombardment, constituted much more than the facilitation of the principle of surprise—it embodied both a stroke of genius and sheer moral courage.

But Gona would leave a bitter, lingering anguish with a commander who was to be awarded a Distinguished Service Order for that battle. Out of the triumph that was Gona, the chivalrous soldier saw in certain others dishonour, self-service, and the unforgivable denial of an Australian legend.

11

THE KOITAKI FACTOR

For a generation of postwar Australians, names such as Gallipoli, Passchendaele, the Somme, El Alamein, Tobruk and Long Tan are identified, if at times vaguely, with significant events in a proud heritage. Despite a late 20th century surge in the desire by Australians to commemorate and to understand more about their nation's experience of war, the terms Isurava, Brigade Hill, Milne Bay, Gona, Buna and Sanananda remain unknown to the vast majority of those same Australians. Why?

The answers should be examined on three levels—the conduct of Generals MacArthur and Blamey; how their perceptions of the Papuan campaigns affected the conduct of operations; and ultimately how those two factors have influenced the place in Australian history of the Papuan campaigns. In all this, Lieutenant-Colonel Ralph Honner's views on the above points are most worthy of examination, as they portray many of the front line commanders' perceptions of the Australian Papuan experience.

David Horner, Blamey's most recent—and searching—biographer, has stated that:

As Commander Allied Land Forces, Blamey's record is one of some outstanding achievements and also errors. Like Mac-Arthur he can be criticised for not reinforcing New Guinea adequately in mid-1942, especially after signals intelligence revealed Japanese plans to advance over the Owen Stanley Range. His dismissal of Rowell relates as much to his and

220

MacArthur's faulty strategic appreciations, the ambiguity of his own position and the government's inexperience as to any supposed rivalry with Rowell. As Commander New Guinea Force in late 1942 he was hamstrung by MacArthur's close direction, and his dismissals of Allen and Potts were a continuation of the pressures that had resulted in Rowell's dismissal. The address to the 21st Brigade at Koitaki was an error of judgement which demonstrated Blamey's lack of rapport with soldiers. In all, the events of October and November 1942 showed Blamey's ruthless determination to preserve his own position.

Blamey did not, at this stage, fully understand the problems of jungle warfare. Unnecessary casualties were incurred at Buna, Gona and Sanananda through a desire for speed. MacArthur was the chief culprit but Blamey must share some of the blame.[1]

Horner's succinct passage provides a framework for discussion.

Both MacArthur and Blamey's failure to recognise the Kokoda Trail as a potential battleground for the defence of Port Moresby has been well documented, and needs neither further condemnation nor comment; Horner's point regarding the inexperience of the Curtin government—its total acquiescence to MacArthur's wishes at the expense of the counsel of its own Army Commander-in-Chief—is also entirely accurate; and the fact that the casualties at the beachhead were an end result of the 'desire for speed' is also unarguable.

MacArthur's desire for speed at the beachhead was purely a matter of securing a quick victory in Papua to enable a greater share of his government's resources for his South-West Pacific theatre of operations. In this, MacArthur was in direct competition with the American Navy's progress in the South Pacific theatre and its claim to those same—and limited—resources. Ralph, on the 'desire for speed':

I do not know what pressure there was for a quick solution, but no pressure for a quick solution would justify gung-ho attacks without reconnaissance, without planning, without concentration, without coordination, without support. There had to be better use of reconnaissance to gain all possible information of enemy strengths and positions, of possible approaches, to succeed by concentrating our strength where it would be most effective, and not attacking enemy strength where it could be most effective. This is where the approach to Gona was faulty. We did not use our military knowledge on the ground in the hands of the local commanders who could use it . . .[2]

MacArthur, Blamey and Herring repeatedly used the ploy of an imminent Japanese reinforcement of the beachhead as a further means of hurrying events. Ralph Honner:

> I didn't need to be told about this, there is always such a possibility . . . that there might be some pressure to get a quick solution before enemy reinforcements could arrive. But none of this could justify unmilitary procedure of attacking without proper preparation.[3]

The salient point is that MacArthur and Blamey could have had their speedy beachhead victory, and that MacArthur could thereby have secured his desired resources. The lesson of the Gona–Buna–Sanananda beachhead during November–January 1942/43 is that a desire for speed in military operations is all the more reason to conduct a battle in a thorough, military manner and secure the objective the first time—or even the second—rather than commit a force to uneducated, repeated and futile attacks which cause unnecessary casualties rather than attainable progress.

In November 1929 Liddell Hart wrote one of his succinct 'thoughts on war'. He might well have been predicting—thirteen years before the battle—the chain of events at Gona Mission:

> To 'throw good money after bad' is foolish. But to throw away men's lives where there is no reasonable chance of advantage, is criminal . . . But the real indictment of leadership arises when attacks that are inherently vain are ordered merely because if they could succeed they would be useful.[4]

But Horner's point that the Koitaki Parade 'was an error of judgement which demonstrated Blamey's lack of rapport with soldiers' falls short of a fair assessment of the impact of Blamey's ill-chosen Koitaki words.

The truth is that General Blamey's Koitaki diatribe had two critical consequences at Gona. The first was that Brigadier Dougherty was given an unfair impression of his battalion commanders. Those commanders were not consulted on tactics at Gona; their operations were constantly interfered with by a brigadier who did not reconnoitre the ground, and did not allow his commanders time to conduct their battles sensibly; and, critically, when the progress of events became repeatedly hamstrung and those officers complained to him concerning the slaughter, his poisoned perception of those officers' ability convinced him to sack them rather than listen to them with an open mind.[5] At the junior leadership level (company and platoon commanders), and at the private soldier level, Blamey's words caused a determination to prove him wrong—at almost any cost.

In 1992, a year after the publication of the author's *Those Ragged Bloody Heroes*, Ralph Honner committed his thoughts on the Koitaki Parade to paper. His article is not only a legitimate reaction to that parade but an illuminating insight into the chivalrous soldier's view of the men of the 21st Brigade, its commander Brigadier Arnold Potts and, most importantly, the nobility of the Australian soldier who fought along the Kokoda Trail and at the beachhead. It is reproduced here in full.

The Koitaki Factor
(On looking into Brune's *Those Ragged Bloody Heroes*)

Nearly two and a half thousand years ago Leonidas and his Spartan band braced themselves to perish for their country's sake on a little hillock clear of the hot springs of their narrow pass under the brow of the wooded hillside from which the encircling Persians poured. Thermopylae, the Hot Gates, became the gates of death—and of immortality. 'Since that time,' wrote Charlotte Yonge, 'how many hearts have glowed, how many arms have been nerved at the remembrance of the Pass of Thermopylae!'

Fifty years ago another outnumbered and devoted band stood on a hillside at Isurava to hold another narrow pass against the enemy erupting from the surrounding jungle. 'Unawed in the gates of death' is the fitting title of the chapter in Peter Brune's *Those Ragged Bloody Heroes* recording Maroubra Force's first major battle. It would have been pointless for the defenders to perish to the last man—they had an overriding duty to deny the Japanese passage to Port Moresby. But the shining example of their gallant dead invigorated the grim living to complete the task. Who amongst them could fail to be uplifted by the recollection of the sustained valour of Bruce Kingsbury and 'Butch' Bisset and their peers at Isurava, or of the unflinching courage of Claude Nye and 'Lefty' Langridge and 'Bluey' Lambert and the scores of the bravest of the brave slain beside them on Butcher's Hill [Brigade Hill]? As Peter Brune records:

> Langridge passed his identity discs and paybook to a friend and then inspiringly led the forlorn foray . . . That hor- rendous Brigade Hill action typified the spirit of Maroubra Force—not just blindly reckless but calmly brave, and faithfully accepting the duty that often meant death.

Maurice Treacy and Bob Dougherty of the 2/14th Battalion and countless others repeatedly demonstrated that same spirit through their next campaign—the culpable tragedy and costly triumph of Gona. But, for some, there was an added spur that goaded them beyond the utmost bounds of duty. What had changed?

Against all the odds Maroubra Force had saved Port Moresby by an ill-starred but still brilliant fighting withdrawal that finally halted the Japanese at Ioribaiwa; and, for reward, its magnificent leader, Arnold Potts, was dismissed from the com- mand of the 21st Brigade. Then, on the day of infamy at Koitaki, his beloved battalions, grieving for their lost brothers, were told by an unknowing and uncaring commander-in-chief that they had run like rabbits. Even his war-long closest colleague, Lieutenant-Colonel Carlyon, in 'I Remember Blamey', could not excuse him:

> I was there when those fine soldiers lined up . . . He told them that they had been defeated . . . In future he expected no further retirement, but advance at all costs. He concluded with a remark which I think was particularly ill-chosen and unfair. 'Remember', he said, 'it is not the man with the gun that gets shot, it's the rabbit that is running away.' It amazed me that Blamey should deal so insensitively with the men of such a well-proven brigade.

The dark cloud of Koitaki shadowed the brigade to Gona. Canberra and Brisbane tactics demanded that the troops be thrown, piecemeal as they arrived, into frontal attacks without adequate reconnaissance, planning, concentration, coordination or support—over the protests of divisional, brigade and battal- ion commanders alike. It was the competent commanders at battalion level, already Koitaki branded, who were removed because of their resistance to the wanton waste of their men. For them their command careers were shattered; for their men, it was their lives that were destroyed, not merely at random on the perilous path of duty but, for many, beyond it on some remoter byway of inevitable death with honour.

At Koitaki they had acutely perceived the unjust slighting of both their dead heroes and their living battalions. Some of them reacted by resolving, jointly or individually, never again to withdraw from the untenable, never again to draw back from the unattainable. It was as if they had already written their names in the roll of the already dead; they had taken on themselves the unbearable burden of injustice—the injustice of the Gods in a Greek tragedy, pursuing them with the relentless momentum of the Furies to their destined fate amongst the friendless bodies of unburied men. As in Greek tragedy, the death of the hero is the end of the action; but the pain of his passing leaves an unforgettable impression.

The normally undemonstrative and unprofane Charlie White of the 2/16th Battalion was reported as launching the doomed dawn attack along Gona beach in which he was first wounded, then killed, with the exhortation, 'Let's show the bastard!' It can only be conjectured what Koitaki-fuelled fires of resentment, defiance and pride forced that hot anger and combined with cold courage to conquer the terror of death. But the sacrificial witness of others spoke more eloquently of the demon that drove them than could any battle-cry.

In the 2/27th Battalion's first beach action the company that had swung left, to forge ahead through thin cover, turned right across open ground to attack a heavily armed post, only to be mown down by withering fire. The only two unwounded officers, company commander Joe Cuming and second-in-command Justin Skipper, could see no military option but to withdraw the company to its former cover to avoid further casualties. But, for themselves, there was no drawing back. Cuming, followed by Skipper, their weapons blazing—diverting enemy fire from the retrieval of the wounded—charged across the enfiladed inferno into the tunnelled stronghold they could not capture. When it ultimately fell, their bodies were discovered there, ringed by enemy dead. Such was the burrow to which they had run.

Two days later, beyond the 2/27th's left flank, the man the 2/16th's R.M.O., 'Blue' Steward, remembered as 'Smiling Johnny O'Neill' faced an even more awesome task—a fourth attack on the so-far impregnable Mission hut area protected by a barren no man's land against assault from the kunai grass and scrub cover to its east and south. From that cover Miller's 2/31st Battalion (with the Chaforce 2/14th company under command) had attacked unsuccessfully on the 19th and 22nd of November, losing one hundred and thirty-two killed and wounded. For the third attack, on the 23rd, strength was doubled with the 2/25th Battalion coming in on the right but, despite Miller's covering fire, suffering sixty-four casualties and making little headway across the extended killing-ground. Mission impossible was abandoned.

The next day Brigadier Eather counted over nine hundred men in his four battalions and, with the assistance of Chaforce, he could still commit a thousand to the attack. But he concluded that he was not strong enough to capture Gona; he could only contain it.

One week later, O'Neill attempted the seeming impossible with just one company of the 2/16th and one platoon of the 2/27th, both far under strength and further weakened by the previous day's fighting. The 3rd Battalion, from Eather's nearby command, had been programmed to safeguard his vulnerable left flank and triple his numbers but it had failed to arrive. He looked across the clean shaven killing ground and saw no victory; he looked around at his ill-shaven heroic few and saw no defeat; 'advance at all costs'—so be it! Jack Breakey of the 2/27th remembered:

> We started to walk and then the Western Australians started to run and they were doing this yelling out, so I began doing it with them.

On the left Peter Gorrie's men were obliterated except for the few wounded fortunate enough to find refuge in shell-holes beneath the merciless fusillade that had cut them down. In the centre Leo Mayberry and five others of his eighteen-man platoon survived both the charge through the curtain of death and the fire-fight to blast out the close defences; they were joined by three South Australians.

O'Neill and his nine companions had attained the unattainable but they had little opportunity to consolidate. Their supporting artillery put down a ten-minute barrage on the already captured objective, persuading its new garrison to seek a surer, if little calmer, life elsewhere. There could be no turning back. As they continued their advance, in the direction of Gona Creek, the barrage lifted and the Japanese converged from the surrounding cover. In the running fight that followed Lloyd Morey was killed, A.G. Sage, wounded in the barrage, was hit again, this time mortally, and O'Neill, too, was struck down. The seven others crossed Gona Creek under the guns of Haddy's Chaforce 2/16th company watching on its western bank; but for smiling Johnny O'Neill, lying desperately wounded beside its eastern shore, it was only his life that was running out. In the dark of the night two of Haddy's intrepid men swam across the creek, evaded the enemy posts they marked for future attention and brought O'Neill back on a punt. He was four days in his dying. He will live for evermore.

'Blue' Steward regarded Alan Haddy as 'the very embodiment of all the great virtues of the Australian infantryman —great-hearted, laconic, loyal.' Early in the day O'Neill died Haddy led twenty volunteers from his malaria ridden company west to the mouth of the Amboga River, resuming a standing patrol to give timely warning of any further incursion, from the north-west, of newly-landed Japanese forces heading for Gona. Peering into the downpour for forty hours the patrol detected little movement; but towards a rain-driven midnight on the 6th of December, the Japanese closed in with a grenade attack; a sentry was killed and Haddy was wounded. He sent three other wounded back, along with a request for reinforcement.

The searching light of day discovered the enemy coming in hundreds. The early-warning post had forestalled the surprise of the Gona besiegers; it was no longer needed and it could not be held. Haddy instructed his patrol to retire slowly and silently while he covered their withdrawal. He was reported variously, as saying that he would 'stay to the last' or that he would 'follow the last man'. They expected that he would follow as a rearguard—he always chose the point of danger for himself. He did not follow. While he lived, all that he was going to run out of was ammunition; and, even then, the mayhem he inflicted, on the last of the in-rushing foe he committed to the cordon of dead around him, attested the ferocity of the cornered tiger.

What else but the fatally magnified edict, 'no more retirement', could have driven the cool, resourceful, pragmatic veteran of many battles to refuse to surrender the worthless post he could not hold and yet to yield what he must have held most dear—his hopes, his dreams, his life? Lifeless, he lives with the legends—young Casabianca, steadfast on L'Orient's exploding deck; proud Roland, the last to fall at the Pass of Roncesvalles. What minstrel will sing the song of Alan?

The Furies have faded from the scene; the heroes are dead; the tragedy is finished. The consuming critic of Koitaki is silenced now; his words can wound no more; but the

Lieutenant-Colonel F.H. Sublet,   *Ralph Honner, 1992.*
2/16th Battalion.

unforgotten deeds of the valiant he defamed proclaim their
constant courage to all posterity.

Ralph Honner, 1992[6]

Ralph Honner was not the only Maroubra Force officer to
maintain that Blamey's slur influenced the 21st Brigade's soldiers' actions at Gona. Lieutenant-Colonel F.H. Sublet, 2/16th
Battalion:

> Well I'd tackle it this way. Many of the young officers who
> were killed at Gona weren't on the Owen Stanley track
> anyway. But those officers who were at Koitaki and heard
> Blamey's speech were very, very incensed and they were really
> carrying on about it. Almost mutinous in their feelings! What
> I did see at Gona was that a number of the young officers and
> sergeants who had not taken part in the Kokoda Trail were
> determined to show their mettle at Gona, because they knew
> what the battalion had gone through on the Kokoda Trail and
> they'd been left out of battle; they were determined to redeem
> the battalion; put the battalion back on its mantle.[7]

And Sublet observed a similar attitude in others in the 21st
Brigade:

I can quote one! Stan Bisset used to jump up and down with
rage every time he talked about it. Stan was absolutely ropable
because his own brother had been killed up there. And a great
bloke Stan! A strong man, strong in will; strong in resolve;
strong in every way. Actually the whole brigade was in a mood
to show the commander-in-chief. And of course the opportunity arose at Gona.[8]

Brigadier Arnold Potts, although now serving in Darwin, had
been kept in touch with events through letters from his former
brigade officers. In a letter to his wife he wrote:

> Don't blame Dougherty. He was given to understand that he
> had a dud crowd to handle (I gather) and a bowler hat would
> be his if he didn't do the job. Nice atmosphere . . .
>   Hugh [Lieutenant-Colonel Hugh Challen, CO 2/14th Bat-
> talion] sent me a precis of his (T's) [Blamey's] speech to the
> old team and to the officers. Hells Bells, it was a cowardly bit
> of work and untrue in every detail. I'll fry his soul in the next
> world for that bit of 'passing the buck'. Surely a man in his
> position is big enough to carry his own mistakes.[9]

Ralph Honner's feeling for the 21st Brigade went further
than a chance observation of them along the Kokoda Trail and
at Gona. He had witnessed first-hand the performance of the
2/14th Battalion at Isurava; he had seen the 2/16th's performance along the Kokoda Trail; and he had observed both the
degree of difficulty of the operation and the magnificent bravery
of the 2/16th and 2/27th Battalions at Gona Mission and the
2/14th at Haddy's Village. Further, a number of the soldiers of
the 2/16th were Ralph's former pupils at Hale School. Honner
thus knew the calibre of the defamed.

In October 1992 the South Australian United Service Institute invited the author to address its monthly luncheon. The
topic was 'Australian Operations on the Kokoda Trail'. Unbeknown to the author, the Institute recommended to the Field
Marshal Sir Thomas Blamey Fund that the speech be awarded
the Blamey Oration for 1992 in South Australia. Some time
after that oration, the author was told of the selection. And
some time after that, he was informed that the Blamey Fund
had refused the application as being 'inappropriate'.[10] Obviously
the content of the author's *Those Ragged Bloody Heroes* was a
contentious issue.

If the reaction of the Blamey Fund to the nomination was a surprise to the author, then Honner's reaction was more of a shock. When the author phoned Ralph to tell him the news, his cutting reply followed a sarcastic laugh: 'Peter, why would you want a medal perpetuating Monash's pot-bellied clerk!' During a highly valued and privileged working relationship and friendship spanning eight years, it was the *only* time the author can remember Ralph Honner being anything other than the polite, diplomatic and measured man that he was.

12

THIS IS NOT A MOB!

As soon as Haddy's Village fell, malaria-ridden troops, who had hung on until the fighting was over, staggered to the RAP for special treatment. Next day we were relieved by a fresh garrison and went back to Gona Mission . . .

And on our first day of rest many of us had our first wash for three weeks; and many who saw their sodden feet for the first time in twenty days—red-raw and white-swollen—hobbled weakly about in bandages instead of boots.

Ralph Honner, 'The 39th at Gona'[1]

On 21 December 1942, the 39th Battalion was ordered to march to Soputa and its CO to 7th Division Headquarters. Major Anderson, the 39th's 2/IC, led the battalion from Gona at 12.15 pm but made very slow progress, as the majority of the troops were sick and the track muddy and slow.

Ralph returned to his men at Soputa with the news that the 39th was to march to Sanananda for a further fight. On the morning of 22 December General Vasey visited the unit. Shortly after his departure, Ralph suffered a severe malaria attack and was evacuated to the Advanced Dressing Station. In his absence, Major Anderson was to march the battalion to Sanananda.

During peacetime, there were three practicable landward lines of approach to Sanananda: the eastern approach, from Buna Village along the coast via Siwori–Tarakena–Giruwa; the western approach, from Gona, via Basabua–Garara–Surirai–Cape Killerton–Wye Point; and the inland approach, via Soputa, along a 4-metre-wide road of some 10 kilometres in length. A little over halfway between Soputa and Sanananda Point, the narrow Killerton Track ran from the road to Cape Killerton. Near the Sanananda Road–Killerton Track junction, the remaining portion of the road to the coast was of corduroy construction.

The ground in the region was of three types. Scattered patches of kunai grass were prevalent, particularly around the Killerton Track area, while very thick scrub dominated the remaining landscape. However, nearly all of the territory bounded by the triangle Cape Killerton, Tarakena and the Killerton Track–Sanananda Road junction was swampland. The swamps were mainly freshwater and their depths depended largely on the tides—shallow when the tide was out and deeper when it was in. The incoming tide stopped the flow of waters from sources inland, but after heavy rain the swamps deepened rapidly. At the time of the struggle for the beachhead, the wet season was at its zenith. Thus, when tropical downpours of rain occurred—and that was frequently—the numerous patches of kunai grass were subject to flooding.

The beach along the Sanananda coast was about five metres wide and ran up to a bank, which was higher than the immediate hinterland. The ground for a short distance inland was covered by reasonably tall tropical growth and the occasional coconut palm and banyan tree, before falling away to the scrub–kunai grass–swamp conglomeration.

It will be remembered that when General Vasey's 25th and 16th Brigades debouched from the confines of the Owen Stanley Range in early November 1942, Brigadier Eather's 25th Brigade had been assigned the task of capturing Gona, while Brigadier Lloyd's 16th Brigade had been allocated the capture of Sanananda.

The Japanese defences at Sanananda were deployed in four main localities. The first was the main base area, stretching in a semicircle from Wye Point around to about halfway between Giruwa and Tarakena. The second was on the fourth small track junction back from the coast along the main road. The third was stationed about 1 kilometre back from the Killerton Track–Sanananda Road junction, while the fourth was situated around that position.

The Japanese Sanananda fire plan relied on the familiar mutually supporting beachhead bunkers and an abundant number of snipers. But there was one striking defensive feature at Sanananda that was far more imposing than at Buna and Gona. The vast sheets of swampland narrowed the Japanese defensive localities to the road, and access to the Killerton Track at the junction. The ability of any attacker to force a penetration of the Japanese defences was thus contingent on concentrated movement along the road and the Killerton Track—well protected by strong enemy positions. Any inclination to move through the swamp areas was prejudiced by the obvious frustration of slow movement, the difficulty of concentration of force, and the density of fire from camouflaged Japanese positions in the scrub line. The Official Historian estimates that at the onset of the fighting there were about 5500 Japanese troops in the Sanananda area, of which approximately 1800 were hospital patients.[2]

It is little wonder that, from the beginning of the battle, Sanananda provided General Vasey with more casualties and frustration than progress. By early December, after about two weeks of tough fighting in the area, it was clear that the 16th Brigade's long campaigning from the Kokoda Trail up to and including the beachhead had taken its toll. Dudley McCarthy:

> It was clear that this spent formation, willing though it still was, could do no more to affect the course of events along the Sanananda Track. Between 3rd October and 6th December (when its relief by the 30th Brigade began) it lost about 29 officers and 576 men in action. Fifty-six officers and 922 men had been evacuated through sickness.
>
> The total of these figures represented approximately 85 per cent of the strength with which it had set out on the campaign.[3]

McCarthy's mention of the relief of the 16th Brigade by the 30th Brigade identifies the point when Ralph's 39th Battalion had attempted a coastal march to Sanananda with the 2/14th Battalion, but had failed and returned to fight at Gona. The remaining two battalions of the 30th Brigade, the 55th/53rd and the 49th, had then relieved the 16th at Sanananda.

During their first fruitless attacks in the Sanananda area on 7 December, the 55th/53rd Battalion suffered 130 battle casualties, eight of them officers, while the 49th Battalion lost a staggering total of fourteen officers and 215 other ranks—nearly 48 per cent of the battalion strength. Within the following fortnight the 55th/53rd sustained 75 further casualties, including six officers, and the 49th increased its total of killed, wounded and missing by 55.

The early addition of two American battalions of the 126th Regiment to the battle proved of little or no worth. During nine days of indecisive probing rather than concerted fighting, the precarious Huggins Roadblock (named after Captain Meredith Huggins)—about 800 metres north of the Killerton Track–Sanananda Road junction—was their only significant gain. During a frustrating duplication of events at Buna, the Americans at Sanananda were handicapped by their soft physical condition, their lack of high-quality infantry tactical training and, most of all, by uninspired and bewildered leadership.

Thus, when the malaria-ridden and depleted 39th Battalion arrived at Sanananda on 22 December 1942, the position of the Australians and Americans at the beachhead was still most delicately poised. The 21st Brigade War Diary for that day:

> **1300 hrs**. Brig I.N. DOUGHERTY with HQ 21 Aust Inf Bde, K Sec Sigs, 39 Bn and ninety native carriers moved forward with guide from 30 Inf Bde to HUGGINS road block via track through 49 Bn area EAST of main SOPUTA–SANANANDA track.
>
> **1625 hrs**. The relief of US troops was commenced and 39 Bn with portion of 7 Aust Div Cav were in small perimeter defence around 21 Bde HQ.[4]

Dougherty's force was a rather interesting one. His remnant 21st Brigade force—the 2/14th, 2/16th and 2/27th Battalion Gona survivors—was to remain at that village to provide a blocking role, under the command of Lieutenant-Colonel Hugh Challen, while Dougherty was to command the 39th and 49th Battalions of the 30th Brigade and elements of the 2/7th Cavalry Regiment in the Huggins Roadblock area. The 39th Unit Diary:

> **22 Dec**. The Huggins area was contained within a perimeter (oval) one hundred and fifty yards at its widest part. The unit arrived at 16.30 hrs after passing a hut with about twelve long-dead enemy in the vicinity. The situation within the perimeter at time of arrival appeared to be chaotic. American troops whom the Bn was relieving, details from 2/7 Cav

collecting rations, and native carriers wandered all over the area. The Bn was dispersed to posns on the perimeter with such speed as circumstances permitted after which the other troops departed. While final arrangements were being made to the defensive posns Lieut Whelan was killed and one other wounded by a sniper who had approached the area under cover of the jungle.[5]

Sergeant Jack Boland, D Company, 39th Battalion:

Huggins was about 95% surrounded by Japs. When we arrived there my section consisted of myself and one rifleman, and I was to relieve a section post of eight 'Yanks'. Anyway, Company HQ managed to get me two more men and the four of us relieved the eight 'Yanks' who were so glad to be getting out that they gave us all their 'candies' and cigarettes.

Next morning we were ordered to move forward about twenty yards and dig new positions. We couldn't dig very deep because after a depth of about 18 inches water started to seep in. The 'Yanks' had dug a number of holes about two feet deep to get drinking water and had dug other holes for latrines—but the problem was to work out which were which! So we filled in all the 'Yank' holes and dug fresh ones.[6]

Given that the 39th was few in number and that the 49th, 'reduced to a skeleton',[7] was deployed in the bush about 200 metres to their southeast, the role given to Dougherty was to hold Huggins, build up reserves of ammunition and food, and patrol aggressively.[8] The 39th's story at Huggins Roadblock during 23–27 December 1942 was one of constant vigilance and patrolling:

23 Dec. 1230 hrs. 49 Bn report no change.
1730 hrs. 39 Bn patrols report—
(1) Patrol moved WEST of SOPUTA–SANANANDA track observed enemy posns extending for approx 70 yds EAST of track. Posns protected by tangled sig cables and rattles.
(2) Patrol moved 600 yds to WEST from perimeter along old L of C to HUGGINS. No enemy but many tracks . . .
2340 hrs. Patrol from 39 Bn reported. It had moved NE along WEST side SOPUTA–SANANANDA track and grenaded Jap post approx 150 yds from HUGGINS perimeter. Japs opened fire with MMGs, LMGs and bomb throwers . . .
24 Dec. Brig I.N. Dougherty ordered that 39 Bn supply standing patrol at posn 500 yds WEST from perimeter on old

L of C to HUGGINS. From infm supplied by 39 Bn 'A' patrol,
Brig I.N. Dougherty decided 39 Bn should establish listening
post near track and estimate enemy strength. Further patrol
ordered to move SOUTH along EAST side of SANANANDA–
SOPUTA track to contact 49 Bn and return to HUGGINS
along WEST side of SANANANDA–SOPUTA track . . .
1545 hrs. Patrol from 39 Bn investigated Jap posns and lean-tos
. . . Reported that they were unoccupied.
1615 hrs. Message conveying Christmas greetings from Maj-Gen
G.A. Vasey GOC 7 Aust Div was received. All informed . . .
2100 hrs. Patrol from 39 Bn, which was ordered to move on
EAST side of SOPUTA–SANANANDA track in an attempt
to contact 7 AUST DIV CAV forward, struck Japs in position
(behind wire entanglements) that hadd [sic] previously been
unoccupied. Patrol was engaged with grenades and was forced
to withdraw.[9]

Ralph returned to assume command of the 39th Battalion at
Huggins Roadblock at 1 pm on 27 December 1942.[10] His bout
of malaria had cost him five days at the Advanced Dressing
Station. In the morning he had felt sufficiently fit to have risen,
washed, shaved and excused himself from his carers.[11]

By this time it was clear to Generals Vasey and Herring that
the fall of Sanananda could not be achieved with the available
resources. It was therefore determined that the role of the forces
at Sanananda would be one of containment of the enemy,
pending a victory at Buna. And with that victory the 18th
Australian Brigade and the Americans could be swung over to
Sanananda to allow for a significant injection of not only
concentration of numbers but also experience and training.

On 31 December 1942, the CO of the 163rd United States
Regiment made a recce of the Huggins Roadblock positions,
and on 2 January—the very day that Buna fell to the Allies—
the 39th was relieved by that formation. On the afternoon of
that day the 39th came under command of the 30th Brigade
(Brigadier Porter), and moved to 30th Brigade HQ near Soputa.
The 39th Battalion was now down to 150 all ranks, and was
therefore organised into three groups of 50 with the role of
holding a position between a detachment of the Americans and
the 49th Battalion. The 39th Unit Diary:

> Owing to evacuations through sickness it was found necessary
> to divide the Bn into two groups instead of three. Each group

to have 48 hrs in the line and 48 in reserve. Capt Gilmore therefore relieved Capt Bidstrup at 2000 hrs. The probable number of enemy killed was twelve.[12]

On 23 January, the day that hostilities ceased at the beachhead, the 39th, now at a strength of seven officers and 25 other ranks, was ordered to march to Dobodura airfield and take a flight to Port Moresby.

Perhaps a realistic measure of the spirit of the 39th Australian Infantry Battalion is given by its CO. In an interview with the author at Headquarters Training Command over 51 years after the event, Lieutenant-Colonel Ralph Honner proudly described the battalion's march to Dobodura and into immortality:

> Down to this point, the war was almost becoming a farce for us; we were only a remnant, and we were malaria-ridden. But as we marched back towards Soputa, we were told that we were to march to Dobodura the next day to the airfield to be evacuated.
>
> Our RMO reported to brigade that some of our troops were not capable of marching to Dobodura and would have to have transport, because they were tottering with malaria— they could hardly stand let alone walk. The edict from brigade was that transport would be provided to pick up all stragglers, but the battalion would march to Dobodura. I said, 'The 39th Battalion won't have any stragglers, you won't need to pick any of them up'.
>
> We marched to Dobodura. It was a hot day, a long march. We marched all the way, but mostly we marched in columns of three, two blokes supporting one bloke in the middle. And truckloads of cheering troops went past us. These were the stragglers, who hadn't seen, many of them, much campaigning and less fighting.
>
> When we got to Dobodura, we made an effort, we went back into parade ground formation—one single file . . . We marched across Dobodura airfield and the spectators came out to see this unusual sight . . . and one of them said, 'What mob's this?' And we ignored them, looking straight ahead and marching at attention. But my 2/IC marching at the end of the line barked, 'This is not a mob, this is the 39th!'[13]

The last entry in the 39th's War Diary for January 1943:

25 Jan. All ranks were at the emplaning point at 0730 hrs and during the morning were flown to Ward's Drome [near Port

Moresby]. MT [motor transport] met the planes and moved personnel to the rest camp at Donadabu. This portion of the unit remained resting in that area until the end of the month. During this period personnel returning from hospital were sent to B Ech [Echelon] area at 17-mile from where they went on daily route marches. All personnel were placed on 72 hrs notice for embarkation for Australia.[14]

During its distinguished Papuan campaigning (the Kokoda Trail, Gona and Sanananda) the 39th Battalion lost 117 men killed in action, nine died of wounds, and 258 wounded in action.

On 12 March 1943 the 39th Battalion embarked on the *Duntroon* and arrived at Cairns the following night. From Cairns the unit entrained for Wondecla in the Atherton Tablelands where some days later Brigadier Porter held a parade to congratulate the 30th Brigade on its Papuan campaigning. During that parade he announced that the brigade would in future comprise the 39th, 49th and 3rd Battalions; further, that the 30th Brigade was now a part of the 6th Division.

On 24 March 1943 the soldiers of the 39th Battalion were granted fourteen days' leave. For Ralph, the task of dealing with various administrative responsibilities had to be undertaken before leave. He would later be disappointed that Brigadier Porter chose to limit the number of his recommendations for awards. The point is that the 39th Battalion had been attached to the 21st Brigade during almost its entire Papuan service— Ralph felt that Porter found it difficult to acknowledge his most tried and tested battalion, which had served under another formation and its commanders.[15]

Little is known of Ralph's subsequent leave in Nedlands, Perth, with Marjory, but it is highly likely that 'her Ralphie' was a much reduced physical specimen of the one that had left her in August of the previous year. It is interesting to note that Ralph maintained that the Kokoda Trail campaign was fought by the troops on a very reduced ration due to the paucity of supply. The soldiers were therefore always hungry, and that hunger, and subsequent weight loss, was compounded by the tough physical nature of the campaign. However, at the beach-head the problem was not the availability of food—a plentiful supply of bully beef and biscuit—but the severe influence of the heat and disease on the men's appetite for that food.

When Ralph returned to the unit in late April 1943 the

39th began the task of reorganising and training. On 1 July the Officers' Mess was formally opened. The next night that mess was used for a wake. On 2 July 1943 Ralph received news that the 39th Battalion was to be disbanded. He may have told the senior officers, but the platoon commanders were not aware of the news. Ralph Honner's relinquishing of his normally quiet, formal deportment—and frugal drinking habits—therefore came as quite a revelation. Lieutenant A.W. 'Kanga' Moore:

> . . . and that one night he [Honner] got stuck into the grog. And it was the only time he was ever known to have more than a couple. Those old tents . . . half way up the slope they had a sort of opening . . . with a little canopy that came out over them and he went up the pole and he dived through that opening to slide down the other side.[16]

The 39th Battalion Unit Diary:

> **3 July 0945.** 39 Bn marched onto 30 Bde parade addressed by Lt-Gen Morshead who announced the disbandment of 30th Brigade and the amalgamation of its units with the 2/1, 2/2, and 2/3 Bns.
> **1030.** 30 Bde marched past Lt-Gen Morshead.
> **1115.** CO addressed the Bn for the last time.[17]

Lieutenant-Colonel Ralph Honner, 'usually so impassive, had difficulty in containing his emotion'.[18] Lieutenant A.W. 'Kanga' Moore:

> And the thing he told us on that parade, he said, 'Before you march into other units I want you to take off your 39th Battalion colour patches; it would break my heart if any 39th man was told to remove his colour patches'.[19]

On 3 July 1943 the 39th Australian Infantry Battalion ceased to exist, its personnel scattered far and wide in random groups large and small throughout a number of AIF and militia units. The militia personnel, who had steadfastly refused to join the AIF—under any circumstances—were sent to the 36th Militia Battalion; A Company, 39th Battalion, went to compose almost the entire strength of 9 Platoon, 2/2nd Battalion; D Company, 39th Battalion, made up the majority of 16 Platoon, 2/2nd Battalion; B and C Companies were similarly absorbed into their corresponding companies of the 2/2nd; about twelve men were transferred to the 2/8th Battalion; and three officers, Lieutenants French, Moore and Plater, were transferred to the 2/6th Battalion.[20]

While one 39th soldier later stated that 'our reception was cool but correct',[21] Lieutenant A.W. 'Kanga' Moore had a different experience:

> It was something that was alot stronger than many people realise, in fact, when I went over to the battalion that I joined in the 6th Division, 17th Brigade [2/6th Battalion], I suffered the indignity of the company commander . . . the first morning I was there, parading me in front of his company and saying, 'Oh we've got an officer whose joined us from the chocos!' And then when we were being re-photographed for our paybooks and things and we had the numbers hanging around our neck in front of about fifty men, he said, 'God! Look at that! It's like the population of India!' This was my VX number. He was a very good soldier, a decorated soldier, but he wasn't a very nice man!
> . . . I finished up with his rank leading his company. It was that sort of feeling that made the 39th what it was to a degree.[22]

Given the 39th Battalion's abominable lack of training both before and during its Port Moresby garrison days, and its early experience in losing its CO and a company commander at and near Kokoda respectively, the historian—and the reader—are left to ponder the reasons for its startling Papuan success. In a videoed interview with the author only months before his death, Ralph addressed the issue:

> I think the 39th Battalion's success had its roots in its formation. It was largely composed of young volunteers who had been conscripted into military service the year in which they were to turn eighteen . . . Some of them had been rejected for AIF service because the AIF was fully manned and needed no more volunteers . . .
> When the 39th Battalion was specially raised from volunteers for tropical service, these youngsters flocked to the 39th as their chance of adventure or duty or whatever it is that drove them. So they had the right spirit to start with. They were fortunate enough to have among their ranks a few old soldiers with experience from the First War, and a few leaders with some sense of military *esprit de corps* from the First War. And some how or other among good raw material, raw as it

was, there was something to work with, with people who were willing to go to war, willing to take on the unknown. When they got to Port Moresby of course, they were misused as labourers; they were not trained as soldiers; they were militarily almost entirely unskilled; they had obsolete weapons; they were suddenly thrown into a campaign without training; they were given new weapons they'd never seen before . . . but they had the immense advantage of having built up a mateship among themselves of, if you like, kindred young spirits, who seemed somehow or other united by being thrown together in difficult circumstances. And also suddenly having added to them some experienced AIF officers to buttress the quite good leadership they had among their own rather superior militia officers and NCOs who were a good lot—if you like, a select few out of the many that were offering in Australia.

. . . the ingredients came together in battle with already a foundation of trust in each other . . . and when they found that it worked in battle, and when they found that they could handle the Japanese . . . They were just applying common sense, and a lot of military tactics is just applied common sense to the circumstances around you, they learnt, and they learnt fast . . . where there's nothing like saving their skins to motivate them!

I think they grew into a formidable military force mentally and spiritually more than they did physically and, if you like, militarily skilfully . . .

When it went to Gona it was still militarily untrained, it was skilled in one facet of warfare only, that is close quarter fighting, where you can't see the enemy, where you can't see beyond the close screen that is within your vision, but where you have learnt to trust your mates around you, and trust that if anything goes wrong, someone will be backing you up.[23]

The 39th Battalion's inspiring Australian story had a further crucial attribute—Lieutenant-Colonel Ralph Honner.

In the military sense, Honner brought a wealth of varied and critical war knowledge to Isurava. It was as if Libya, Greece and Crete had nurtured in him an ability to cope with both the diversity and pressure of battle. He had practised the fighting withdrawal in Greece; he had operated under the stress of the set-piece defence on Crete; he had worked the attributes of fire and movement in the coordinated Libyan offensives; and he had witnessed the potential of movement under one's own artillery barrage, and applied it brilliantly at Gona Mission. However, amongst those military qualities, the essential soldier possessed the succinct and searching mind of the lawyer; the breadth of mind and sense of history of the scholar; and, perhaps most importantly, the moral courage and faith, hope and trust of the Christian ideals that underpinned his entire existence.

In the spiritual sense, the 39th Battalion and Ralph Honner were made for each other, and the two together became the stuff of which legends are made.

13

THE INEVITABLE LAST ACT

A change in command took place on 9th July, when Lt-Col. Ralph Honner, D.S.O., M.C., took over from Lt-Col. Challen, who had been seconded to a senior staff appointment on Corps Headquarters . . .

Lt-Col. Honner was one of the most capable, courageous and versatile officers in the Second A.I.F. . . .

The Battalion welcomed him as an old friend, so that from the start there existed that implicit mutual confidence between C.O. and Unit which is essential to an infantry battalion.

W.B. Russell, The Second Fourteenth Battalion [1]

B rigadier Ivan Dougherty had moved quickly. Within six days of the disbandment of the 39th Battalion, he had secured a commanding officer for his vacant 2/14th Battalion command whose credentials from Bardia to Gona were both impeccable and entirely known to him.[2]

The feeling was mutual. Ralph Honner needed no introduction to the accomplishments of the 2/14th Australian Infantry Battalion and its brigade commander. He was acutely aware of the 2/14th's distinguished Papuan campaigning and the high performance of both its senior and junior leadership during that campaign. Further, Brigadier Ivan Dougherty was well known to him. He therefore regarded his posting to the 2/14th as not only a 'plum' job but familiar territory.

Much had happened to the 2/14th after its return to Australia in late January 1943.

While Ralph and his 39th Battalion—and the 21st Brigade—had been immersed in their fighting at the beachhead, General MacArthur had been planning his next move in the South-West Pacific theatre of operations. By late February 1943, plans had been prepared for a double thrust for the capture of Rabaul: one in the South-Pacific theatre through the Solomons (Admiral Halsey), and the second through the Huon Peninsula in New Guinea (General MacArthur). The spearhead of MacArthur's offensive was to be the 2nd Australian Corps (Lieutenant-General Morshead), consisting of the AIF 6th, 7th and 9th Divisions. The Australians' objectives were the capture of Lae and Madang and air bases in the Huon Peninsula–Markham Valley region. These objectives were to be seized by a combination of 'airborne, overland and overwater operations'.[3]

After fourteen days' leave during March 1943, the 7th Division began to reform in the Atherton Tablelands in Queensland. The choice of this area had a number of advantages: while humid, the climate was not oppressive; jungle terrain for training purposes was nearby; some base facilities had been built prior to the division's arrival; the area was reasonably isolated and therefore lacked the distraction of other areas and their amenities; and, given that the next operation was to be in New Guinea, the troops were stationed not far from that theatre. The 7th Division was stationed at Ravenshoe, about 50 kilometres south of Atherton.

General Vasey was faced with two challenges during this period of training. The first was the fact that his division, although now jungle experienced, had been gravely depleted by its Papuan campaigning and needed to be substantially reinforced. The second was that the Papuan veterans within its ranks took some time to recover from their continual bouts of malaria, which inhibited the continuity of that training. Nonetheless, the quality of the 7th Division's training in the Ravenshoe area was first-class. Captain Gerry O'Day, OC D Company, 2/14th Battalion:

> The AIF had learnt its lessons after Papua 1942. An awareness of the effects of diseases such as malaria and dysentery, the need for good hygiene levels in the tropics was driven home

continuously to all ranks. Clothing was dyed green, 'shorts' were removed and long U.S. gaiters appeared. Equipment was lightened wherever possible . . . machetes were made available for jungle slashing . . . and the steel helmet left in the kit stores.

Leadership at company level was emphasised, including stress on platoon/patrol level command. Quick deployment and battle drills to counter Japanese tactics were taught and practised. The 'fox hole' had replaced the trench and contact at close range practised until it became second nature.[4]

Thus, during July 1943, Ralph Honner and his battalion trained extremely hard, and, unlike that preceding the Owen Stanley campaign, the training was applied with the decisive knowledge of previous jungle experience.

Captain Keith Lovett had proved an adjutant of great worth, and had developed a relationship of trust and respect with Ralph during their time with the 39th Battalion. A similar relationship quickly developed between Ralph and his new adjutant. Captain Stan Bisset, Adjutant, 2/14th Battalion:

> I had met Ralph at Isurava, and on the 29th August '42, he and I were ordered back by Arthur Key to recce. and select a suitable ambush position for the withdrawal planned for that night . . . I also had had several contacts with Ralph at Haddy's Village.
>   . . . he got on well with officers and NCOs and his performance with the 39th Bn. was known to most troops. His training, academic and military, plus campaign experience, enabled him to instil confidence and trust into his officers and ORs. His open, friendly but firm manner, helped in achieving good relationships. I never observed him at any time as being out of control. He and I had an excellent relationship and respect for each other.[5]

The fact is that Ralph Honner and Stan Bisset had much in common: both men had been athletes before the war, Ralph as a league footballer and sprint champion, and Bisset as a prominent rugby union player;[6] both took great pride—and friendly competition—in their physical endurance in the field, although Bisset was a more imposing physical specimen in terms of height and weight; both had a lofty and admirable sense of service, Honner through his Catholicism and the nature of his education, and Bisset through his highly principled participation in the

*Captain Stan Bisset, Adjutant
2/14th Battalion.*

Lord Somers Camp and Power House movement. Peter Dornan, in *The Silent Men*:

> The Camp system was modelled on a movement begun in 1921 by Prince Albert, the Duke of York, in England, in an attempt to bring together boys from the workforce with Public School boys in the hope that they would develop a common understanding and a sense of mutual appreciation and loyalty . . .
>
> Probably the more important function of the movement found expression in the institution known as Power House. It was here that a boy began fully to learn the spirit of service and duty and to understand that he had responsibilities, both to himself and to others.[7]

For the significant number of new officers and other ranks who were new to the battalion—or those 2/14th officers and other ranks who had missed the Papuan campaign—the new CO's restrained style of leadership took some time to fathom. Captain Gerry O'Day, OC D Company, 2/14th Battalion, was one of the latter:

> Of medium height, well-built but spare physically, with a piercing glance. No obvious signs of the previous campaigning, moving quietly but with purpose. To the unit a quietly determined character, to a degree shy, but with a gentle smile which had the firmness behind it. He did not display the

charisma of some COs . . . but won respect by his consistently fair dealings. He was treated warily at first despite his experience, as the unit after Kokoda had a fairly ineffectual CO, but that soon passed and he was accepted as the one to lead the battalion successfully.

Ralph worked almost exclusively through his company commanders. He gave clear orders often reading them from the back of a letter from his wife, with his wire-rimmed glasses, and hence his orders were concise. He expected orders to be carried out with every assistance from him but with minimal interference. It took him time to develop a firm relationship with his officers being by nature shy. The other ranks respected him and admired his leadership.

In battle he was 'as cool as a cucumber' and out of it he handled any pressure with logical reasoning.[8]

On 31 July 1943, Ralph and half of the 2/14th Battalion embarked from Townsville on the *Duntroon* bound for Port Moresby, while the remainder of the unit left on the *Taroona* six days later.[9] On arrival in Port Moresby, the 2/14th was deployed in tents at Austin's Crossing, which became known as 'Bootless' because of its close proximity to Bootless Inlet. Captain Stan Bisset:

> The training carried out at Bootless was a continuation of the lessons learnt on The Track and at Gona, mainly giving all Section and Platoon Comds. the opportunity to work together as a unit, perfect their teamwork and dependence on one another. 2 inch and 3 inch mortars were used extensively in the Ramu Valley operations demonstrating the effectiveness of the training at Bootless. My recollections are that higher intelligence work which was lacking in the Kokoda and Gona campaigns had come a long way and the Nadzab operation was very successful. The Battalion was ready![10]

In late July 1943 detailed planning had begun in Port Moresby for the capture of the Huon Peninsula. The plan had, as its first objective, the capture of Lae. This involved General Wootten's 9th Division landing by sea to the east of that town, while Vasey's 7th Division was to trek overland from the Wau–Bulolo area down the Markham Valley, cross the wide Markham River and then move on Lae. The river crossing was to be assisted by a parachute battalion drop at Nadzab, which would facilitate a reinforcement by air at that airfield and an overland reinforcement via the Bulolo Valley. While those two operations were in progress, General Milford's 5th Division was to continue its advance towards Salamaua with the task of drawing enemy forces away from the Lae operation. The aim of landing Vasey's division in the Markham Valley was to facilitate a blocking of any enemy attempt to reinforce Lae from Madang and, further, to enable airfields to be built in the Markham Valley for the 5th Airforce.

General Vasey, in typical fashion, expressed his disapproval: 'They've got a dog's breakfast of a plan to capture Lae!'[11] Vasey fought hard to change the plan to allow for a parachute regiment to capture the Nadzab airfield (instead of a battalion), and for his two brigades (the 25th and 21st) to be landed at that airfield. Vasey won the day. W.B. Russell, in *The Second Fourteenth Battalion*:

> On 8th September the issue of maps, photographs and pamphlets on an unbelievably liberal scale, coupled with reports of bull-dozers, jeeps and field guns being prepared for plane-loading, dispelled any forebodings that there was another Owen Stanley campaign ahead. Sand-table lectures on Lae, Nadzab and the Markham Valley told what the theatre of operations was to be. Emplaning practice followed, and the Unit was put on a twelve hours' notice to move. The twelve hours' notice was never given. At 9.30 p.m. on the evening of 14th September, the Battalion, much of which was spread over the countryside at American picture shows, two-up schools and 'jungle-juice' depots, was ordered to move in four hours' time . . .
>
> At 2.15 a.m. on the morning of the 15th the first convoy left for Ward's Drome and at 6.30 a.m. the first plane was away. By 10 a.m. the last of the forty-two plane loads had safely arrived at the landing strip at Nadzab in the Markham Valley.[12]

The 25th Brigade had spearheaded the 7th Division thrust. On 16 September 1943, the 7th and 9th Divisions entered Lae. Vasey's task was to now move as quickly as possible towards Boana, through which the retreating Japanese must pass. To this end, Brigadier Dougherty and his 2/14th Battalion and one company of the 2/16th were landed at Nadzab on 15 September. The remainder of the 2/16th was unable to emplane from Port Moresby because of poor weather. With orders to commit his first-arrived battalion to the chase, Dougherty sent Ralph and his 2/14th out towards Boana with orders to secure that village as a patrol base. David Dexter, the Official Historian:

> While the 2/16th Battalion had been attempting to trap an enemy who had already escaped along the tracks north of Lae, the 2/14th was attempting a similar task along the tracks north of Nadzab. Resuming their advance on 16th September, the Victorians marched steadily north up Ngafir Creek all day. It was the same story on the 17th, except that the track into the Saruwaged mountains was steeper and signs of the enemy's hasty and recent use of it were more numerous. For the night the battalion camped on a kunai ridge one and a half miles south-east of Gumbuk.[13]

At around 10 am on 18 September, with D Company (Captain O'Day) in the van, Lieutenant Simmons and his 18 Platoon crossed the Busip River west of its junction with the Bunbok. As the platoon approached the Bunbok, it was fired on from three directions by a Japanese rearguard which was protecting the site of a wire bridge which it had destroyed. 18 Platoon withdrew under covering fire.

Ralph now ordered a standing patrol about 450 metres west of the river junction, while two companies prepared to cut tracks north from the crossing along the east bank of the Busip, keeping the opposite side of the Bunbok under observation for a possible crossing point. The 2/14th, despite the numerous geographical limitations placed on its advance, must have been within close range of the enemy, as Japanese could be seen on the far bank of the Bunbok River.

Late on the morning of 19 September, a patrol led by Captain Bisset found a likely crossing place about two-and-a-half kilometres north of the river junction. The patrol found that about half of the river was fordable, while the remainder might be bridged by the felling of a likely looking tree. By about 6.30 pm that evening the tree had been felled, but it fell just short of the required distance.[14] With the failed attempt by the 2/14th to bridge the river, the Japanese were able to distance themselves considerably from the Victorians.

As Ralph's soldiers were thus occupied, Brigadier Dougherty was becoming concerned about the 2/14th's pursuit role. Perhaps his main anxiety was the lack of reliable communication with his

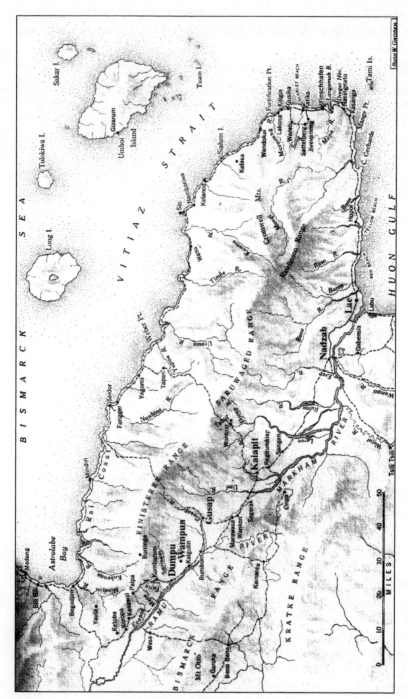

Huon Peninsula.

forward battalion. The new radio set, known as the 'Handy-talky'[15] or '536' set, was light and mobile but, at this stage, still unreliable. Further, the laying of a signal line in this terrain would not be a match for the speed of the 2/14th's advance. Dougherty therefore sent a liaison officer, Captain Holley, to communicate to Ralph his desire to gain Boana as soon as possible and cut the likely enemy withdrawal through Lumbaip, Bambok or Kemen.[16] David Dexter, the Official Historian:

> By 10.30 a.m. on the 20th the 2/14th succeeded in getting a bridge across the deep channel of the Bunbok. As the main body of the battalion was crossing Dougherty's signal cancelling the battalion's present role and ordering its return to Nadzab was received . . .
>
> By 3.30 p.m. on 21st September the battalion was back at Camp Diddy. The 2/14th Battalion had been hotter on the trail than any other unit engaged in the pursuit and, had it continued through Boana, it might have caught the retreating enemy.[17]

The decision to pull back just as a crossing had been achieved disappointed Ralph and the 2/14th Battalion, as it was felt that contact with the enemy and the subsequent chance of achieving their original orders had been a distinct possibility.[18] W.B. Russell, in *The Second Fourteenth Battalion*:

> After washing, bathing and cleaning arms and equipment, the Unit emplaned on the 24th and 25th September for Kaiapit. The reason for the changed role was now made clear. Intelligence had discovered that the enemy's plan was to unite the remnants of the Japanese 51st Division, which had escaped from Lae, with a force moving overland from Madang. This combined force was to seize Kaiapit and halt any move up the Markham Valley.[19]

The fact that the 2/14th Battalion was able to land at Kaiapit—after the arrival of the 2/16th and then the fresh 2/27th from Port Moresby—was the result of a brilliant and brave assault by the 2/6th Independent Company. Such was the level of this unit's daring and aggressive fighting spirit that the Japanese were not only evicted from that village but subjected to a withering counterattack when they sought to regain Kaiapit from the much smaller Australian force.

Vasey was reluctant to allow the 21st Brigade to push further through the Markham Valley until his 25th Brigade was flown into Kaiapit. When this had been achieved by 29 September, the 2/14th pressed ahead. On 1 October 1943, the battalion entered the roughly 16-kilometre-wide Ramu–Markham Valley which, bordered by steep, jungle-clad ranges, was covered by tall kunai grass punctuated only by an occasional line of trees signalling a tributary riverbed, or a collection of palms which indicated the presence of a village. When the soldier entered this sea of tall grass the heat became oppressive. W.B. Russell, in *The Second Fourteenth Battalion*:

> The pace was a cracker, especially for the rear of the column. The C.O., Lt-Col. Honner, and the Adjutant, Capt. Bisset, were both athletes: and in the improved war of 1943 a native carrier was allotted to carry some equipment for each, so that they would have greater freedom of action and more energy for co-ordinating and planning during the night . . .
>
> On 2nd October, the Unit reached the Gusap River, a fast flowing tributary of the Ramu. This had to be bridged. The 2/14th Battalion assisted the Engineers in the task while the 2/16th pushed forward to Kaigulan and Namaput, where small engagements took place.[20]

On 4 October 1943, the 2/14th moved out on the right flank towards Wampun and the 2/16th on the left towards Dumpu. By 2 pm Captain McInnes' A Company had reached Wampun and found it clear of the enemy. After occupying that village, Ralph was faced with a pressing problem—water. The nearby perennial Pompuquato River was found to be dry. Ralph's soldiers, who had endured a long, hot day's march, now possessed only the bare minimum in their water bottles.[21] His native carriers, similarly disposed, needed water for both drinking and their rice meal—the first for the day.

Ralph therefore ordered Captain McInnes to push his A Company towards Koram to ascertain whether the region was clear of the enemy and to find water. If none was found, he determined that the battalion would bivouac at Wampun and have water brought up by jeep. Ralph further ordered B Company (Captain Christopherson) and D Company (Captain O'Day) to move east and north respectively with the same purpose—clear the area of the enemy and find water. Neither was found.

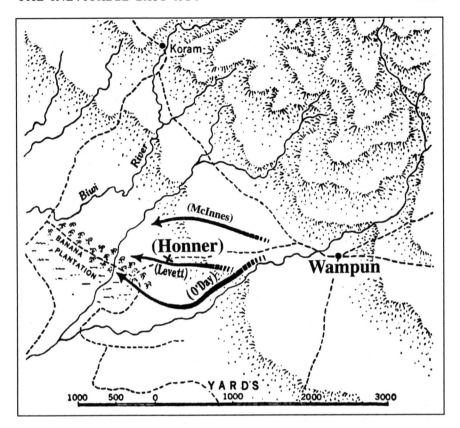

The 2/14th Battalion, 4 October 1943.

In the meantime, Ralph moved out with Private Bennet and decided to follow in A Company's path. This decision did not impress his adjutant. Captain Stan Bisset, 2/14th Battalion:

> Ralph insisted, against my protests, in going forward to look for water or possible signs of the Japs—I could never understand how or why he advanced past the spot where 'A' Coy. had left the track to occupy higher ground.[22]

At the point where A Company had left the track, Captain O'Day assigned Sergeant Pryor and three men of D Company to accompany the CO.[23] The six men moved on, with Honner and Pryor eventually setting such a pace that the two had, after about 1600 metres, far outstripped the rearward four. Ralph and Sergeant Pryor then observed troops in a 'banana plantation and a belt of timber running south-east from it'.[24] The distant troops seemed to disregard their approach, giving Honner the impression that they were A Company, 2/14th Battalion.

The distant soldiers were Japanese. At 'about one hundred and thirty yards range',[25] the Japanese opened up with machine-gun and small-arms fire. A machine-gun bullet shattered Ralph's left ball-and-socket hip joint and exited through his right buttock. Sergeant Pryor was hit in the chin and chest. With both men bleeding profusely, Pryor began dragging his CO back along the narrow track. Despite a determined combination of Pryor's dragging and Honner's crawling, the two were making little progress while leaving a discernible blood trail—and a rapidly closing enemy. Ralph Honner:

> So I told him to get back. I'd stay where I was in the kunai grass. I couldn't go any further. And he'd just have to get back and get the news to the battalion to come up quickly and if I was still there, well, I'd be right. I did have an official bodyguard, a lad named Bennet and I thought he'd gone back with the others when I said they had to go back, because it would be stupid to have me carried out and then be caught with me.[26]

Bennet was one of the four soldiers bringing up the rear behind Honner and Pryor. He refused to leave. Ralph Honner:

> . . . we dodged off a bit to the side from the trail of blood that we'd made and which Pryor had carried on with him when he left, and there were some trees not far away and the Japanese got up in these trees to look down on the kunai grass where we'd disappeared . . . we could see them but they couldn't see us. We were looking through the veil of the kunai grass; we could hear them chattering away at each other and they marched past on either side of us, beating through the kunai grass—spread out like an Emu walk . . .[27]

Both Bennet and Honner contemplated the next move. Bennet prepared himself for a solitary sacrificial charge that might disguise Honner's presence. Ralph Honner:

> I was still making up my mind whether I should . . . I had a pistol and some grenades . . . whether I should die fighting . . . or whether I should risk that they might be stupid enough and let me live if I didn't put up a show of resistance and looked helpless.
>
>   But they didn't see us . . . they turned back and we heard

them go back past us on either side . . . the chattering in the trees started again and we just laid doggo . . .[28]

Meanwhile, the wounded Pryor had arrived back at his D Company. Lieutenant Avery (who had been involved in the action at Isurava with Private Kingsbury when the latter had won his VC) was immediately despatched with a patrol to bring Ralph in. W.B. Russell, in *The Second Fourteenth Battalion*:

> The patrol reached him, but brought considerable fire on itself. The Colonel, however, was able to use Lieut. Avery's '536' wireless set to issue orders through Capt. O'Day, to the Adjutant. He [Ralph] ordered D Company . . . to attack with two platoons, and C Company, commanded by Lieut. Levett, to follow in, via the trees on the right, to roll up the enemy's left flank. He refused to allow the stretcher party to come forward for fear of endangering the men's lives, but when D Company attacked from the left the stretcher-bearers came forward, dressed his wounds, and got him to safety after more than two hours spent within shouting distance of the enemy.
>
> D Company pushed home the attack with great speed and determination. The enemy were driven back in disorder, leaving twelve dead. Of the others who were driven back across C Company's front, eleven were killed and about a dozen wounded . . .
>
> For his courage and leadership on this and other occasions during the campaign, Capt. O'Day was mentioned in despatches.[29]

Captain Stan Bisset:

> I saw and spoke to him briefly after he was carried out. It was a tragedy in my view that we had to lose a great C.O. in that manner. I knew that he was seriously wounded. I would have been honoured to continue service with him for much longer as we were good mates and with his guidance, knowledge and experience, I would have benefited greatly. His loss was a severe blow to the Bn but fortunately when Phil Rhoden was given command some two weeks later, great leadership was once again established.[30]

As a company commander at Derna, Ralph Honner had run under fire to pick up mortar bombs and bring them back to his troops; in Crete, after losing a number of his men under withering fire in attempts to relay a message to headquarters,

Damien Parer on his last leave, taken by Max Dupain. (Print Jill White)

he had tied that message to his wrist and performed the task himself; at Isurava, as a battalion commander, he had journeyed 45 minutes down the track to his standing patrol; and at Wampun he had gone forward looking for water, a task which could—and should—have been performed by a trusted corporal and his section.

Experienced battalion commanders should never be unnecessarily eliminated from their battles and therefore from their valued service to the hundreds of soldiers they serve. Thus, Ralph Honner's Wampun sojourn was not an isolated indiscretion but the almost inevitable last act of the chivalrous soldier's paradox—his exalted sense of duty to his faith, his nation and his soldiers had driven his demise.

The fateful meeting between Ralph Honner and Damien Parer at Derna only two years before had signalled the beginning of a parallel attitude in the war cameraman. After experiencing continual frustration in his dealings with the Australian Department of Information, Parer journeyed to the island of Peleliu in September 1944—a little under a year after Ralph's wounding—to film the American marine landings. His biographer Neil McDonald wrote:

> Parer decided to go with the men following the lead tank. Brennan would follow with the second. He caught a brief glimpse of Damien as the squad moved halfway across the isthmus. Using the tank for cover, Damien started to walk backwards to film the faces of the advancing troops. Then a burst of machine-gun fire from a concealed pill box ripped into him. The camera spun out of his hands as he crashed to the ground.
>
> It was late the following afternoon before a distraught John Brennan discovered Damien's body. Souvenir-hunting Marines had plundered the corpse. The camera had been opened and around Damien's body were the reels of his unspooled film and empty cans.[31]

Thus, by 16 September 1944, two years to the day since the last elements of Maroubra Force had gone into reserve near Ioribaiwa on the Kokoda Trail, two of the great characters of the Australian Kokoda legend were gone from the war. One was dead and the other disabled for life.

14

LEAVE MY WINDOW OPEN

By the time Ralph had been carried back to Wampun, he had endured severe pain and lost a considerable amount of blood. From Wampun he was taken by jeep (equipped to carry three stretchers) to Gusap, where a holding station had been established and a surgeon deployed on 1 October.[1] The Official Historian (Medical) has described the preparations for such a journey:

> Where a severely wounded man had perforce to be moved before further treatment could be undertaken, injection of morphine (1/2 grain) combined with hyoscine (1/100 grain) was found valuable. This not only relieved pain but produced an amnesic state which greatly lessened distress.[2]

When his condition had been stabilised, Ralph was flown from Gusap to Nadzab and then to Port Moresby. After arriving in Brisbane, Ralph paid the price for his Western Australian place of residence—a series of lengthy, tedious hospital stays and railway trips through Sydney, Melbourne, Adelaide and finally across the Nullarbor to Perth and its Hollywood Repatriation Hospital.[3]

Richard and Brian Honner remembered visiting their father on a regular basis, and also recall a major operation there, as a metal plate was inserted into their father's hip joint. Ralph and Marjory's third child was born during this time (Margaret Cecile Honner, 4 December 1943). Mary Jeffs, Ralph's sister:

When Ralph came out of hospital, he was told that he would have to wear a calliper on his shoes to help his walking, but he was adamant that he would not have such a contrivance on his shoes. And he used to do everything he could to make his leg strong. He even took dancing lessons with Marjory to strengthen up the muscles. We went to the pictures one night with him . . . we walked from Stanley Street in Nedlands to the Windsor Theatre . . . it was quite a walk . . . he sat on every little fence along the way, but he was determined that he was going to walk . . . without any callipers.[4]

Ralph won his battle—there would be no callipers; but a walking stick and a pronounced limp would henceforth become part of the Honner persona.

Lieutenant-Colonel Ralph Honner's last army posting occurred in the second half of 1944 in Melbourne as General Staff Officer 1 Directorate of Military Training, G Branch, Land Headquarters. The production of various training manuals ensued, but the period (at least in Ralph's eyes) was highlighted by his determination to circumvent certain rules when the chance to apply common sense and help others occurred. An example was General Blamey's policy of sending recently promoted soldiers from officer cadet training units to a new unit rather than posting them back to their original formation (this policy had caused many soldiers to avoid promotion, because they were reluctant to leave their original battalions). Ralph Honner:

You shouldn't have to risk your life amongst strangers when your own men who are used to you . . . trust you without you doing anything stupid. This was a terrible thing . . . in the 2/14th there was a lad named Bear who was naturally called 'Teddy Bear'. He had a DCM and an MM and he'd won them many times over, but every campaign he fought in, winning these decorations, he was wounded and he'd go to hospital and he'd be out of hospital in time to get back into the next action . . .

I spoke later to a psychologist and they had to vet these people, and he said, 'we got Bear's record and it was so outstanding, we were looking for the flaw because obviously he should have been commissioned three years before he went to OCTU and we thought there must be something wrong here' . . . I by this time, had been wounded . . . I was back in Melbourne Headquarters and I came across Bear with his pips just up and I said, 'What are you doing?' He said, 'Oh

well, I can't go back to the 2/14th, so I'm going into Z
Special.' I said, 'That's a shame, I know you'll probably have
a lot of fun but don't you want to go back to your mates?'
He said, 'Of course I do, but they won't let you go back to
your own unit' . . .

I got onto his brigade commander [Dougherty] . . . and
I said, '. . . see if you can circumvent Blamey on this'. What
they did was they posted him to 21st Brigade Headquarters
and seconded him as a liaison officer to the 2/14th Battalion
where he served as a platoon commander . . .

But of course, you had to have a special case. You couldn't
do it too often or there would be hell to pay![5]

Ralph Honner left the army in late 1944 to become Chairman of the No. 3 War Pensions Assessment Appeal Tribunal.
At 40 years of age he felt that the task of re-establishing a law
career, while not beyond him, would prove difficult. Besides,
here was a career path where his skills as a lawyer could be put
to good use; which gave him an opportunity to further serve
both the men he had fought alongside and the nation; which
offered excellent remuneration; and, critically, that required a
knowledge of the nature of the conditions under which ex-
servicemen had served. In this last prerequisite, he was, given
his varied war record, extremely well qualified.

Two of his former comrades remembered his demeanour
during tribunal sittings. Major Keith Lovett, Ralph's former
39th Battalion Adjutant:

> . . . I applied for assistance through the repatriation department
> for high blood pressure and a few problems internally, which
> I was entitled to. Like most of those things, you make the
> application and then they make you appeal, go before a
> tribunal. And when I went down there to the tribunal, there
> was the RSL bloke who was going to represent me, and I
> said, 'Who's on the tribunal today?' And he said, 'Colonel
> Ralph Honner is the chairman of the tribunal today.' And I
> said, 'He was my CO, this is going to be embarrassing.' I said,
> 'I'd like you to let Colonel Honner know that I'm here and
> that I'm most embarrassed and . . . I'm prepared to wait for
> another tribunal' . . . and the chap came back with a smile
> on his face and said, 'Colonel Honner said to tell you he'd be
> delighted to see you.'
>
> He didn't put me through any questions . . . he said, 'I don't

need to know that about Captain Lovett, he served me well
during the war and I think he's entitled to some consideration.'[6]

And when one of his former 2/11th Battalion C Company
platoon commanders appeared before him, the reception was
friendly but correct. Lieutenant K.T. Johnson:

> . . . just as a matter of interest I was given the large percentage
> of ten per cent, and everyone says at that stage post war, 'You
> must appeal!' I filled in the piece of paper and I went down
> to the Repat. in due course to this appeal tribunal. And who
> should be present as the chairman but one Ralph Honner. And
> there were two doctors on the board and it was an old
> weatherboard building with a verandah. And we were talking
> as man to man . . . we went inside to that board room and
> he sat at one end of the table and I sat at the other, and he
> did not know me from a bar of soap. And he asked me to
> 'State my case Mr Johnson'. He increased it to 15 per cent.[7]

. . .

> He always came to see me at work and more often than not
> we'd go off and have a light lunch . . . he was an ordinary
> everyday individual, never demonstrated his wealth or ability
> over others. I know that he asked McRobbie or told
> McRobbie that there was a vacancy on the tribunal and he
> ought to apply for the job, but he never did. And another
> Major out of the unit, Heagney, subsequently applied for and
> got a job, and he told me that in such tribunal hearings Honner
> used to sum up the answer in no time, never took a file home,
> always seemed to finish up with near the right answer as is
> possible, and he said, 'I used to take files home and sit up to
> ten or eleven at night sweating over them trying to be sure
> that I had arrived at the right decision, whereas the Honner
> brain summed it up in a quarter of the time'.[8]

As there were no set times for tribunal hearings, Ralph often
managed to conduct his work in capital cities when such
activities coincided with an athletics meeting or perhaps a
football grand final.[9]

If Ralph's decision was a sound one in terms of employment,
from a family perspective it was unfortunate. Marjory was
destined, during her children's formative years, often to play
the role of sole parent to their four children while Ralph was

away (John Roderick Honner had arrived on 1 May 1946).
John Honner:

> And I get a sense that that was the time, the 40s and the 50s,
> where this growing love and realising that being human is
> about giving, not being walked on, but giving and under-
> standing and supporting, became Mum's choice.
>
> As we know, my father was a man of firm opinion, to put
> it mildly, and mum was as soft as butter. And yet she got her
> way sometimes and Dad got his way a lot of the time. But
> they grew together.[10]

Marjory's concept of family led her to the decision to attempt
to join the Catholic Church during the late 1940s. Margaret
Honner:

> . . . she went down to the local Parish Priest and said she
> wanted to talk to him about becoming a Catholic. He said,
> 'Oh, go and talk to the Nuns.' She said, 'I don't want to go
> and talk to the Nuns, I want to talk to you!' And he said,
> 'Oh no, go and talk to the Nuns!' So she walked off in a huff
> and that was the end of that attempt! The second attempt was
> also in Perth . . . and Dad said that . . . he'd go with her.
> They went up, the two of them, and Mum said they sat around
> while Dad and the priest talked football non-stop, and then
> suddenly the priest (Dad took a breath, or the priest took a
> breath) turned around and said, 'Now, what's this about you
> wanting to become a Catholic, why would you want to do
> that?' And Mum said she got such a shock that they'd stopped
> talking football, she couldn't think, and she said, 'I thought it
> would be good for the family.' And he said, 'That's a silly
> reason', and went back to talking football! That was the second
> attempt.[11]

By late 1949 Ralph and Marjory took the decision to move
to Sydney where the length (but not the frequency) of Ralph's
travelling might be reduced, thus allowing more time with his
family. From 1950 until his retirement in 1968, Ralph held the
position of Chairman of the No. 2 War Pensions Assessment
Appeal Tribunal. The family settled at Seaforth in Sydney,
which overlooked the Spit Bridge. Richard was thirteen years
of age, Brian twelve, Margaret six and John four.

Ralph's child-rearing qualities were, to a large measure,

governed by the experience of his own childhood and the influence of his mother. Richard Honner:

> . . . he was very quiet and never made much noise. My mother would do her block and yell at me. A lot of the time he wasn't there . . . because he had this war pensions stuff that was his job, and then several nights a week he'd fill in with things like the Liberal Party and the United Nation's Association and other things . . . that used to irritate my mother I think. He was around on the weekends usually, doing gardening and pottering about. He bought this house with a huge garden and so we all used to get dragooned into putting in weekends gardening which used to drive us nuts. My mother liked it.
>
> Emotionally he was very controlled . . . I'm sure he was emotional but he didn't show it. There weren't too many father and son chats.[12]

Brian Honner:

> He was certainly not demonstrative, certainly not. He was very calm and quiet. I cannot recall him ever raising his voice against any of us, and, I guess it was part of the times that Mum sort of ran the family.[13]

Margaret Honner:

> A lot of my memories to do with dad are related to books. When he went away and then came back the presents would be books. Books that were on special or second hand, but books and chocolates . . . books, there were books in the house, I remember him reading to us and I can remember him encouraging us to read.[14]

John Honner:

> My memories of dad in the 1950s are first of all of his painstaking and patient devotion to thorough detail, whether it was mending our shoes, covering books, sewing carpet, teaching us to write, tying the laces on our football boots. Dad was away a lot . . . mum always lamented that he was off again to save the world. On the occasions when the family needed him, however, he was always there, and a tower of strength.[15]

Ralph Honner's contribution to 'saving the world' was largely as President of the New South Wales Division of the

United Nations Association (1955–57), and as an active member
of the Liberal Party (since 1945), culminating in his presidency
of the NSW Branch 1961–63. Little is known of his term with
the United Nations Association[16] and, surprisingly, there has
been a paucity of scholarship regarding that period in NSW
politics.

Ralph Honner the political figure based his philosophy on
his faith. His beliefs were so emphatic, so ordered and detailed
that he felt compelled to record them—to formally declare
them. Just prior to his election as president of the party in 1961,
Ralph compiled his political manifesto, 'Approach to Politics',
an exhaustive handwritten collection of documents comprising
119 pages and approximately 20 000 words.[17]

His political philosophy embodied the belief that courage,
hope, fortitude and endurance are all nurtured by conviction.
The strong and united community is supported by a continuity
of a great tradition. He believed that it is not wealth and power
and organisation that hold a society together but its Christian
faith. And the message he took to the NSW Catholic electorate
was that such Christian faith was Catholic in its origins.

A decisive thrust of 'Approach to Politics', therefore, was an
attempt to influence the Catholic vote in NSW.[18] Further, it
would seem that his potential sway in this area was partly
responsible for his election as president in 1961. Katherine West,
in *Power in the Liberal Party*:

> On merit, he [Honner] was a natural successor to R.C. Cotton,
> although some claimed that he was elected unopposed chiefly
> because he was a prominent Catholic layman—a fact that was
> published in the Sydney press before the Executive elections
> took place at the end of 1960.[19]

In hindsight, perhaps one of the most interesting aspects of
Ralph's 'Approach to Politics' is his preoccupation, in part, with
the menace of socialism and, by extension (according to conser-
vative politics of the time), communism. Such a philosophy was
a not uncommon one for the 1950s and early 60s: the formation
of the so-called 'Iron Curtain' in eastern Europe, the perceived
communist expansion during the Korean War, and, in Australia,
concern over increased communist infiltration of the union
movement, the Petrov affair, and the split in the Australian Labor
Party resulting in the formation of the Democratic Labor Party,

collectively conspired to provide the Menzies federal government with more than enough political ammunition with which to attack the Labor Party.

If the formation of the DLP in Victoria and Queensland had sent the ALP into political obscurity in those states for some years, the DLP had not enjoyed a similar influence in NSW. In fact, as the election of January 1962 approached, the Labor Party in NSW had been in continuous government for 21 years. Katherine West, in *Power in the Liberal Party*:

> Indeed, the majority of Catholic Labor voters in New South Wales continued to support the A.L.P.: this was partly, no doubt, a reflection of their Cardinal's personal attachment to a Party securely in office, right-wing and sympathetic to the Catholic point of view. In 1959, the Liberal Party attributed its electoral defeat to a well organised personal canvass of Catholic voters in the key metropolitan electorates of Sydney, Rockdale, Ryde and Concord.[20]

Mrs Ralph Honner would not have been one of them, as Marjory's third attempt to become a Catholic in 1958 had been successful.

One of the most contentious issues of the times was state aid to church schools. Ralph became a passionate advocate for such aid. Prior to the election campaign of 1962 both the ALP and the Liberals showed signs of adopting limited forms of state aid. The Liberals retained their opposition to direct state aid, but pledged free travel for all students and higher funding for books. Perhaps with the perceived propensity for large Catholic families in mind, the Labor Party pledged free travel for only the fourth and subsequent children in any one family.[21] From a Liberal perspective the issue was exceedingly difficult, as the Country Party had openly advocated substantial state aid. The leader of the Liberal Party, Robin Askin, sought to appease all factions within the party, and as late as ten minutes before his policy speech during the 1962 election, the controversy and the pressure continued—from Ralph Honner. Ian Campbell, in *The New South Wales State Election, 1962*:

> If the roneoed copy of Askin's policy speech, compiled before it was delivered, is compared with the printed copy, published after, there is a significant difference in the paragraphs regarding education. According to the roneoed copy: 'We do not think

it would be in the best interests of the community as a whole, or indeed of the private schools which would lose their independence, to support direct state aid such as per capita payments, capital loans, or interest subsidies.' The printed copy merely says: 'But we do not support direct aid such as per capita payments, capital loans, or interest subsidies.'[22]

As Askin and the party dignitaries prepared to go on stage, Ralph saw his speech. This was war. There could be no weakness and no compromise—Ralph threatened Askin with the president of the party's departure from the stage the moment he heard the words 'the best interests of the community as a whole'.[23] Askin was seen to accomplish some rapid revision of his typed speech and, as a consequence, its verbal delivery.

In the event, Ralph's stand proved a shallow victory, as Askin's roneoed version of his speech had been released to the press. Following the election a majority of Liberal state parliamentary members rejected the party's Joint Standing Committee's proposal that the party should advocate state aid for interest loans for capital building programs in independent schools. Ralph might well have viewed the exercise from a military standpoint: a temporary withdrawal or defeat does not constitute the winning or losing of the war. Ian Campbell, in *The New South Wales State Election, 1962:*

> An urgent crisis developed in July 1962 when the Catholic schools in Goulburn were closed down, and their pupils sent to state schools, which almost collapsed under the strain. This tactic was adopted deliberately by some Catholic leaders to demonstrate the fact that if no Catholic schools existed, the entire State system would be unable to cope, and the resulting costs to the public revenue would be enormous. The crisis was eventually settled, while Cardinal Gilroy announced a five point program of aid as his ultimate object. By October 1962 it was reported that the Liberal sub-committee was in favour of state aid by an 8 out of 14 margin. This 8 included Catholics R.O. Healey (MLA, Wakehurst), Party President Ralph Honner, and future Attorney General McCaw.[24]

During the 1963 federal election, Prime Minister Menzies announced a scheme for government subsidies to be given to independent schools for the building of science blocks. This federal initiative gave the NSW branch of the Liberal Party more confidence, and many more within its ranks were converted to the state aid cause.

Ralph relinquished his position at the end of his term in 1963. His successor, Brigadier 'Jock' Pagan, and John Carrick were among a number of continuing powerful advocates of state aid as being first a matter of principle, and second a palatable issue for electors. In his policy speech during the 1965 election, Askin announced a comprehensive state aid plan.

Ralph Honner's term as President of the NSW branch of the Liberal Party (1961–63) was seen as a period of consolidation for the party. Sir John Carrick remembered him as 'a private man who didn't sell himself in any way, of immense character and widely respected'.[25] Along with the considerable efforts of such people as Sir John Carrick, John Howard and R.C. Cotton, Ralph Honner is remembered within the party as a champion of state aid to independent schools; the first Catholic president of the NSW branch of the party; a man instrumental in the broadening of the party support base across all social classes; and, in a measure typical of the man, the person who proposed, advocated and then won a motion that a prayer be adopted for all meetings of the State Council, the State Executive, the State Convention and other important meetings of the Liberal Party of Australia in NSW. The prayer:

> O God, grant us in our deliberations the aid of Thy divine wisdom that we may see clearly, speak with truth, and act with courage and justice, so that in all our works Thy will may be done.[26]

During the 1960s the career paths of Ralph and Marjory's children were resolved: by 1961 Richard Honner had graduated from medical school and would later become a highly successful hand surgeon; Brian Honner entered Duntroon in February 1956 and served during the Malayan Emergency as a lieutenant in command of an infantry platoon, in Vietnam (1968–69) as a major in command of an infantry company, and in 1978 left the army and worked in public employment in Canberra; Margaret Honner joined the Loreto Sisters and gained a BA (Hons) and a DipEd; and John Honner joined the Jesuit Order in 1964, gained his PhD in Boston, left the Order in 1999, and is currently working in welfare.

In 1960 Richard Honner, Ralph's father, died at the age of 95 and Eleanor Honner died in 1965 at the age of 99.

Ralph Honner retired from his employment in 1968 to become Australian Ambassador to Ireland. On 22 July 1968 a prominent Australian newspaper ran the headline:

Outsider Envoy Defends his Job

SYDNEY—The newly appointed Australian Ambassador to Ireland, Mr Ralph Honner, said today he could not see why members of the Diplomatic Corps should be upset by his appointment . . .

In Canberra today, diplomatic sources could not give any special reasons which might qualify Mr Honner for his appointment. They said the new appointment was regarded as a 'one shot' job. Mr Honner was not likely to get a further appointment.

The reporter, having woven his/her web of shock, horror and bewilderment and described Honner's impressive war, public and political record, then saved the last three paragraphs for the perfectly logical reasons as to why Ralph Honner had been appointed. Under the heading of 'Outsiders', the article finished with:

Diplomatic sources said today that 'plum' diplomatic posts are going to people from outside the Department of External Affairs because of a big shortage of diplomats.

The shortage is caused by a rise in the number of new diplomatic posts being opened by Australia. And it's being aggravated by the fact that some top officials who would make first-class ambassadors are being kept in Canberra to work on policy and evaluation reports.[27]

The family home at Seaforth was sold before their departure and provided a magnificent insight into the extreme measures Ralph was prepared to go to adhere to his principles: Marjory was appalled to find him showing prospective buyers a minor leak in the garage roof by means of spraying it with water from a hose.

When Ralph and Marjory Honner arrived at their residence at Killiney, just outside Dublin, the significance of the Honner family history must have been uppermost in Ralph's mind. Just 110 years after John and Mary Honner had emigrated to South Australia aboard the *Utopia*, full of hope and enthusiasm for a life that might provide them a modest chance to own their own land, one of their great-great-grandchildren had returned to their native land in a manner they could not have dreamt of.

As with all else in his life, Ralph Honner took to his new task with the same level of faith, integrity and work ethic that had so characterised the teacher, lawyer, soldier, political figure and public servant. For Marjory Honner here was a busy, action-packed existence, with 'her Ralphie' to herself. In essence, she regarded this period in her life as a hard-working but priceless second honeymoon.[28] Ralph relished his chance to represent Australia in the land of his forebears. No invitation to represent his country by way of attendance at any conceivable function, no matter how seemingly insignificant, was rejected.[29] Guests from Australia, be they official, family or old war comrades, were struck by the Honners' hospitality—warm, gracious and always approachable. Ralph felt great pride in the fact that he had met and knew personally all four presidents of Ireland up to and including that period.

One of Marjory's favourite stories from their time in Ireland occurred when Ralph and Marjory met Lord Louis Mountbatten at a formal function in Dublin. As Mountbatten strolled along the line of dignitaries, all immaculately turned out and wearing their civil and military awards, he stopped in turn to talk to nearly all of them. When he paused to converse with the Honners, he glanced at Ralph's DSO and MC and commented, 'Ah, a real soldier!'[30]

When Ralph's term as Ambassador to Ireland ended in 1972 the couple went into retirement at Beauty Point in Sydney. In 1978 the Honners toured Europe using Spain as their base and in 1981 travelled to Crete to commemorate the fortieth anniversary of the battle for that island. For Ralph the pilgrimage provided an opportunity to renew old acquaintances among the villagers who had been so generous to him years before. Marjory wrote to their daughter Margaret on 27 May 1981:

> Two of the boys of the family who gave the party were 9 &
> 10 yrs old during the fighting & they had been sent out by
> their mother with food & drink for the soldiers (father & one
> elder brother killed) & they remember Ralph. So he (with his
> garland) had to perform with these fellows & their small son.
> I could go on forever—tales I'll never forget . . . but it all
> ended & and we set off exhausted for the pilgrimage Ralph

has long dreamed of—to go to the tiny village & see the people who fed & kept him safe for 3 months.

We took a bus to the south side—through lovely valleys of grape vines & olive trees, huge mountains, still snow covered—& four hours later drove into a tiny fishing port, found somewhere to stay & immediately set about trying to find a way to the village. Ralph threatened me with a donkey ride, but after complicated phone calls, found the village serviced by bus, water & electricity laid on & the people had got the paper reporting on Ralph, their village & families mentioned (which we had realised—all in Greek of course) & so then we were welcomed by the oldest old men (one actually produced a snap of Ralph) with more tales. But it was to the widow of the man who organised the people, that Ralph went. A daughter (married) had come across the island that morning to act as interpreter & give her mother support. Her father had retold the tales so often she knew the names & places where the men were kept hidden.

Widow I leave to last, although we met her first—a tiny little bundle of dirty black (grey with age) rags—no teeth, with outstretched arms of welcome—out of an old door in a wall. The house was 2 rooms joined by a courtyard—vine covered, full of fowls, 2 goats, pigeons & obvious signs of a donkey. She refused to leave the old house when husband & one son were killed. The other children moved on, but come back each weekend to help her. We all cried and hugged her—she gave us the usual greeting of wine & sweet bread—none for herself or daughter.

We went on a tour to the cemetery; to the library where we gave children's books from the battalion [the 2/11th], called in at at least a dozen other homes—more sweet bread and wine—& back to the widow who had killed & cooked a fowl for us. We sat & ate in utter filth—eventually made her sit with us but she wouldn't eat—and when we left we were laden with goats cheese (she'd made that morning), almonds and wine. We saw all the family photos, all husband's letters & records of the boys he'd saved; addresses of nearest in case plans went wrong. She showed us them all so proudly, so sadly; her poor little hands like claws. She is 1 year older than I am. We still feel humble & overwhelmed.

Ralph is the original iron man [Ralph was approaching his 77th birthday at this time]. He keeps very fit. We miss you all—but we are happy and thankful to be together.
Mother, with love.[31]

During the early 1980s Ralph and Marjory moved to an apartment on Sydney Harbour at Fairlight. Although Marjory's gardening was now curbed somewhat, she managed to produce an extensive and impressive potplant collection along their lengthy balcony.

I first met Ralph Honner on 1 September 1986 for the purpose of an oral history interview for my book, *Those Ragged Bloody Heroes*. At the time he was enduring a course of chemotherapy for a cancer condition. Despite this, I was met at the door by a straight-backed man wearing grey pants, black polished shoes, white shirt and tie, and cardigan. His soon-to-be familiar limp and walking stick were noticeable as he led me into a spacious lounge room leading to a stunning view of Sydney Harbour and its Heads. Marjory Honner impressed me as a sprightly, intelligent lady whose hospitality was quickly felt. During the interview in his den (which contained a spacious library indicative of a well-read scholar), I found Ralph to have an extraordinary memory for detail, to possess the deliberate mind of the lawyer and diplomat, and to be extremely self-effacing. The interview was a long and fruitful one, and I departed with the pledge that I would send him draft chapters of the work for his comment regarding the participation of the 39th Battalion during the Kokoda Trail and Gona campaigns. It was the start of a working relationship and a friendship that I shall always treasure.

After reading the first chapter, Ralph offered his services for the entire manuscript. I accepted gratefully but did not appreciate the consequences. Ralph Honner's proofreading involved a meticulous examination of the work, but was always prefaced by 'I suggest', rather than blunt, impersonal instructions. All suggestions were accompanied by a detailed grammatical explanation, or why a proposition might need more examination, and, critically, Ralph did not once interfere in the shaping of the conclusions I drew from that research. But perhaps the attribute I admired most in Honner was his assertion that Maroubra Force should be the thrust of the book and not just the 39th Battalion. Of all the veterans I have interviewed, Ralph Honner undoubtedly possessed the most incisive and formidable sense of history.

The correspondence always ended with 'Bless the work, Ralph', or 'It's been a long day, I'm beginning to fall asleep over the work, Cheers, Ralph'. Ralph Honner the teacher had formally resigned from the Western Australian Education Department before the Depression, but continued to teach until his death. Margaret Honner:

> I think he was a born teacher . . . he taught you . . . he taught us too, up until the last time he saw us . . . he was still teaching us . . . he loved helping people and educating and teaching them.[32]

Ralph Honner resented the fact that many military historians had tended to take the easy way out and concentrated purely on documents at the Australian War Memorial, rather than balancing those sources against the experiences of the participants. In an interview with Neil McDonald in 1985, he provided an example:

> Gavin Long wrote the first book of the official history without asking me about Bardia . . .
> I was never asked for a report on that. My Brigade didn't have a report so that's why Long didn't know it happened. When I heard the first story was coming out I wrote to him and I said 'Look, what are you doing about Bardia?' He did ask me about Derna . . . but he hadn't asked me about Bardia . . . so I wrote to him and I said . . . 'Did you know that the 2/11th was involved and that my company played a role?' He said, 'Oh, we've only got the official records.' I said that no one had ever asked me for a report, so how could anyone know? And he said that it was too late now, it had gone to press. Perhaps we will get a revised edition later on.[33]

After a long illness Marjory Honner died in 1990. John Honner:

> When mum became sick, dad looked after her with exquisite care—washing her every day, washing her bed clothes, even when she could no longer recognise him. She used to say, 'That can't be my Ralphie, he's too nice that man.' And I said to dad once, 'It must be difficult for you, constantly having to be beside mum, when she can't even recognise you.' And he said quite simply, 'After all that Marjory has given me this is the very least that I can do.'[34]

Perhaps a letter written by Ralph on 5 May 1990 best portrayed his love for Marjory:

> Dear_____
> Thank you for your thoughtful letter. Don't be too sorry for me. Of course I'm sad at losing Marjory and the sweet smile that never failed her even when her memory had gone and she was a trusting, wondering child again. But any sadness is far outweighed by an immense gladness for having loved and been loved by her for 65 years—9 of them before we could afford to marry. Still, there are times at night when I almost reach out a hand for her hand that is not there. I do not think she can be far away while she is in our hearts and thoughts and prayers and I am grateful to you for keeping her in yours, Love Ralph[35]

Despite Marjory's prolonged illness and the long hours spent in nursing her, Ralph had insisted that the proofreading of *Those Ragged Bloody Heroes* continue. When I received correspondence from him, I noticed his practice of sending me back the same envelopes I had sent him with a label with my address glued to the front. I also recall his comment, 'You may ring me STD if you choose, but I won't be ringing you, the socialists aren't getting my money!' And they didn't—they got mine. At the time I attributed this to his experience during the Depression, but its origins clearly lay in his childhood in Three Springs, Western Australia. Nor did the dreaded socialists lay their hands on other accumulated monies. Towards the end of his life Ralph took to making large donations to charities at the end of each financial year.[36]

Yet the same man was a most gracious host, whose hospitality knew no bounds: when I visited him from Adelaide he insisted I stay with him; he often took me to his favourite seafood restaurant in Manly and always insisted on paying, and on each occasion he discreetly placed in a young waitress's hand a 10-dollar note which had been momentarily placed under the tablecloth. The act was crisp in execution—the ritual had obviously been enacted on many occasions. I once impertinently suggested that the young lady was far too young for him and should cost him a lot more than 10 dollars. Ralph produced a wry smile and then described his struggling days at university. An understanding and generous man.

Such sojourns were always undertaken in his Mercedes-Benz.
On the first occasion I drove with him, I anticipated a lengthy
trip at perhaps 25 kilometres an hour. I was repeatedly to be
treated to a seemingly confident, fast ride of short duration. A
number of similar speedy trips were taken together to locations
as far away as Mosman. Four years after Ralph's death I interviewed his eldest son, Richard. Part of that discussion caused me
to break out in a cold sweat:

> He failed one test. And they wouldn't let him have his driving
> licence back until he passed the test. So he virtually memorised
> the whole of the area, and he got through the test because he
> knew there was a 30 kilometre per hour zone, he knew there
> was a give way sign or something, but he didn't see it too
> well. I spoke to his local doctor and I tried to have him banned
> from driving, because I thought he was going to injure himself
> or injure someone else. And I said, 'Look, all you've got to
> do is keep failing him on his eyesight and he won't be able
> to renew his licence.' And the local doctor wouldn't do it.
> And this was when he was about 85. But they foolishly sent
> him a ten-year licence and he signed up.[37]

Those Ragged Bloody Heroes was launched in Melbourne in
October 1991—a fitting place and time, as many veterans of
the 39th Battalion had gathered for the battalion's celebration
of the fiftieth anniversary of the unit's formation. Ralph, with
Lieutenant-Colonels Rhoden and Sublet (former COs of the
2/14th and 2/16th Battalions respectively), launched the book.
Ralph wrote, memorised and subsequently recited three six-page
speeches for the weekend commemorations. He was driven to
Spencer Street Railway Station on the following Monday morning by one of his former 39th Battalion platoon commanders.
Lieutenant Don Simonson:

> I wished him a good trip back, and looked forward to him
> coming down again, and he said, 'You're always part of my
> family, of course I'll be down to see you. You're one of my
> sons'.[38]

When my book *Gona's Gone!* was launched in Sydney in
1994 (by Ralph and Lieutenant-Colonel Geoff Cooper), Ralph
met Lieutenant Hugh Dalby, one of his 39th platoon commanders, for the first time since Gona. Although ill, Dalby
relished the opportunity to see his former CO. When Hugh

'Old infantrymen' at the launch of Gona's Gone! *Left to right: Geoff Cooper, Ralph Honner, the author, Captain Hugh Dalby, Captain Ron Plater.*

Dalby and I returned to Adelaide, Hugh wrote to thank Ralph and received the following reply:

Dear Hugh,
Thankyou for your letter from 'an old infantryman'. I still think of you as the young dasher who spearheaded the captures of Gona Mission and Gona Village—since called Haddy's Village after another platoon commander of heroic mould, deprived of 52 years of living to look back on the time of his testing.

It is the young infantryman leading the section, the platoon or the company in critical action on whom a battalion's reputation is built; and history will ever have you in the front rank of those whom the 39th owes its fame.

Such thoughts thronged my mind during the comfort and joy of seeing you again after long parting. And with our farewells came deeper thoughts for which I could find no words. I was thinking of the last part of Tennyson's 'Ulysses'—'It may be we shall touch the Happy Isles'.

I look forward to seeing you again but, if not before this world fades, then in another—the Happy Isles, Valhalla, Heaven or wherever old infantrymen may go to share the Eternal Light.

With proud recollections of the great, and the daunting days of old and warmest wishes for happy years ahead from an older infantryman,

Ralph Honner[39]

On Saturday 14 May 1994, Ralph rose at about 7 am and showered and dressed. At around 8 am he made his way to the front lawn of his apartment building and, with Sydney Harbour and its distant Heads as a background, raised the Australian flag—the last act of a great patriot. Soon afterwards Ralph must have felt distressed, or at least ill, as he then made his way inside. But along that path he left telltale signs that all was not well. His electronically operated garage door was left partly open, and after reaching his front door he stepped over his copy of the *Sydney Morning Herald*. Margaret Honner:

> He knows he's dying, he's not going to fall down as a heap on the floor . . . fully dressed, no one's going to find him in his jarmys . . . nobody's going to find him with his bed not made . . . there are people who would have helped him, but I don't think he would have been able to die peacefully if he'd been worrying about what other people, you know, like if we'd been there, he'd still be trying to look after us, whereas he was able to die in peace.[40]

The circumstances of Ralph Honner's passing were therefore, in many ways, not unlike his youth and its foundations and his later life—independent, in a sense private, and perhaps at times lonely. His last years had been punctuated by the recurring pain of cancer and its equally painful radiotherapy treatment. Ralph Honner had quite simply had enough. And, critically, his concept of death and its aftermath brought no fear, as his unshakeable faith could not have contemplated an end—merely a new journey.

After noticing his still-ungathered paper, his next-door neighbour entered the apartment. Ralph Honner lay on his bed at peace. He was 89.

When three of his children gathered at the apartment they found his proposed funeral arrangements, his last will and testament, and all other matters of business neatly arranged in a top drawer of his desk. There was a book written in his impeccable handwriting of his translations of French and German and Italian poetry. Also among these papers was a collection of poems written by Ralph. One of those pieces of verse was apt:

Leave My Window Open

When I die leave my window open wide.
A boy plucks mulberries. I see him eat them from
my window. When he runs, bright-eyed, my window
lets me hear his hurrying feet.
Soft to my window birds chant from the stream
Where veiling vines immure them, cloister-cool;
Through clement airs drift drowsy clouds; I dream
that I don't dream within the sleeping pool.
Clear from my window I can see a tower;
I feel myself as tower and window too; the
aspiring steeple, earth-chained, chimes man's
hour, reminding me my day will soon be through.
The sea-wind wafts a will-o'-the-wisp of calls;
The shore is shrill with shrieks; the ebbing tide
turns golden pages on sun-gilded walls.
When I die leave my window open wide.

Lieutenant-Colonel Ralph Honner, DSO, MC, had his last parade at St Mary's Church, North Sydney, on 20 May 1994, and was laid to rest beside Marjory Honner at Northern Suburbs Cemetery.

The history of a nation is composed of the spiritual, cognitive and emotional energy of its citizens, both in the individual and collective sense, implanted into the building blocks of momentous events. John Honner, during his eulogy for his father:

> We celebrate a life that spans every generation of this century. Dad belonged to that absolutely wonderful generation of Australians, many of whom are here today, who recovered from the First War, who survived the Depression, who fought the Second War, and who built our prosperity in the 1950s.
> . . . it is a life of grace. It's a life that was lived for some higher dream—some higher vision. It's the only way to make sense of Dad's life.[41]

Ralph Honner, 1941.

Lieutenant-Colonel Ralph Honner's deeds in the Western Desert, Greece, Crete, along the Kokoda Trail, at Gona and in the Ramu–Markham Valley have earned him a distinguished place in Australian history and in its mythology. His name has been, and will continue to be, an inspiring example of what is expected of a first-class Australian commander.

We search for his epitaph. His daughter Margaret suggested Horatio, in the last act of *Hamlet*:

Now cracks a noble heart, goodnight sweet prince,
And flights of angels sing thee to thy rest.

NOTES

1 BORN OF THE GREAT HUNGER

1 Liddell Hart, *Thoughts on War*, p. 152.
2 Taken from an unpublished Honner family history. Copy most kindly given to the author by Brian Honner 1994, referred to hereafter as 'Honner family history'.
3 ibid.
4 ibid.
5 ibid.
6 ibid.
7 ibid.
8 *The Southern Cross*, Adelaide, Friday, 6 July 1928. Copy of the article, 'An Appreciation of a Noble Life: The late Richard Honner Sen., Maitland, R.I.P.'. Copy given to the author by Brian Honner.
9 John Honner, nephew to Ralph, letter to the author, 23 March 1999.
10 From papers found in Ralph Honner's files. The handwriting is clearly Ralph's.
11 Copy, from Ralph Honner papers.
12 ibid.
13 ibid.
14 Ralph Honner papers.
15 Mary Jeffs, taped questionnaire reply, conducted by her son, Peter Jeffs, Albany, Western Australia, 12 March 1995.
16 Patrick O'Farrell, *The Catholic Church and Community: An Australian history*, p. 254.
17 ibid., p. 257.

18 Ralph Honner papers.
19 Letter from John Honner, Ralph's nephew, who worked on the farm, 23 March 1999.
20 Ralph Honner papers. A copy of his father's police service record.
21 Clem Honner's documents. Copy from his son John Honner, 23 March 1999.
22 ibid.
23 ibid.
24 Mary Jeffs, taped questionnaire reply, conducted by her son Peter Jeffs, Albany, Western Australia, 12 March 1995.
25 Rita Quartermaine, Ralph's niece, letter 23 March 1999.
26 ibid.
27 Letter, Mary Jeffs to Margaret Honner, undated.
28 Mentioned on a number of occasions in conversation between Ralph Honner and the author.

2 LIFE IN EPIC TERMS

1 Liddell Hart, *Thoughts on War*, p. 153.
2 Documents written by Ralph's brother Clem confirm Ralph's entrance exam in 1915 aged eleven.
3 Ralph's Perth Modern School records show his transfer from Perth Boys to Perth Modern School and his prior lodgings. A copy of his Perth Modern School records was most kindly sent to the author from Carol Stabb of the Perth Modernians Society, December 1998. Ralph's papers provide only one fleeting mention of Perth Boys School. Future reference to his Perth Modern School records will be shown as 'school records'.
4 Ralph made a number of references to the Great War casualties in conversations with the author.
5 School records.
6 A copy of the Perth Modern School booklet for 1918 was kindly sent to the author by Carol Stabb of the Perth Modernians Society, December 1998.
7 ibid.
8 ibid.
9 Mary Jeffs, interview 12 March 1995. Also article written by Ronald Monson, a fellow Perth Modern School student. The date of the article is unknown. Copy given to the author by Brian Honner, Ralph's son.
10 Richard Honner, Ralph's eldest son, interview Sydney, 11 January 1999.
11 Mary Jeffs, interview 12 March 1995.
12 John and Margaret Honner, interview 16 July 1995.
13 School records.
14 ibid.
15 ibid.

16 Rita Quartermaine (Ralph's niece), letter to the author, received from Narrogin, Western Australia, 25 March 1999. Rita had been told this during conversations with Ralph's mother.
17 A copy of the certificate was found in Ralph's papers. Kindly lent to the author by Brian Honner.
18 School records.
19 Copy of Richard Honner's police service record from Ralph's papers.
20 Mary Jeffs, interview 12 March 1995.
21 ibid.
22 Letters, Rita Quartermaine and John Honner, Clem Honner's children.
23 Copy of Richard Honner's police service record from Ralph's papers.
24 A copy of Ralph's University of Western Australia academic record and course material was kindly sent to the author by Mr Colin Halbert, Archives and Central Records, Office of the Registrar, University of Western Australia, November 1998.
25 Mr Humphrey Tranter, interviews 8 February, 23 March, 6 April 1999.
26 Prestage, E., *Chivalry: Its historical significance and civilising influence*, p. 2.
27 Tranter interview.
28 ibid.
29 John Honner, Clem's son, letter 21 March 1999.
30 ibid.
31 ibid.
32 John Honner, letter 21 March 1999.
33 Mary Jeffs, interview 12 March 1995.
34 Ian Bennett, interview Perth, 13 November 1994.
35 ibid.
36 Mary Jeffs, interview 12 March 1995.
37 John Honner, from his eulogy at his father's funeral. Taped copy given to the author by Richard Honner.
38 Richard Honner, interview Sydney, 11 January 1999.
39 Mary Jeffs, interview 12 March 1999.
40 Letter Honner to Edgar, 1 August 1992. Copy given to the author by Edgar, November 1994.
41 Mr Owen Burges, boarder at Hale School in Ralph's time, letter from Perth, 15 April 1999.
42 ibid.
43 ibid.
44 Dr J.B. Craig, boarder Hale School, letter 15 April 1999.
45 Mr Keith Prescod, student Hale School, letter 6 November 1995.
46 AWM 76 B249, Honner, letter to a Mr Bazley, 17 May 1956.
47 Ralph Honner, letter to K.T. Johnson, 6 June 1992. Copy given to the author by Mr Johnson.
48 Mary Jeffs, interview 12 March 1995.
49 ibid.

3   IT'S A CONFIDENCE BUSINESS

1   Neil McDonald interview with Honner, Sydney, 8 January 1985.
2   Long, *To Benghazi*, pp. 47–53.
3   The 2/11th (City of Perth) Australian Infantry Battalion, 1939–45, pp. 1–2. An unpublished collection of stories/experiences. Honner's copy most kindly lent to the author. Referred to hereafter as '2/11th collection'.
4   ibid., pp. 1–2.
5   Captain Darrald McCaskill, 2/11th Battalion, interview Perth, 13 November 1994
6   2/11th collection, p. 9.
7   Lieutenant K.T. Johnson, phone con. 9 April 1999.
8   Lieutenant K.T. Johnson, interview Perth, 11 November 1994.
9   ibid.
10 In conversations with the author on numerous occasions, Honner maintained that his C Company was the best he had seen during the war, in terms of fitness, training and junior leadership.
11 Private Harry Johnson, 2/11th Battalion, interview Perth, 11 November 1994.
12 Corporal Cecil Rogers, 2/11th Battalion, interview Perth, 11 November 1994.
13 Corporal Bernie Rogers, 2/11th Battalion, interview Perth, 11 November 1994.
14 Private Harry Johnson, 2/11th Battalion, interview Perth, 11 November 1994. Confirmed, C. Rogers, B. Rogers, 11 November 1994.
15 Lieutenant K.T. Johnson, 2/11th Battalion, interview Perth, 11 November 1994.
16 2/11th collection, p. 10.
17 AWM 76 B249. Letter from Honner to a Mr Bazley.
18 2/11th collection, p. 11.
19 ibid., p. 12.
20 ibid., p. 15.
21 Corporal Bernie Rogers, C Company, 2/11th Battalion, interview Perth, 11 November 1994.
22 2/11th collection, p. 20.
23 Lieutenant K.T. Johnson, 2/11th Battalion, interview Perth, 11 November 1994.
24 2/11th collection, p. 23.
25 ibid., p. 24. Confirmed by Lieutenant K.T. Johnson, C Company platoon commander, who 'captured' the said officer on the last of the three occasions. Phone con. 13 April 1999.
26 Private Harry Johnson, C Company, 2/11th Battalion, interview Perth, 11 November 1994.
27 Gavin Long, *To Benghazi*, pp. 147–8.

28 ibid., p. 196.
29 Ralph Honner, 'The Last Day at Bardia', in *Stand To*, July–August 1962.
30 Ralph Honner's letters were examined by the author in Canberra at his son Brian's residence. Copies were then sent to the author in Adelaide. These letters will henceforth be referred to as 'Honner letters'.
31 Honner letters, Bardia.
32 ibid.
33 Lieutenant K.T. Johnson, phone con. 3 May 1999.
34 Honner letters, Bardia.
35 Gavin Long compiled an equipment and clothing list of what the 16th Brigade took/wore into battle. It was at some variance with that of the 2/11th. Lieutenant K.T. Johnson was read this list during a phone con. on 14 January 1999, and supplied the 2/11th list.
36 Honner letters, Bardia.
37 Honner, 'The Last Day at Bardia'.
38 Lieutenant K.T. Johnson, C Company, 2/11th Battalion, phone con. 14 April 1999.
39 Honner, 'The Last Day at Bardia'.
40 Lieutenant K.T. Johnson, phone con. 14 April 1999.
41 Honner, 'The Last Day at Bardia'.
42 Honner letters, Bardia.
43 Honner, 'The Last Day at Bardia'.
44 Private Harry Johnson, C Company, 2/11th Battalion, interview Perth, 11 November 1994.
45 Honner letters, Bardia.
46 David Horner, *General Vasey's War*, p. 80.
47 Gavin Long, *To Benghazi*, p. 190.
48 2/11th collection, p. 28.
49 Gavin Long, *To Benghazi*, p. 209.
50 ibid., p. 210.
51 ibid.
52 Honner letters, Bardia.
53 2/11th collection, p. 32.
54 Ralph Honner, interview 1 September 1986.

4 THESE WAR CORRESPONDENTS AMUSE US

1 Gavin Long, *To Benghazi*, p. 242.
2 ibid., p. 241.
3 Ralph Honner, 'The Capture of the Drome at Derna', printed in *Australia at Arms*. The author's copy is from the 2/11th collection, pp. 63–4.
4 ibid., p. 64.
5 ibid.
6 ibid.

7 Lieutenant K.T. Johnson, C Company, 2/11th Battalion, interview Perth, 11 November 1994.
8 Honner letters, Derna.
9 Lieutenant K.T. Johnson, C Company, 2/11th Battalion, interview Perth, 11 November 1994.
10 2/11th collection, p. 40.
11 Ralph Honner, 'The Capture of the Drome at Derna'.
12 Gavin Long, *To Benghazi*, p. 246.
13 2/11th collection, p. 42.
14 Honner letters, Derna.
15 Gavin Long, *To Benghazi*, p. 244.
16 AWM 52 8/3/11, the 2/11th Battalion Unit Diary, the February Diary 1941.
17 Honner letters, Derna.
18 Neil McDonald, *War Cameraman: The story of Damien Parer*, p. 76.
19 ibid., p. 78.
20 Honner letters, Derna.
21 Gavin Long, *To Benghazi*, p. 272.
22 Honner letters, Derna.
23 ibid.
24 Honner papers.
25 Honner letters, Derna.

5 THE MORNING HATE

1 Gavin Long, *Greece, Crete and Syria*, pp. 6–7.
2 David Horner, *Blamey: The Commander-in-Chief*, pp. 168–74.
3 ibid., p. 187.
4 Gavin Long, *Greece, Crete and Syria*, p. 29.
5 ibid., p. 30.
6 2/11th collection, p. 54.
7 Honner letters, Greece.
8 Gavin Long, *Greece, Crete and Syria*, pp. 40–1.
9 Honner letters, Greece.
10 David Horner, *General Vasey's War*, pp. 90–3.
11 ibid., p. 99.
12 Honner letters, Greece.
13 Lieutenant Arthur McRobbie, letter to his mother, 29 April 1941, copy given to the author by Lieutenant K.T. Johnson, December 1994.
14 Honner letters, Greece.
15 ibid.
16 ibid.
17 ibid.

18 Lieutenant K.T. Johnson, 2/11th Battalion, interview Perth, 11 November 1994.

19 David Horner, *General Vasey's War*, p. 103.

20 Honner letters, Greece.

21 ibid.

22 ibid.

23 Lieutenant Arthur McRobbie, letter to his mother, 29 April 1941, copy given to the author by Lieutenant K.T. Johnson, December 1994.

24 Captain Darrald McCaskill, 2/11th Battalion, interview Perth, 13 November 1994.

25 AWM 52 8/3/11, the 2/11th Battalion Unit Diary, the April Diary 1941.

26 Lieutenant K.T. Johnson, 2/11th Battalion, interview Perth, 11 November 1994.

27 Gavin Long, *Greece, Crete and Syria*, p. 183.

6 GROPERS ALBANY

1 Liddell Hart, *Thoughts on War*, pp. 89–90.

2 In his Crete letters to Marjory, Ralph merely mentions 'the destroyer', but in his elaboration of his letters just after the war he writes, 'p. 4 last line destroyer "Hasty"'.

3 Gavin Long, *Greece, Crete and Syria*, pp. 161, 179.

4 Shortly after the war Ralph added key information to the sequence of the letters for posterity. The letters were numbered in sequence from his first Middle East letters: 7. 29 April 1941 G for Greece (pp. 1–4). C1, C2 for Crete (pp. 5–6). p. 5. 'Monday April 28 . . . village' = Neon Khorion 8. Undated—end of p. 3 and top of p. 4 of a letter from Palestine about late August or early September 1941. It contains reference to letters in which I had described Crete and Cretans—before the deluge. The letters never reached their destination. C3 C4 just indicate the Crete sequence, continued. 9. Undated—pp. 2–4 of another letter are marked C5 C6 C7 carrying on the Crete sequence. 10. Undated—map C8 and pages marked C9 to C16 to complete the Crete sequence. The complete postwar notes of elaboration were kindly lent to the author by Brian Honner. The Crete letters will hereafter be referred to as 'Honner letters, Crete'.

5 From Iven Chapman, *Transcriptions of Interviews for the 40th Anniversary of the Battle of Crete*. The analogy is Chapman's while interviewing Lieutenant-Colonel Ian Campbell, 1981. Copy of the interviews with Honner and Campbell given to the author by Neil McDonald, June 1999.

6 The description of Crete's geography and facilities is taken from Gavin Long's *Greece, Crete and Syria*, pp. 202–3, and participant interviews.

7 Gavin Long, *Greece, Crete and Syria*, p. 205.

8 Gavin Long, *Greece, Crete and Syria*, p. 211, and David Horner, *General Vasey's War*, pp. 110–11.

9 General Freyberg's description of these units cited from Gavin Long, *Greece, Crete and Syria*, p. 212.

10 A description of the units and their deployment on Crete is to be found in Gavin Long's *Greece, Crete and Syria*, pp. 218–19.

11 ibid., p. 214.

12 ibid., p. 216.

13 From General Freyberg's Crete report, Gavin Long, *Greece, Crete and Syria*, p. 216.

14 ibid.

15 Gavin Long, *Greece, Crete and Syria*, p. 228.

16 Honner letters, Crete.

17 AWM 52 8/3/11, the 2/11th Battalion Unit Diary, the May Diary 1941.

18 Campbell's 2/1st Battalion and 4th and 5th Greek Battalion dispositions are taken from the map on p. 258 of Gavin Long's *Greece, Crete and Syria*, and his accompanying narrative.

19 Honner letters, Crete.

20 The 2/11th's dispositions are taken from Ralph Honner's Crete letter (p. 5), and confirmed by Lieutenant K.T. Johnson (OC 13 Platoon) and the Official Historian.

21 Private Harry Johnson, C Company, 2/11th Battalion, interview Perth, 11 November 1994.

22 Corporal Cecil Rogers, C Company, 2/11th Battalion, interview Perth, 11 November 1994.

23 Honner letters, Crete.

24 Gavin Long, *Greece, Crete and Syria*, p. 258.

25 Ralph Honner, 'Paratroops in Crete', in *Australia at Arms*, by Norman Bartlett. This article is hereafter referred to as 'Ralph Honner, "Paratroops in Crete"'.

26 Ralph Honner, 'Paratroops in Crete'. The story is confirmed by Lieutenant K.T. Johnson, 2/11th Battalion, interview Perth, 11 November 1994.

27 Ralph Honner, 'Paratroops in Crete'.

28 Sandover, in 2/11th collection.

29 Ralph Honner, 'Paratroops in Crete'.

30 ibid.

31 Gavin Long, *Greece, Crete and Syria*, p. 264.

32 Honner letters, Crete.

33 Gavin long, *Greece, Crete and Syria*, footnote p. 266.

34 Ralph Honner, 'Paratroops in Crete'.

35 ibid.

36 ibid.

37 Lieutenant K.T. Johnson, C Company, 2/11th Battalion, interview Perth, 11 November 1994.

38 Ralph, 'Paratroops in Crete'.
39 Honner letters, Crete.
40 AWM 52 8/3/11, the 2/11th Battalion Unit Diary, the May Diary 1941.
41 Honner letters, Crete.
42 ibid.
43 ibid.
44 ibid.
45 Honner letters, Crete.
46 ibid.
47 ibid.
48 Gavin Long does not mention this meeting, and infers in his narrative that the attack was Sandover's idea. Further, Long does not mention the role(s) of Roberts and the Greeks. See Long, *Greece, Crete and Syria*, p. 269. Honner mentions the meeting, and the complete roles for the attack. Honner letters, Crete.
49 Gavin Long, *Greece, Crete and Syria*, p. 269.
50 AWM 52 8/3/11, the 2/11th Battalion Unit Diary. A report written by the adjutant, Lieutenant Dowling.
51 Gavin Long, *Greece, Crete and Syria*, p. 270.
52 Ralph Honner, 'Paratroops in Crete'.
53 Honner letters, Crete.
54 ibid.
55 Gavin Long, *Greece, Crete and Syria*, p. 272, note.
56 Honner letters, Crete.
57 Lieutenant K.T. Johnson related McRobbie's fate to the author, phone con. 27 June 1999.
58 Lieutenant K.T. Johnson, 2/11th Battalion, interview Perth, 11 November 1994.
59 Gavin Long, *Greece, Crete and Syria*, p. 275.
60 Ralph Honner, 'Paratroops in Crete'.
61 Honner letters, Crete.
62 Brigadier R.L Sandover, 'Escape from Crete', the 2/11th collection.
63 ibid.
64 Honner letters, Crete.
65 ibid.
66 Brigadier R.L. Sandover, 'Escape from Crete', the 2/11th collection.
67 ibid.
68 ibid.
69 ibid.

7 SOME UNTIDY THINGS

1 Brian Honner, letter to the author, June 1999.
2 National Library of Australia, Vasey Papers MS 3782.

3 ibid.
4 The author cannot claim a taped interview or a piece of writing with regard to this matter, but can vividly remember Honner expressing this view on a number of occasions.
5 Gavin Long, *Greece, Crete and Syria*, p. 65 and note on same page.
6 David Horner, *General Vasey's War*, pp. 116–31.
7 Honner made his assessment of Sandover to the author on a number of occasions.
8 AWM 76 B249. Honner letter to Mr Bazley.
9 Colonel Patrick Shanahan, 2/11th Battalion, phone con. 12 July 1999. Shanahan was posted with Ralph to that unit.
10 Richard Honner, interview Sydney, 11 January 1999.
11 AWM 76 B249. Honner letter to Mr Bazley.
12 Brian Honner, letter to the author, June 1999.
13 ibid.
14 AWM 76 B249. Honner letter to Mr Bazley.
15 Ralph Honner, letter to Mary Breslim, dated 25 January 1942. Copy given to the author by John Honner.
16 Sergeant K.J. Irwin, letter 20 March 1989.
17 David Horner, *Crisis of Command*, p. 304.
18 ibid., p. 303.
19 AWM 39th Battalion Unit Diary, 49th Battalion Unit Diary, AWM 53rd Battalion Unit Diary. The names of the 30 officers were traced. The 53rd had the smallest number and, significantly, a number of new militia officers.
20 Dudley McCarthy, *South-West Pacific Area: First year*, p. 130.
21 Lieutenant A.G. Garland, 39th Battalion, interview Melbourne, 7 June 1986.
22 Wilkinson's diary, p. 3. Copy lent to the author by the late H.T. 'Bert' Kienzle, 1989.
23 For a detailed analysis of the battle to retake Kokoda, see Peter Brune, *Those Ragged Bloody Heroes*, ch. 5.
24 AWM 76 B249. Honner letter to Mr Bazley.
25 The author cannot be certain of Honner's travel log, as it was described by him verbally and was not recorded. The place sequence is therefore from the author's memory.

8 A SOLDIER'S CALVARY

1 Liddell Hart, *Thoughts on War*, p. 223.
2 AWM 52, the 39th Battalion Unit Diary, the August Diary 1942.
3 Captain Keith Lovett, 39th Battalion, interview Horsham, Victoria, 5 October 1998.
4 Ralph Honner, 'The 39th at Isurava'.
5 H.D. Steward, *Recollections of a Regimental Medical Officer*, p. 108.

6 Ralph Honner, videotaped interview by the author for Headquarters Training Command, Australian Army, February 1993.

7 The reader is referred to Liddell Hart's quotation at the beginning of this chapter.

8 Ralph Honner, interview Sydney, 1 September 1986.

9 Sergeant Jack Sim, taped reply to questionnaire, from New South Wales, October 1997.

10 Peter Brune, *Those Ragged Bloody Heroes*, p. viii.

11 The appreciation cited is based on a letter written by Honner to the author in November 1988.

12 AWM 52, the 39th Battalion Unit Diary, the August Diary 1942.

13 Ralph Honner, interview Sydney, 1 September 1986.

14 Captain Keith Lovett, 39th Battalion, interview Horsham, Victoria, 5 October 1998.

15 Ralph Honner, 'The 39th at Isurava'.

16 Peter Brune, *Those Ragged Bloody Heroes*, p. 84.

17 Dudley McCarthy, *South-West Pacific Area: First year*, pp. 145–6.

18 Given that Captain Sam Templeton's assessment at the onset of the fighting was adopted (1500–2000), the additional 4000 estimation would have given the Japanese a force of 6000–7500 short of the actual number.

19 Ralph Honner, 'The 39th at Isurava'.

20 Captain Keith Lovett, 39th Battalion, interview Horsham, Victoria, 5 October 1998.

21 Victor Austin, *To Kokoda and Beyond*, p. 150.

22 ibid., p. 151.

23 Ralph Honner, 'The 39th at Isurava'.

24 Captain Keith Lovett, 39th Battalion, interview Horsham, Victoria, 5 October 1998.

25 ibid.

26 Major M.L. Bidstrup, 39th Battalion, interview Adelaide, 14 January 1986.

27 Captain Keith Lovett, 39th Battalion, interview Horsham, Victoria, 5 October 1998.

28 Ralph Honner, 'The 39th at Isurava'.

29 ibid.

30 ibid.

31 ibid.

32 ibid.

33 'Report into Operations, 21st Brigade, Owen Stanley Campaign', p. 7. There were, in fact, two reports written. The first was sent to Army HQ in Brisbane shortly after the campaign. It was returned with orders to condense its contents and emphasis. The 'edited' version is to be found in the AWM. A copy of the original was lent to the author by Lieutenant-Colonel Ken Murdoch, who was Potts' Staff Captain Learner during the Kokoda campaign.

34 Major J.E. Gwillim, 2/14th Battalion, letter July 1987.
35 Ralph Honner, 'The 39th at Isurava'.
36 For a detailed account of the 2/14th's fighting at Isurava, see Peter Brune, *Those Ragged Bloody Heroes*, ch. 8.
37 Captain Keith Lovett, 39th Battalion, interview Horsham, Victoria, 5 October 1998.
38 Dudley McCarthy, *South-West Pacific Area: First year*, p. 206.
39 Lieutenant-Colonel F.H. Sublet, letter from Perth, 10 July 1987.
40 ibid.
41 ibid.
42 Ralph Honner, 'The 39th at Isurava'.
43 AWM 52, the 39th Battalion Unit Diary, the August Diary 1942.
44 ibid.
45 ibid.
46 ibid.
47 Victor Austin, *To Kokoda and Beyond*, p. 168.
48 AWM, the 39th Battalion Unit Diary, the September Diary 1942.
49 ibid.
50 Neil McDonald, *War Cameraman: The story of Damien Parer*, p. 153.
51 ibid., p. 155.
52 Victor Austin, *To Kokoda and Beyond*, p. 174.
53 Major M.L. Bidstrup, 39th Battalion, interview Adelaide, 11 June 1986.
54 Neil McDonald, *War Cameraman: The story of Damien Parer*, p. 155.
55 ibid., p. 156.
56 ibid.
57 Captain Keith Lovett, 39th Battalion, interview Horsham, Victoria, 5 October 1998.
58 Neil McDonald, *War Cameraman: The story of Damien Parer*, p. 160.
59 Peter Brune, *Those Ragged Bloody Heroes*, p. 151.
60 Sergeant Jack Sim, 39th Battalion, taped reply to questionnaire, October 1997.
61 Neil McDonald and Peter Brune, *200 Shots: Damien Parer George Silk and the Australians at war in New Guinea*, p. 57.
62 Neil McDonald, *War Cameraman: The story of Damien Parer*, p. 160.
63 Peter Brune, *Those Ragged Bloody Heroes*, p. vii.
64 Neil McDonald, *War Cameraman: The story of Damien Parer*, pp. 157–8.
65 Victor Austin, *To Kokoda and Beyond*, p. 175.
66 ibid., p. 176.
67 Victor Austin, *To Kokoda and Beyond*, p. 255.

9   ENERGISING THE SITUATION

1 For a detailed examination of the battle for Brigade Hill and the subsequent plight of the 2/27th Battalion, see Peter Brune, *Those Ragged Bloody Heroes*, chs 11 and 12.

2 For a detailed examination of the fighting leading up to the relief of 21st Brigade, see Dudley McCarthy, *South-West Pacific Area: First year*, pp. 223–8.

3 Minutes of Advisory War Council Meetings, vol. V., Minute nos 870–1073, 1 April–17 September 1942, pp. 510–645, Australian Archives, Canberra, CRSA. 2682/1 Minute no. 1067.

4 Neil McDonald, interview Ralph Honner, 8 January 1985. Transcript given to the author.

5 Dudley McCarthy, *South-West Pacific Area: First year*, p. 227.

6 Victor Austin, *To Kokoda and Beyond*, p. 177.

7 Dudley McCarthy, *South-West Pacific Area: First year*, pp. 227, 229, 241, 244. Lovett, interview 5 October 1998. Victor Austin, *To Kokoda and Beyond*, p. 177.

8 Dudley McCarthy, *South-West Pacific Area: First year*, p. 241.

9 Captain Keith Lovett, 39th Battalion, interview Horsham, Victoria, 5 October 1998.

10 This was not recorded in interview with Honner, but was stated to the author.

11 Victor Austin, *To Kokoda and Beyond*, pp. 177–82.

12 ibid.

13 D.M. Horner, *Crisis of Command*, p. 171.

14 For a detailed account of the command crisis in New Guinea and Australia during this period, see D.M. Horner, *Crisis of Command*, ch. 8.

15 For a detailed account of the removal of Brigadier Potts, see Peter Brune, *Those Ragged Bloody Heroes*, pp. 194–8.

16 For a detailed account of Allen's fighting on the Kokoda Trail and his removal from command, see Dudley McCarthy, *South-West Pacific Area: First year*, chs 8 and 9.

17 For a detailed account of the conclusion of 21st Brigade's fighting on the Kokoda Trail and the Koitaki Parade, see Peter Brune, *Those Ragged Bloody Heroes*, ch. 13.

18 Norman Carlyon, *I Remember Blamey*, p. 111.

19 Captain H.J. Katekar, 2/27th Battalion, interview Adelaide, 13 August 1988.

20 Major-General Sir I.N. Dougherty, interview Sydney, 12 November 1988.

10   ONCE MORE UNTO THE BREACH

1 Liddell Hart, *Thoughts on War*, p. 223.

2 Milner, *Victory in Papua*, pp. 138–9; Gavin Long, *The Six Years' War*, p. 235.

3 The descriptions of the ground at Gona and the Japanese defences are

taken from interviews with the 21st Brigade and 39th Battalion veterans, for the author's *Those Ragged Bloody Heroes* and *Gona's Gone!*

4 For a detailed description of Vasey's 7th Division campaigning from Kokoda to Gona, see Dudley McCarthy, *South-West Pacific Area: First year*, ch. 10.

5 Major H.J. Katekar, 2/27th Battalion, interview Adelaide, 4 April 1989.

6 AWM 52, the 39th Battalion Unit Diary, the November Diary 1942.

7 Victor Austin, *To Kokoda and Beyond*, pp. 194–5.

8 'Report on Operations 25 November 1942–14 January 1943', by Brigadier I.N. Dougherty, Commander 21 Aust. Inf. Bde (with appendixes). A copy of this report was most kindly lent to the author by Major-General Dougherty in Sydney, 12 November 1988. The report is hereafter referred to as 'The Dougherty Report'.

9 Victor Austin, *To Kokoda and Beyond*, pp. 196–7.

10 In February 1993, the author interviewed Ralph Honner at Headquarters Training Command, Australian Army, at Georges Heights, Sydney. A videotape was made of the interview. This interview is hereafter referred to as 'Honner, Headquarters Training Command interview'.

11 Ralph Honner, 'The 39th at Gona'.

12 ibid.

13 Major-General Sir I.N. Dougherty, interview Sydney, 12 November 1988.

14 The official history, for example, shows an aerial photograph of Gona dated July 1942.

15 Major M.L. Bidstrup, 39th Battalion, interview Adelaide, 25 August 1986.

16 The author does not have a record of Honner's objection to Brigadier Dougherty in writing or on tape, but the issue was discussed with the author on a number of occasions.

17 Honner, Headquarters Training Command interview.

18 Lieutenant D.I.H. McClean, 39th Battalion, interview Melbourne, 29 March 1993.

19 Honner, Headquarters Training Command interview.

20 Major M.L. Bidstrup, 39th Battalion, interview Adelaide, 1 March 1989.

21 Honner, Headquarters Training Command interview.

22 The Dougherty Report, p. 9.

23 Captain M.L. Bidstrup, 39th Battalion, interview Adelaide, 1 March 1989.

24 Lieutenant A.W. Moore, 39th Battalion, interview Melbourne, 23 March 1993.

25 Private C. Bloomfield, 2/16th Battalion, letter from Western Australia, March 1993.

26 Lieutenant A.W. Moore, 39th Battalion, interview Melbourne, 23 March 1993.

27 Captain Keith Lovett, 39th Battalion, interview Horsham, Victoria, 5 October 1998.

28 Ralph Honner, interview Sydney, 1 September 1986.

29 ibid.

30 Honner, Headquarters Training Command interview.

31 Lieutenant Hugh Kelly, 39th Battalion, interview Melbourne, 29 March 1993.

32 Captain Hugh Dalby, 39th Battalion, interview Adelaide, 23 March 1993.

33 Honner, Headquarters Training Command interview.

34 Major-General Sir I.N. Dougherty, interview Sydney, 12 November 1988.

35 Private B.J. O'Connor, 2/27th Battalion, interview Mount Gambier, 24 March 1993.

36 Lieutenant-Colonel F.H. Sublet, 2/16th Battalion, interview Adelaide, 6 August 1988.

37 Corporal J.L. Hardie, 39th Battalion, interview Melbourne, 27 March 1993.

38 Lance-Corporal E.G. Pannell, 2/27th Battalion, interview Mount Gambier, 24 March 1993.

39 Sergeant Jack Sim, 39th Battalion, taped reply to questionnaire, October 1997.

40 Lieutenant A.W. Moore, 39th Battalion, interview Melbourne, 23 March 1993.

41 Lieutenant-Colonel F.H. Sublet, interview Adelaide, 6 August 1988.

42 Ralph Honner, 'This is the 39th'.

43 The Dougherty Report.

44 Honner, Headquarters Training Command interview.

45 Ralph Honner, 'The 39th at Gona'.

46 ibid.

47 Lieutenant A.W. Moore, 39th Battalion, interview Melbourne, 27 March 1993.

48 Lieutenant Hugh Dalby, 39th Battalion, interview Adelaide, 23 March 1993.

49 Ralph Honner, 'The 39th at Gona'.

50 Lieutenant E.F. Sheldon, 2/14th Battalion, letter July 1987.

51 Ralph Honner, 'The 39th at Gona'.

11   THE KOITAKI FACTOR

1 David Horner, *Blamey: The Commander-in-Chief*, p. 565.

2 Honner, Headquarters Training Command interview.

3 ibid.

4 Liddell Hart, *Thoughts on War*, pp. 208–9.

5 See Peter Brune, *Those Ragged Bloody Heroes*, chs 15 and 16.

6 Honner's 'The Koitaki Factor' was reproduced in a number of the 21st Brigade's ex-servicemen's journals and the 39th's *Good Guts*. The author has Honner's handwritten original.

7 Lieutenant-Colonel F.H. Sublet, 2/16th Battalion, interview Adelaide, 6 August 1988.

8 ibid.

9 Bill Edgar, *Warrior of Kokoda*, p. 233.

10 As a member of the SA United Services Institute, the author was entitled to view the correspondence between that organisation and the Blamey Fund.

12   THIS IS NOT A MOB!

1 Ralph Honner, 'The 39th at Gona'.

2 Dudley McCarthy, *South-West Pacific Area: First year*, p. 394.

3 ibid., pp. 407–8.

4 The 21st Brigade War Diary, 1 December–31 December 1942. A copy of this document was lent to the author by Brigadier Dougherty in 1988 and a photostat copy made (AWM 52 8/2/21).

5 AWM 52, the 39th Battalion Unit Diary, the December Diary 1942.

6 Victor Austin, *To Kokoda and Beyond*, pp. 218–19.

7 Dudley McCarthy, *South-West Pacific Area: First year*, p. 505.

8 ibid.

9 AWM 52 8/2/21, the 21st Brigade War Diary.

10 ibid.

11 Ralph Honner related the story to the author of his dismissing himself from the ADS, early on the morning of 27 December 1942, on a number of occasions.

12 AWM 52, the 39th Battalion Unit Diary, the December Diary 1942.

13 Honner, Headquarters Training Command interview.

14 AWM 52, the 39th Battalion Unit Diary, the January Diary 1943.

15 Ralph discussed this issue with the author on a number of occasions when asked to give his impressions of Brigadier Porter.

16 Lieutenant A.W. Moore, 39th Battalion, interview Melbourne, 27 March 1993.

17 AWM 52, the 39th Battalion Unit Diary, the July Diary 1943.

18 Victor Austin, *To Kokoda and Beyond*, p. 233.

19 Lieutenant A.W. Moore, 39th Battalion, interview Melbourne, 27 March 1993.

20 Victor Austin, *To Kokoda and Beyond*, pp. 233–4.

21 ibid., p. 234.

22 Lieutenant A.W. Moore, 39th Battalion, interview Melbourne, 27 March 1993.

23 Honner, Headquarters Training Command interview.

13   THE INEVITABLE LAST ACT

1   W.B. Russell, *The Second Fourteenth Battalion: A history of an Australian Infantry Battalion in the Second World War*, p. 220.

2   Major-General Sir I.N. Dougherty, interview Sydney, 12 November 1988. Dougherty did not elaborate on whether Lieutenant-Colonel Challen was seconded to the school before or after the 39th's disbandment, but made it absolutely clear that he requested Honner as the new CO of the 2/14th as soon as he learned of the 39th's demise.

3   David Horner, *General Vasey's War*, p. 240.

4   Colonel G.O. O'Day, 2/14th Battalion, questionnaire received from Buderim, Queensland, 5 October 1999.

5   Captain S.Y. Bisset, 2/14th Battalion, questionnaire received from Sunshine Beach, Queensland, 5 October 1999.

6   Peter Dornan, *The Silent Men: Syria to Kokoda and on to Gona*, pp. 3–4.

7   ibid., p. 6.

8   Colonel G.O. O'Day, 2/14th Battalion, questionnaire received from Buderim, Queensland, 5 October 1999.

9   W.B. Russell, *The Second Fourteenth Battalion*, p. 220.

10   Captain S.Y. Bisset, 2/14th Battalion, questionnaire received from Sunshine Beach, Queensland, 5 October 1999.

11   David Horner, *General Vasey's War*, p. 258.

12   W.B. Russell, *The Second Fourteenth Battalion*, p. 223.

13   David Dexter, *The New Guinea Offensives*, p. 399.

14   ibid. Confirmed by Captain Bisset, phone con. 8 October 1999.

15   W.B. Russell, *The Second Fourteenth Battalion*, note p. 222.

16   David Dexter, *The New Guinea Offensives*, p. 399.

17   ibid., p. 400.

18   Captain S.Y. Bisset, 2/14th Battalion, phone con. 6 October 1999.

19   W.B. Russell, *The Second Fourteenth Battalion*, pp. 225–6.

20   ibid., pp. 226–7.

21   Colonel G.O. O'Day, 2/14th Battalion, questionnaire received from Buderim, Queensland, 5 October 1999.

22   Captain S.Y. Bisset, 2/14th Battalion, questionnaire received from Sunshine Beach, Queensland, 5 October 1999.

23   Colonel G.O. O'Day, 2/14th Battalion, questionnaire received from Buderim, Queensland, 5 October 1999.

24   W.B. Russell, *The Second Fourteenth Battalion*, p. 228.

25   ibid.

26   Neil McDonald, interview with Ralph Honner, Sydney, 8 January 1995.

27   ibid.

28   ibid.

29   W.B. Russell, *The Second Fourteenth Battalion*, pp. 228–9.

30 Captain S.Y. Bisset, 2/14th Battalion, questionnaire received from Sunshine Beach, Queensland, 5 October 1999.
31 Neil McDonald, *War Cameraman: The story of Damien Parer*, p. 242.

14 LEAVE MY WINDOW OPEN

1 Allan S. Walker, *The Island Campaigns (Medical)*, pp. 201–2.
2 ibid., p. 219.
3 Ralph related this story to the author on a number of occasions.
4 Mary Jeffs, taped questionnaire reply, conducted by her son Peter Jeffs, Albany, Western Australia, 12 March 1995.
5 Neil McDonald, interview with Ralph Honner, Sydney, 8 January 1985.
6 Captain Keith Lovett, 39th Battalion, interview Horsham, Victoria, 5 October 1998.
7 Lieutenant K.T. Johnson, 2/11th Battalion, interview Perth, 11 November 1994.
8 ibid.
9 Related to the author by Honner on a number of occasions.
10 Taken from John Honner's eulogy to his father. Copy most kindly given to the author by Richard Honner.
11 Margaret Honner, interview Melbourne, 16 July 1995.
12 Richard Honner, interview Sydney, 11 January 1999.
13 Brian Honner, interview Canberra, 11 January 1995.
14 Margaret Honner, interview Melbourne, 16 July 1995.
15 John Honner, interview Melbourne, 16 July 1995.
16 The author contacted the NSW division of the United Nations Association and was told by both its office staff and a former president, Mr Suter, that records had not been kept and scholarship regarding that organisation was unknown to them.
17 A copy of this document was given to the author by Brian Honner. It is hereafter referred to as 'manifesto'.
18 Clearly stated in his preface.
19 Katherine West, *Power in the Liberal Party*, p. 150.
20 ibid., p. 133.
21 ibid., p. 178 note. Also Ian Campbell, *The New South Wales State Election, 1962*, pp. 14–16.
22 Ian Campbell, *The New South Wales State Election, 1962*, p. 16.
23 ibid.
24 Chris Puplick, *The New South Wales State Election, 1965*, p. 28.
25 Sir John Carrick, phone con. 17 October 1999.
26 The prayer is cited in Ralph's manifesto.
27 A copy of the newspaper report appears in the Honner papers.
28 Margaret Honner, interview Melbourne, 16 July 1995.
29 ibid.

30 John Honner, interview Melbourne, 16 July 1995.
31 The Honner papers.
32 Margaret Honner, interview Melbourne, 16 July 1995.
33 Neil McDonald, interview with Ralph Honner, Sydney, 8 January 1985. Copy of the transcription kindly given to the author.
34 From John Honner's eulogy to his father. A tape of the service was given to the author by Richard Honner.
35 Honner papers.
36 Copies of Ralph's last three tax returns were given to the author by his son Richard. His donations were substantial.
37 Richard Honner, interview Sydney, 11 January 1999.
38 Lieutenant Don Simonson, 39th Battalion, interview Melbourne, 15 July 1995.
39 Copy of the letter kindly given to the author by the late Hugh Dalby, May 1994.
40 Margaret Honner, interview Melbourne, 16 July 1995.
41 Taped copy of John Honner's eulogy to his father given to the author by Richard Honner.

BIBLIOGRAPHY

OFFICIAL RECORDS

Australian Archives
Advisory War Council Minutes Files, CRS A2673 vol. 5, 12
National Library of Australia
Vasey Papers, MS 3782
Australian War Memorial
Advanced Land Headquarters, Weekly Intelligence Summaries AWM 54 423/11/63
Blamey Papers, Field Marshal Sir Thomas, AWM DRL 6643
Headquarters 6 Division, War Diary AWM 52 1/5/12
Headquarters 7 Division, War Diary AWM 52 1/5/14
Headquarters 19 Brigade, War Diary AWM 52 8/2/19
Headquarters 21 Brigade, War Diary AWM 52 8/2/21
Headquarters 30 Brigade, War Diary AWM 52 8/2/30
Long Papers, Gavin Long, the Official Historian (1939–57)
Rowell Papers, Lieutenant-General Sir Sydney, AWM DRL 6763
2/11th Australian Infantry Battalion Unit Diary, AWM 52 8/3/11
2/14th Australian Infantry Battalion Unit Diary, AWM 52 8/3/14
2/16th Australian Infantry Battalion Unit Diary, AWM 52 8/3/16
2/27th Australian Infantry Battalion Unit Diary, AWM 52 8/3/27
39th Australian Infantry Battalion Unit Diary, AWM 52

INTERVIEWS

Bennett, J.I., Perth, 13 November 1994
Bidstrup, Major M.L., 39th Battalion, Adelaide, 9 November 1985, 7 January,
    14 January, 13 March, 11 June, 25 August, 13 November 1986

Cooper, Lieutenant-Colonel G.D.T., 2/27th Battalion, Adelaide, 19 September 1986, 13 August 1988, 4 April 1989
Dalby, Captain H., 39th Battalion, Adelaide, 6 March, 24 April, 27 July, 6 October 1986
Dougherty, Major-General Sir I.N., Sydney, 12 November 1988
Garland, Lieutenant A.G., 39th Battalion, Melbourne, 7 June 1986, 16 July 1995
Grieve, Captain B.R., 2/11th Battalion, Perth, 13 November 1994
Hardie, Corporal J.L., 39th Battalion, Melbourne, 27 March 1993
Honner, Brian, Canberra, 11 January 1995
Honner, John, Melbourne, 16 July 1995
Honner, Margaret, Melbourne, 16 July 1995
Honner, Lieutenant-Colonel R., 39th Battalion, Sydney, 1 September 1986, 11 November 1988, April 1993
Honner, Richard, Sydney, 11 January 1999
Johnson, Private H., 2/11th Battalion, Perth, 11 November 1994
Johnson, Lieutenant K.T., 2/11th Battalion, Perth, 11 November 1994
Katekar, Major H.J., 2/27th Battalion, Adelaide, 13 August, 30 September 1988, 4 April 1989
Kelly, Lieutenant H.H., 39th Battalion, Melbourne, 29 March 1993
Lovett, Captain K.H., 39th Battalion, Horsham, Victoria, 5 October 1998
McCaskill, Captain D., 2/11th Battalion, Perth, 13 November 1994
McClean, Major D.I.H., 39th Battalion, Melbourne, 7 June 1986, 29 March 1993
Moore, Captain A.W., 39th Battalion, Melbourne, 27 March 1993
Mortimore, Lieutenant H.E., 39th Battalion, Melbourne, 28 March 1993, 17 July 1995
Murdoch, Lieutenant-Colonel K., 2/16th Battalion, 21st Brigade HQ, Adelaide, 25 February 1988
O'Connor, Private B.J., 2/27th Battalion, Mount Gambier, South Australia, 24 March 1993
Pannell, Lance-Corporal E.G., 2/27th Battalion, Mount Gambier, South Australia, 24 March 1993
Rogers, Corporal B., 2/11th Battalion, Perth, 11 November 1994
Rogers, Corporal C., 2/11th Battalion, Perth, 11 November 1994
Simonson, Captain D.J., 39th Battalion, Adelaide, 3 July 1988, Melbourne, 15 July 1995
Sublet, Lieutenant-Colonel F.H., 2/16th Battalion, Adelaide, 6 August 1988
Thomas, Lieutenant J.I., 2/11th Battalion, Perth, 13 November 1994
Tranter, H., Senior Lecturer in English, Flinders University, South Australia, 20 March 1999, April 1999

CORRESPONDENCE: LETTERS, QUESTIONNAIRES

Bisset, Captain S.Y., 2/14th Battalion, 28 June 1988, 5 October 1999
Craig, Dr J.B., 15 April 1999

Herbert, C., University of Western Australia, Perth, November 1998
Honner, John (nephew to Ralph), 23 March 1999
Honner, Lieutenant-Colonel R., 39th Battalion, October 1988
Jeffs, Mary, taped reply to questionnaire, 12 March 1995
O'Day, Colonel G.O., 2/14th Battalion, 5 October 1999
Prescod, K., 6 November 1995
Quartermaine, Rita, 23 March 1999
Sim, Sergeant J., 39th Battalion, taped reply to questionnaire, October 1997
Stabb, Carol, Perth Modernians Society, December 1998
Sublet, Lieutenant-Colonel F.H., 2/16th Battalion, 20 July 1987

UNPUBLISHED PAPERS

Honner, Clem, papers from his son John Honner
Honner, Ralph, papers from his son Brian Honner

ARTICLES

Honner, R., 'The 39th at Isurava', *Australian Army Journal*, July 1967
——'The Last Day at Bardia', *Stand To*, July–August 1962
——'This is the 39th', *The Bulletin*, 3 August 1955
——'Paratroops in Crete', *Australia at Arms*, by Norman Bartlett

BOOKS

Austin, V., *To Kokoda and Beyond: The story of the 39th Battalion 1941–43*, Melbourne University Press, Melbourne, 1988
Bourke, D.F., *The History of the Catholic Church in Western Australia*, Archdiocese of Perth, Perth, 1979
Brune, Peter, *Those Ragged Bloody Heroes: From the Kokoda Trail to Gona Beach 1942*, Allen & Unwin, Sydney, 1991
——*Gona's Gone!: The battle for the beachhead 1942*, Allen & Unwin, Sydney, 1994
Burns, J., *The Brown and Blue Diamond at War: The story of the 2/27th Battalion A.I.F.*, 2/27th Battalion Ex-Servicemen's Association, Adelaide, 1960
Campbell, Ian, *The New South Wales State Election 1962*, New South Wales Parliamentary Library, Sydney, 1997
Campion, Edmund, *Australian Catholics*, Penguin, Melbourne, 1988
Carlyon, N.D., *I Remember Blamey*, Macmillan, Melbourne, 1980
Dexter, David, *The New Guinea Offensives*, Australian War Memorial, Canberra, 1961
Dornan, Peter, *The Silent Men: Syria to Kokoda and on to Gona*, Allen & Unwin, Sydney, 1999

Edgar, Bill, *Warrior of Kokoda*, Allen & Unwin, Sydney, 1999

Hart, Liddell, *Thoughts on War*, Faber & Faber, London, 1944

Horner, David, *Crisis of Command: Australian Generalship and the Japanese Threat, 1941–1943*, Australian War Memorial, Canberra, 1978

——*High Command: Australia and Allied strategy 1939–1945*, Allen & Unwin, Sydney, 1982

——*General Vasey's War*, Melbourne University Press, Melbourne, 1992

——*Blamey: The Commander-in-Chief*, Allen & Unwin, Sydney, 1998

Keen, Maurice, *Chivalry*, Yale University Press, New Haven, CT, 1984

Long, Gavin, *To Benghazi*, Australian War Memorial, Canberra, 1952

——*Greece, Crete and Syria*, Australian War Memorial, Canberra, 1953

——*The Six Years War*, Australian War Memorial, Canberra, 1973

McAulay, Lex, *Blood and Iron*, Hutchinson, Melbourne, 1991

——*To the Bitter End: The Japanese defeat at Buna and Gona 1942–43*, Random House, Sydney, 1992

McCarthy, Dudley, *South-West Pacific Area: First year*, Australian War Memorial, Canberra, 1959

McDonald, Neil, *War Cameraman: The story of Damien Parer*, Lothian, Melbourne, 1994

O'Farrell, Patrick, *The Catholic Church and Community: An Australian history*, New South Wales University Press, Sydney, 1985

Paull, Raymond, *Retreat from Kokoda*, Heinemann, Melbourne, 1958

Prestage, Edgar, *Chivalry: Its historical significance and civilising influence*, Kegan Paul, Trench, Trubner and Co, London, 1928

Puplick, Chris, *The New South Wales State Election 1965*, NSW Parliamentary Library, Sydney, 1995

Rowell, S.F., *Full Circle*, Melbourne University Press, Melbourne, 1974

Russell, W.B., *The History of the Second Fourteenth Battalion*, Angus & Robertson, Sydney, 1948

Steward, H.D., *Recollections of a Regimental Medical Officer*, Melbourne University Press, Melbourne, 1983

Tiver, P.G., *The Liberal Party: Principles and performance*, The Jacaranda Press, Brisbane, 1978

Uren, M., *A Thousand Men at War*, Melbourne, 1959

Walker, Allan, S., *The Island Campaigns*, Australian War Memorial, Canberra, 1957

West, Katherine, *Power in the Liberal Party: A study in Australian Politics*, Cheshire, Melbourne, 1965

INDEX

German Airforce, 73, 88
Gilmore, Captain Joe, 204
Goldie River (PNG), 176
Gona (PNG), 49, 130, 143, 174,
181, 194–9, 210–11, 219
effect of General Blamey's
criticism, 222–3
Haddy's Village, 200–3, 214–19
Honner's attack plan, 203–4,
207
Japanese breakout, 207, 209–10
Japanese defences, 186–90
military errors, 222
Gook, Wally, 105–6, 111
Gorrie, Peter, 226
Grace, Albert, 148
Greek campaign, 72–4, 77–9, 84,
241
Brallos Pass, 81–3
evacuation, 114–16, 118–20
Greek soldiers, 77–8
withdrawal from Vevi, 75–7
Guadalcanal, 174

Haddy, Lieutenant Alan, 190,
200–3, 227
Hale School (Perth), 27–9
Hardie, Jim, 193, 209
Hasluck, Paul, 19
Hearman, Major, 199
Heraud, Andy, 218
Herring, Lieutenant-General, 190
Holley, Captain, 251
Honner, Brian (son), 121, 124,
258, 262–3, 267
Honner, Eleanor, 8–10, 13–14, 22,
268
'Honner Force' (PNG), 176–8
Honner, John, 3, 5
Honner, John Roderick (son),
262–3, 267, 272
Honner, Margaret (daughter), 258,
262–3, 267, 271, 276, 278
Honner, Marjory, 31–2, 121, 124,
261–2, 265, 269–73
Honner, Lieutenant-Colonel
Ralph, 11, 271–8
Ambassador to Ireland, 268

Captain's rank, 39
Chairman, War Pensions
Assessment Appeal
Tribunal, 260–2
contribution to 39th Battalion,
241–2
disbandment, 39th Battalion,
239–40
Distinguished Service Order,
219
education, 17, 21
fatherhood, 262–3
final army posting, 259–60
leadership style, 136, 141,
149–50, 153, 245–7
Lieutenant-Colonel promotion,
131
malaria attack, 231, 236
marriage, 31–2
Military Cross, 66, 123
missing in action, 121, 124
move to Sydney, 262, 269
political interests, 263–7
surviving criticism, 181–2
wounded in action, 254–8
writing style, 23–4
Honner, Richard (father), 4–5, 7,
10, 15, 21, 268
Honner, Richard (son), 121, 124,
258, 262–3, 267
Honner, Sarah, 4–5
Horley, Ron, 51
Horrii, General, 144, 154, 159,
173–4, 183, 185
Howson, 'Smokey', 164, 166
Huon Peninsula–Markham Valley
(PNG), 244, 247–8, 251–2
Boana, 248–9, 251
Kaiapit, 251
Nadzab, 248
water shortage, 252–3, 256

Ioribaiwa (Kokoda), 153, 174, 178
Irwin, Keith, 126–7
Isurava (Kokoda), 81, 123, 131,
219, 223, 256
arrival at, 134–5, 137
battle, 147–53, 155 *passim*